Level III CFA® Exam

Welcome

As the VP of Advanced Designations at Kaplan Schweser, I am pleased to have the opportunity to help you prepare for the 2017 CFA® exam. Getting an early start on your study program is important for you to sufficiently **prepare**, **practice**, and **perform** on exam day. Proper planning will allow you to set aside enough time to master the Learning Outcome Statements (LOS) in the Level III curriculum.

Now that you've received your SchweserNotes™, here's how to get started:

Step 1: Access Your Online Tools

Visit **www.schweser.com** and log in to your online account using the button located in the top navigation bar. After logging in, select the appropriate level and proceed to the dashboard where you can access your online products.

Step 2: Create a Study Plan

Create a study plan with the Study Calendar (located on the Schweser dashboard) and familiarize yourself with your financial calculator. Check out our calculator videos in the Candidate Resource Library (also found on the dashboard).

Step 3: Prepare and Practice

Read your SchweserNotes™ Volumes 1–5
At the end of each reading, you can answer the Concept Checker questions for better understanding of the curriculum.

Attend a Weekly Class

Attend live classes online or take part in our live classroom courses in select cities around the world. Our expert faculty will guide you through the curriculum with a structured approach to help you prepare for the CFA® exam. The Schweser On-Demand Video Lectures, in combination with the Weekly Class, offer a blended learning approach that covers every LOS in the CFA curriculum. (See our instruction packages to the right. Visit **www.schweser.com/cfa** to order.)

Practice with SchweserPro™ QBank

Maximize your retention of important concepts by answering questions in the SchweserPro™ QBank and taking several Practice Exams. Use Schweser's QuickSheet for continuous review on the go. (Visit **www.schweser.com/cfa** to order.)

Step 4: Attend a 3-Day, 5-Day, or WindsorWeek™ Review Workshop

Schweser's late-season review workshops are designed to drive home the CFA® material, which is critical for CFA exam success. Review key concepts in every topic, **perform** by working through demonstration problems, and **practice** your exam techniques. (See review options to the right.)

Step 5: Perform

Take a Live or Live Online Schweser Mock Exam to ensure you are ready to **perform** on the actual CFA® exam. Put your skills and knowledge to the test and gain confidence before the exam. (See exam options to the right.)

Again, thank you for trusting Kaplan Schweser with your CFA exam preparation!

Sincerely,

Tim Smaby

Tim Smaby, PhD, CFA, FRM
Vice President, Advanced Designations, Kaplan Schweser

The Kaplan Way for Learning

PREPARE

Acquire new knowledge through demonstration and examples.

PRACTICE

Apply new knowledge through simulation and practice.

PERFORM

Evaluate mastery of new knowledge and identify achieved outcomes.

CFA® Instruction Packages:
> **Premium Instruction Package**
> **PremiumPlus™ Package**

Final Review Options:
> **Live 3-Day Review Workshop**
  (held in select cities)
> **Live Online 3-Day Review Workshop**
> **NYC 5-Day Review Workshop**
> **DFW 5-Day Review Workshop***
> **WindsorWeek™***
> **Live Schweser Mock Exam**
  (offered in select cities worldwide)
> **Live Online Schweser Mock Exam**

*Only offered for June exam

Contact us for questions about your study package, upgrading your package, purchasing additional study materials, or for additional information:

888.325.5072 (U.S.) | +1 608.779.8327 (Int'l.)

staff@schweser.com | www.schweser.com/cfa

CFA-536505

Book 3 – Economic Analysis, Asset Allocation and Fixed-Income Portfolio Management

SCHWESERNOTES™ 2017 LEVEL III CFA® BOOK 3: ECONOMIC ANALYSIS, ASSET ALLOCATION AND FIXED-INCOME PORTFOLIO MANAGEMENT

©2016 Kaplan, Inc. All rights reserved.

Published in 2016 by Kaplan, Inc.

Printed in the United States of America.

ISBN: 978-1-4754-4100-0

READINGS AND LEARNING OUTCOME STATEMENTS

READINGS

The following material is a review of the Fixed Income Portfolio Management, Fixed Income Derivatives, and Equity Portfolio Management principles designed to address the learning outcome statements set forth by CFA Institute.

STUDY SESSION 7

Reading Assignments
Applications of Economic Analysis to Portfolio Management, CFA Program 2017 Curriculum, Volume 3, Level III

STUDY SESSION 8

Reading Assignments
Asset Allocation and Related Decisions in Portfolio Management (1), CFA Program 2017 Curriculum, Volume 3, Level III

STUDY SESSION 9

Reading Assignments
Asset Allocation and Related Decisions in Portfolio Management (2), CFA Program 2017 Curriculum, Volume 3, Level III

STUDY SESSION 10

Reading Assignments
Fixed-Income Portfolio Management (1), CFA Program 2017 Curriculum, Volume 4, Level III

STUDY SESSION 11

Reading Assignments
Fixed-Income Portfolio Management (2), CFA Program 2017 Curriculum, Volume 4, Level III

LEARNING OUTCOME STATEMENTS (LOS)

The CFA Institute learning outcome statements are listed in the following. These are repeated in each topic review. However, the order may have been changed in order to get a better fit with the flow of the review.

STUDY SESSION 7

The topical coverage corresponds with the following CFA Institute assigned reading:

15. Capital Market Expectations

The candidate should be able to:

a. discuss the role of, and a framework for, capital market expectations in the portfolio management process. (page 1)

b. discuss challenges in developing capital market forecasts. (page 2)

c. demonstrate the application of formal tools for setting capital market expectations, including statistical tools, discounted cash flow models, the risk premium approach, and financial equilibrium models. (page 6)

d. explain the use of survey and panel methods and judgment in setting capital market expectations. (page 17)

e. discuss the inventory and business cycles, the impact of consumer and business spending, and monetary and fiscal policy on the business cycle. (page 18)

f. discuss the impact that the phases of the business cycle have on short-term/long-term capital market returns. (page 19)

g. explain the relationship of inflation to the business cycle and the implications of inflation for cash, bonds, equity, and real estate returns. (page 21)

h. demonstrate the use of the Taylor rule to predict central bank behavior. (page 23)

i. evaluate 1) the shape of the yield curve as an economic predictor and 2) the relationship between the yield curve and fiscal and monetary policy. (page 25)

j. identify and interpret the components of economic growth trends and demonstrate the application of economic growth trend analysis to the formulation of capital market expectations. (page 26)

k. explain how exogenous shocks may affect economic growth trends. (page 28)

l. identify and interpret macroeconomic, interest rate, and exchange rate linkages between economies. (page 29)

m. discuss the risks faced by investors in emerging-market securities and the country risk analysis techniques used to evaluate emerging market economies. (page 30)

n. compare the major approaches to economic forecasting. (page 31)

o. demonstrate the use of economic information in forecasting asset class returns. (page 33)

p. explain how economic and competitive factors can affect investment markets, sectors, and specific securities. (page 33)

q. discuss the relative advantages and limitations of the major approaches to forecasting exchange rates. (page 36)

r. recommend and justify changes in the component weights of a global investment portfolio based on trends and expected changes in macroeconomic factors. (page 38)

The topical coverage corresponds with the following CFA Institute assigned reading:

16. Equity Market Valuation

The candidate should be able to:

a. explain the terms of the Cobb-Douglas production function and demonstrate how the function can be used to model growth in real output under the assumption of constant returns to scale. (page 56)

b. evaluate the relative importance of growth in total factor productivity, in capital stock, and in labor input given relevant historical data. (page 58)

c. demonstrate the use of the Cobb-Douglas production function in obtaining a discounted dividend model estimate of the intrinsic value of an equity market. (page 60)

d. critique the use of discounted dividend models and macroeconomic forecasts to estimate the intrinsic value of an equity market. (page 60)

e. contrast top-down and bottom-up approaches to forecasting the earnings per share of an equity market index. (page 63)

f. discuss the strengths and limitations of relative valuation models. (page 64)

g. judge whether an equity market is under-, fairly, or over-valued using a relative equity valuation model. (page 64)

STUDY SESSION 8

The topical coverage corresponds with the following CFA Institute assigned reading:

17. Asset Allocation

The candidate should be able to:

a. explain the function of strategic asset allocation in portfolio management and discuss its role in relation to specifying and controlling the investor's exposures to systematic risk. (page 84)

b. compare strategic and tactical asset allocation. (page 85)

c. discuss the importance of asset allocation for portfolio performance. (page 85)

d. contrast the asset-only and asset/liability management (ALM) approaches to asset allocation and discuss the investor circumstances in which they are commonly used. (page 85)

e. explain the advantage of dynamic over static asset allocation and discuss the trade-offs of complexity and cost. (page 86)

f. explain how loss aversion, mental accounting, and fear of regret may influence asset allocation policy. (page 86)

g. evaluate return and risk objectives in relation to strategic asset allocation. (page 88)

h. evaluate whether an asset class or set of asset classes has been appropriately specified. (page 91)

i. select and justify an appropriate set of asset classes for an investor. (page 114)

j. evaluate the theoretical and practical effects of including additional asset classes in an asset allocation. (page 92)

k. demonstrate the application of mean–variance analysis to decide whether to include an additional asset class in an existing portfolio. (page 93)

l. describe risk, cost, and opportunities associated with nondomestic equities and bonds. (page 95)

m. explain the importance of conditional return correlations in evaluating the diversification benefits of nondomestic investments. (page 98)

n. explain expected effects on share prices, expected returns, and return volatility as a segmented market becomes integrated with global markets. (page 99)

o. explain the major steps involved in establishing an appropriate asset allocation. (page 100)

p. discuss the strengths and limitations of the following approaches to asset allocation: mean–variance, resampled efficient frontier, Black–Litterman, Monte Carlo simulation, ALM, and experience based. (page 100)

q. discuss the structure of the minimum-variance frontier with a constraint against short sales. (page 112)

r. formulate and justify a strategic asset allocation, given an investment policy statement and capital market expectations. (page 114)

s. compare the considerations that affect asset allocation for individual investors versus institutional investors and critique a proposed asset allocation in light of those considerations. (page 120)

t. formulate and justify tactical asset allocation (TAA) adjustments to strategic asset class weights, given a TAA strategy and expectational data. (page 123)

STUDY SESSION 9

The topical coverage corresponds with the following CFA Institute assigned reading:
18. Currency Management: An Introduction
The candidate should be able to:

a. analyze the effects of currency movements on portfolio risk and return. (page 149)

b. discuss strategic choices in currency management. (page 153)

c. formulate an appropriate currency management program given financial market conditions and portfolio objectives and constraints. (page 156)

d. compare active currency trading strategies based on economic fundamentals, technical analysis, carry-trade, and volatility trading. (page 156)

e. describe how changes in factors underlying active trading strategies affect tactical trading decisions. (page 161)

f. describe how forward contracts and FX (foreign exchange) swaps are used to adjust hedge ratios. (page 163)

g. describe trading strategies used to reduce hedging costs and modify the risk–return characteristics of a foreign-currency portfolio. (page 169)

h. describe the use of cross-hedges, macro-hedges, and minimum-variance-hedge ratios in portfolios exposed to multiple foreign currencies. (page 171)

i. discuss challenges for managing emerging market currency exposures. (page 174)

The topical coverage corresponds with the following CFA Institute assigned reading:
19. Market Indexes and Benchmarks
The candidate should be able to:

a. distinguish between benchmarks and market indexes. (page 186)

b. describe investment uses of benchmarks. (page 187)

c. compare types of benchmarks. (page 187)

d. contrast liability-based benchmarks with asset-based benchmarks. (page 188)

e. describe investment uses of market indexes. (page 188)

f. discuss tradeoffs in constructing market indexes. (page 189)

g. discuss advantages and disadvantages of index weighting schemes. (page 190)

h. evaluate the selection of a benchmark for a particular investment strategy. (page 191)

STUDY SESSION 10

The topical coverage corresponds with the following CFA Institute assigned reading:

20. Fixed-Income Portfolio Management—Part I

The candidate should be able to:

a. compare, with respect to investment objectives, the use of liabilities as a benchmark and the use of a bond index as a benchmark. (page 200)

b. compare pure bond indexing, enhanced indexing, and active investing with respect to the objectives, advantages, disadvantages, and management of each. (page 201)

c. discuss the criteria for selecting a benchmark bond index and justify the selection of a specific index when given a description of an investor's risk aversion, income needs, and liabilities. (page 204)

d. critique the use of bond market indexes as benchmarks. (page 205)

e. describe and evaluate techniques, such as duration matching and the use of key rate durations, by which an enhanced indexer may seek to align the risk exposures of the portfolio with those of the benchmark bond index. (page 206)

f. contrast and demonstrate the use of total return analysis and scenario analysis to assess the risk and return characteristics of a proposed trade. (page 209)

g. formulate a bond immunization strategy to ensure funding of a predetermined liability and evaluate the strategy under various interest rate scenarios. (page 211)

h. demonstrate the process of rebalancing a portfolio to reestablish a desired dollar duration. (page 219)

i. explain the importance of spread duration. (page 221)

j. discuss the extensions that have been made to classical immunization theory, including the introduction of contingent immunization. (page 223)

k. explain the risks associated with managing a portfolio against a liability structure including interest rate risk, contingent claim risk, and cap risk. (page 226)

l. compare immunization strategies for a single liability, multiple liabilities, and general cash flows. (page 227)

m. compare risk minimization with return maximization in immunized portfolios. (page 229)

n. demonstrate the use of cash flow matching to fund a fixed set of future liabilities and compare the advantages and disadvantages of cash flow matching to those of immunization strategies. (page 229)

The topical coverage corresponds with the following CFA Institute assigned reading:

21. Relative-Value Methodologies for Global Credit Bond Portfolio Management

The candidate should be able to:

a. explain classic relative-value analysis, based on top-down and bottom-up approaches to credit bond portfolio management. (page 245)

b. discuss the implications of cyclical supply and demand changes in the primary corporate bond market and the impact of secular changes in the market's dominant product structures. (page 246)

c. explain the influence of investors' short- and long-term liquidity needs on portfolio management decisions. (page 247)

d. discuss common rationales for secondary market trading. (page 247)

e. discuss corporate bond portfolio strategies that are based on relative value. (page 249)

STUDY SESSION 11

The topical coverage corresponds with the following CFA Institute assigned reading:

22. **Fixed-Income Portfolio Management—Part II**

The candidate should be able to:

a. evaluate the effect of leverage on portfolio duration and investment returns. (page 259)

b. discuss the use of repurchase agreements (repos) to finance bond purchases and the factors that affect the repo rate. (page 262)

c. critique the use of standard deviation, target semivariance, shortfall risk, and value at risk as measures of fixed-income portfolio risk. (page 264)

d. demonstrate the advantages of using futures instead of cash market instruments to alter portfolio risk. (page 266)

e. formulate and evaluate an immunization strategy based on interest rate futures. (page 267)

f. explain the use of interest rate swaps and options to alter portfolio cash flows and exposure to interest rate risk. (page 272)

g. compare default risk, credit spread risk, and downgrade risk and demonstrate the use of credit derivative instruments to address each risk in the context of a fixed-income portfolio. (page 275)

h. explain the potential sources of excess return for an international bond portfolio. (page 278)

i. evaluate 1) the change in value for a foreign bond when domestic interest rates change and 2) the bond's contribution to duration in a domestic portfolio, given the duration of the foreign bond and the country beta. (page 279)

j. recommend and justify whether to hedge or not hedge currency risk in an international bond investment. (page 281)

k. describe how breakeven spread analysis can be used to evaluate the risk in seeking yield advantages across international bond markets. (page 287)

l. discuss the advantages and risks of investing in emerging market debt. (page 288)

m. discuss the criteria for selecting a fixed-income manager. (page 289)

CAPITAL MARKET EXPECTATIONS

EXAM FOCUS

Combining capital market expectations with the client's objectives and constraints leads to the portfolio's strategic asset allocation. A variety of economic tools and techniques are useful in forming capital market expectations for return, risk, and correlation by asset class. Unfortunately, no one technique works consistently, so be prepared for any technique and its issues as covered here.

FORMULATING CAPITAL MARKET EXPECTATIONS

LOS 15.a: Discuss the role of, and a framework for, capital market expectations in the portfolio management process.

Capital market expectations can be referred to as **macro expectations** (expectations regarding classes of assets) or **micro expectations** (expectations regarding individual assets). Micro expectations are most directly used in individual security selection. In other assignments, macro expectations are referred to as top-down while micro expectations are referred to as bottom-up.

Using a disciplined approach leads to more effective asset allocations and risk management. Formulating capital market expectations is referred to as **beta research** because it is related to systematic risk. It can be used in the valuation of both equities and fixed-income securities. **Alpha research**, on the other hand, is concerned with earning excess returns through the use of specific strategies within specific asset groups.

To formulate capital market expectations, the analyst should use the following 7-step process.

Step 1: Determine the specific capital market expectations needed according to the investor's tax status, allowable asset classes, and time horizon. Time horizon is particularly important in determining the set of capital market expectations that are needed.

Step 2: Investigate assets' historical performance to determine the drivers that have affected past performance and to establish some range for plausible future performance. With the drivers of past performance established, the analyst can use these to forecast expected future performance as well as compare the forecast to past results to see if the forecast appears reasonable.

Step 3: Identify the valuation model used and its requirements. For example, a comparables-based, relative value approach used in the United States may be difficult to apply in an emerging market analysis.

Step 4: Collect the best data possible. The use of faulty data will lead to faulty conclusions. The following issues should be considered when evaluating data for possible use:
- Calculation methodologies.
- Data collection techniques.
- Data definitions.
- Error rates.
- Investability and correction for free float.
- Turnover in index components.
- Potential biases.

Step 5: Use experience and judgment to interpret current investment conditions and decide what values to assign to the required inputs. Verify that the inputs used for the various asset classes are consistent across classes.

Step 6: Formulate capital market expectations. Any assumptions and rationales used in the analysis should be recorded. Determine that what was specified in Step 1 has been provided.

Step 7: Monitor performance and use it to refine the process. If actual performance varies significantly from forecasts, the process and model should be refined.

PROBLEMS IN FORECASTING

LOS 15.b: Discuss challenges in developing capital market forecasts.

As mentioned earlier, poor forecasts can result in inappropriate asset allocations. The analyst should be aware of the potential problems in data, models, and the resulting capital market expectations. Nine problems encountered in producing forecasts are (1) limitations to using economic data, (2) data measurement error and bias, (3) limitations of historical estimates, (4) the use of ex post risk and return measures, (5) non-repeating data patterns, (6) failing to account for conditioning information, (7) misinterpretation of correlations, (8) psychological traps, and (9) model and input uncertainty.

1. There are several **limitations to using economic data**. First, the time lag between collection and distribution is often quite long. The International Monetary Fund, for example, reports data with a lag of as much as two years. Second, data are often revised and the revisions are not made at the same time as the publication. Third, data definitions and methodology change over time. For example, the basket of goods in the Consumer Price Index changes over time. Last, data indices are often rebased over time (i.e., the base upon which they are calculated is changed). Although a rebasing is not a substantial change in the data itself, the unaware analyst could calculate changes in the value of the indices incorrectly if she does not make an appropriate adjustment.

2. There are numerous possible **data measurement errors and biases**. *Transcription errors* are the misreporting or incorrect recording of information and are most serious if they are biased in one direction. *Survivorship bias* commonly occurs if a manager or a security return series is deleted from the historical performance record of managers or firms. Deletions are often tied to poor performance and bias the historical return upward. *Appraisal (smoothed) data* for illiquid and infrequently priced assets makes the path of returns appear smoother than it actually is. This biases downward the calculated standard deviation and makes the returns seem less correlated (closer to 0) with more liquid priced assets. This is a particular problem for some types of alternative assets such as real estate. Rescaling the data based on underlying economic drivers can be used to leave the mean return unaffected but increase the variance.

3. The **limitations of historical estimates** can also hamper the formation of capital market expectations. The values from historical data must often be adjusted going forward as economic, political, regulatory, and technological environments change. This is particularly true for volatile assets such as equity. These changes are known as *regime changes* and result in *nonstationary* data. For example, the bursting of the technology bubble in 2000 resulted in returns data that were markedly different than that from the previous five years. Nonstationarity would mean different periods in the time series have different statistical properties and create problems with standard statistical testing methods.

   Historical data is the starting point for estimating the following capital market expectations: expected return, standard deviation, and correlations. However, it is not obvious how to select the time period of historical data. A long time period is preferable for several reasons.

   - It may be statistically required. To calculate historical covariance (and correlation), the number of data points must exceed the number of covariances to be calculated.
   - A larger data set (time period) provides more precise statistical estimates with smaller variance to the estimates.
   - As a related issue, if the time period is longer for a larger data set, the calculated statistics are generally less sensitive to the starting and ending points selected for the time period.

   However, long time periods also create potential problems.

   - A longer time period is more likely to include *regime changes*, which are shifts in underlying fundamentals. Each regime change creates a subperiod with distinctly different characteristics. For example, the behavior of real estate and virtually every financial asset was different before and after the Financial Market Meltdown of 2008. 1) This creates *nonstationarity*, which invalidates many statistics calculated from time periods starting before and ending after the meltdown. 2) It forces the analyst to use judgment to decide whether the subperiod before or after the meltdown will be more relevant going forward.
   - It may mean the relevant time period is too short to be statistically significant.
   - It creates a temptation to use more frequent data, such as weekly data, rather than monthly data points in order to have a larger sample size. Unfortunately, more frequent data points are often more likely to have missing or outdated values (this is called *asynchronism*) and can result in lower, distorted correlation calculations.

Two questions can be used to help resolve the issue of time period to select:

1. Is there a reason to believe the entire (longer) time period is not appropriate?

2. If the answer to the first question is yes, does a statistical test confirm there is a regime change and the point in the time series where it occurs?

If both answers are yes, the analyst must use judgment to select the relevant sub period.

> *Professor's Note: I hope most candidates recognize the discussions above have been referring to many of the statistical testing issues covered at Level I and II. The focus here is not on performing such tests or even knowing which specific tests to use, but on recognizing times and ways testing can be relevant. Think of a senior portfolio manager who understands the larger issues and when to ask others with relevant technical skills to do further analysis. This is a common perspective at Level III.*

4. Using **ex post data** (after the fact) to determine **ex ante** (before the fact) risk and return can be problematic. For example, suppose that several years ago investors were fearful that the Federal Reserve was going to have to raise interest rates to combat inflation. This situation would cause depressed stock prices. If inflation abated without the Fed's intervention, then stock returns would increase once the inflation scenario passes. Looking back on this situation, the researcher would conclude that stock returns were high while being blind to the prior risk that investors had faced. The analyst would then conclude that future (ex ante) returns for stocks will be high. In sum, the analyst would underestimate the risks that equity investors face and overestimate their potential returns.

5. Using historical data, analysts can also uncover **patterns** in security returns that are unlikely to occur in the future and can produce biases in the data. One such bias is *data mining*. Just by random chance, some variables will appear to have a relationship with security returns, when, in fact, these relationships are unlikely to persist. For example, if the analyst uses a 5% significance level and examines the relationship between stock returns and 40 randomly selected variables, two (5%) of the variables are expected to show a statistically significant relationship with stock returns just by random chance. Another potential bias results from the time span of data chosen (*time period bias*). For example, small-cap U.S. stocks are widely thought to outperform large-cap stocks, but their advantage disappears when data from the 1970s and 1980s is excluded.

To avoid these biases, the analyst should first ask himself if there is any economic basis for the variables found to be related to stock returns. Second, he should scrutinize the modeling process for susceptibility to bias. Third, the analyst should test the discovered relationship with out-of-sample data to determine if the relationship is persistent. This would be done by estimating the relationship with one portion of the historical data and then reexamining it with another portion.

6. Analysts' forecasts may also fail to account for **conditioning information**. The relationship between security returns and economic variables is not constant over time. Historical data reflects performance over many different business cycles and economic conditions. Thus, analysts should account for current conditions in their forecasts. As an example, suppose a firm's beta is estimated at 1.2 using historical data. If, however, the original data are separated into two ranges by economic expansion or recession, the beta might be 1.0 in expansions and 1.4 in recessions. Going forward, the analyst's estimate of the firm's beta should reflect whether an expansion is expected (i.e., the expected beta is 1.0) or a recession is expected (i.e., the expected beta is 1.4). The beta used should be the beta consistent with the analyst's expectations for economic conditions.

7. Another problem in forming capital market expectations is the **misinterpretation of correlations** (i.e., causality). Suppose the analyst finds that corn prices were correlated with rainfall in the Midwestern United States during the previous quarter. It would be reasonable to conclude that rainfall influences corn prices. It would not be reasonable to conclude that corn prices influence rainfall, although the correlation statistic would not tell us that. Rainfall is an exogenous variable (i.e., it arises outside the model), whereas the price of corn is an endogenous variable (i.e., it arises within the model).

    It is also possible that a third variable influences both variables. Or it is possible that there is a nonlinear relationship between the two variables that is missed by the correlation statistic, which measures linear relationships.

    These scenarios illustrate the problem with the simple correlation statistic. An alternative to correlation for uncovering predictive relationships is a multiple regression. In a multiple regression, lagged terms, control variables, and nonlinear terms can all be included as independent variables to better specify the relationship. Controlling for other effects, the regression coefficient on the variable of interest is referred to as the *partial correlation* and would be used for the desired analysis.

8. Analysts are also susceptible to **psychological traps**:
    *   In the **anchoring trap**, the first information received is overweighted. If during a debate on the future of the economy, the first speaker forecasts a recession, that forecast is given greater credence.
    *   In the **status quo trap**, predictions are highly influenced by the recent past. If inflation is currently 4%, that becomes the forecast, rather than choosing to be different and potentially making an active error of commission.
    *   In the **confirming evidence trap**, only information supporting the existing belief is considered, and such evidence may be actively sought while other evidence is ignored. To counter these tendencies, analysts should give all evidence equal scrutiny, seek out opposing opinions, and be forthcoming in their motives.
    *   In the **overconfidence trap**, past mistakes are ignored, the lack of comments from others is taken as agreement, and the accuracy of forecasts is overestimated. To counter this trap, consider a range of potential outcomes.
    *   In the **prudence trap**, forecasts are overly conservative to avoid the *regret* from making extreme forecasts that could end up being incorrect. To counter this trap, consider a range of potential outcomes.
    *   In the **recallability trap**, what is easiest to remember (often an extreme event) is overweighted. Many believe that the U.S. stock market crash of 1929 may have

depressed equity values in the subsequent 30 years. To counter this trap, base predictions on objective data rather than emotions or recollections of the past.

 Professor's Note: Nothing to dwell on here. Just one more discussion of behavioral biases.

9. **Model and input uncertainty.** Model uncertainty refers to selecting the correct model. An analyst may be unsure whether to use a discounted cash flow (DCF) model or a relative value model to evaluate expected stock return. Input uncertainty refers to knowing the correct input values for the model. For example, even if the analyst knew that the DCF model was appropriate, the correct growth and discount rates are still needed.

Tests of market efficiency usually depend on the use of a model. For example, many researchers use the market model and beta as the relevant measure of risk. If beta is not the correct measure of risk, then the conclusions regarding market efficiency will be invalid. Some believe that market anomalies, which have been explained by behavioral finance, are in fact due to the actions of investors who are rational but use different valuation models (which include the human limitations of cognitive errors and emotional biases).

FORECASTING TOOLS

LOS 15.c: Demonstrate the application of formal tools for setting capital market expectations, including statistical tools, discounted cash flow models, the risk premium approach, and financial equilibrium models.

The use of formal tools helps the analyst set capital market expectations. Formal tools are those that are accepted within the investment community. When applied to reputable data, formal tools provide forecasts replicable by other analysts. The formal tools we examine are statistical tools, discounted cash flow models, the risk premium approach, and financial equilibrium models.

Statistical Tools

Descriptive statistics summarize data. **Inferential statistics** use the data to make forecasts. If the past data is **stationary**, the parameters driving the past and the future are unchanged. Therefore, the historical estimates are reasonable estimates of the future.

Return estimates can be based on the arithmetic or geometric average of past returns.

To estimate the return in a single period, the arithmetic average is used. For example, if a portfolio has a 50/50 chance of making or losing 10% in any given period, there is an equal chance $100 will increase to $110 or decrease to $90. Thus, on average, the portfolio is unchanged at $100 for a 0% return, the arithmetic average of the + and −10% returns.

Over multiple periods, the geometric average is generally preferred. Unannualized, the geometric return of the portfolio is $(1.10)(0.90) − 1 = −1.0\%$. This reflects the most likely value of the portfolio over two periods, as the $100 could either increase 10% to $110 and then decline 10% to $99, or decrease 10% to $90 and then increase 10% to $99. Under either path, the most likely change is −1%.

Another approach is to use the historical equity risk premium plus a current bond yield to estimate the expected return on equities.

Alternatively, a **shrinkage estimate** can be applied to the historical estimate if the analyst believes simple historical results do not fully reflect expected future conditions. A shrinkage estimate is a weighted average estimate based on history and some other projection.

For example, suppose the historical covariance between two assets is 180 and the analyst has used a model to project covariances and develop a **target covariance matrix**). If the model estimated covariance is 220 and the analyst weights the historical covariance by 60% and the target by 40%, the shrinkage estimate would be 196 (= 180 × 0.60 + 220 × 0.40). If conditions are changing and the model and weights are well chosen, the shrinkage estimate covariances are likely to be more accurate.

Time series models are also used to make estimates. A time series model assumes the past value of a variable is, at least in part, a valid estimator of its future value. Time series models are frequently used to make estimates of near term volatility. **Volatility clustering** has been observed where either high or low volatility tends to persist, at least in the short run. A model developed by JP Morgan states that variance in the next period (σ_t^2) is a weighted average of the previous period variance and the square of the residual error. The two weights sum to 1.0 and can be denoted as β and $1 − \beta$.

 Professor's Note: Some authors use θ rather than β to denote the weights. β is a generic symbol used to denote weight or exposure to a factor.

$$\sigma_t^2 = \beta\sigma_{t-1}^2 + (1-\beta)\varepsilon_t^2$$

For example, suppose β is 0.80 and the standard deviation in returns is 15% in period $t − 1$. If the random error is 0.04, then the forecasted variance for period t is:

$$\sigma_t^2 = 0.80(0.15^2) + 0.20(0.04^2) = 0.01832$$
$$\sigma_t = \sqrt{0.01832} = 0.1354 = 13.54\%$$

The forecasted standard deviation of 13.54% is close to the historical standard deviation of 15% because the historical standard deviation is weighted so heavily.

Multifactor models can be used in a top down analysis to forecast returns based on sensitivities (β) and risk factors (F). A two-factor model would take the form:

$$R_i = \alpha_i + \beta_{i,1}F_1 + \beta_{i,2}F_2 + \varepsilon_i$$

In this two-factor model, returns for an asset i, R_i, are a function of factor sensitivities, β, and factors, F. A random error, ε_i, has a mean of zero and is uncorrelated with the factors.

A rigorous approach can be used to work through a sequence of analysis levels and a consistent set of data to calculate expected return, covariance, and variance across markets. For example, Level 1 may consider the factors which affect broad markets, such as global equity and bond. Level 2 then proceeds to more specific markets, such as market i, j, k, l. In turn, further levels of analysis can be conducted on sectors within each market (for example, within market l).

The advantages of this approach include the following:

- Returns, covariances, and variances are all derived from the same set of driving risk factors (betas).
- A set of well-chosen, consistent factors reduces the chance for random variation in the estimates.
- Such models allow for testing the consistency of the covariance matrix.

The choice of factors to consider and levels of analysis is up to the analyst.

> *Professor's Note: The following example illustrates this analysis method. This type of hard core statistical calculation is not common on the exam. The CFA® text has one similar example but no end of chapter questions on the topic.*
>
> *In this reading you will see "inconsistencies" of scale. Do not let them throw you off. The key issue **within any one question is to be consistent using only whole numbers or decimal versions for standard deviation, covariance, and variance.***
>
> *For example, in shrinkage estimators, covariance is presented as the whole number 220. It can also be shown as 0.0220. In the time series discussion, standard deviation was expressed as the decimal 0.15 (for 15%). In the following example and in the corresponding CFA example, decimals are used with 0.0211 for variance and 0.0015 for covariance. It is up to you to know the material well enough to interpret the scale of the data in a given question. For example, 15% standard deviation and its variance can be expressed as 15 and 225 in whole numbers or as 0.15 and 0.0225 in decimal numbers.*

Example: Two-Level Factor Analysis

Thom Jones is a senior strategist examining equity and bond markets in countries C and D. He assigns the quantitative group to prepare a series of consistent calculations for the two markets. The group begins at Level 1 by assuming there are two factors driving the returns for all assets—a global equity factor and a global bond factor. At Level 2, this data is used to analyze each market. The data used is shown in Figures 1 and 2:

Figure 1: Factor Covariance Matrix for Global Assets

	Global Equity Factor	*Global Bond Factor*
Global equity factor	$0.0211 = \sigma_{F1}^2$	$0.0015 = cov(F_1, F_2)$
Global bond factor	$0.0015 = cov(F_1, F_2)$	$0.0019 = \sigma_{F2}^2$

Figure 2: Factor Sensitivities for Countries

Country	*Global Equity*	*Global Fixed Income*
C	$0.90 = \beta_{C1}$	$0.00 = \beta_{C2}$
D	$0.80 = \beta_{D1}$	$0.00 = \beta_{D2}$

The 0.00 sensitivities to global fixed income in country markets C and D indicate both markets are equity markets. (Note that this does not mean the pairwise correlation between each market and the global bond market is zero. It means that, once the effect of the equity market is controlled for, the *partial correlation* of each market and the global bond factor is zero.)

Estimate the covariance between markets C and D:

$$Cov(C,D) = \beta_{C,1}\beta_{D,1}\sigma_{F_1}^2 + \beta_{C,2}\beta_{D,2}\sigma_{F_2}^2 + (\beta_{C,1}\beta_{D,2} + \beta_{C,2}\beta_{D,1})Cov(F_1,F_2)$$

$$Cov(C,D) = (0.90)(0.80)(0.0211) + (0)(0)(0.0019) + [(0.90)(0) + (0.00)(0.80)]0.0015 = 0.0152$$

Estimate the variance for market C:

$$\sigma_C^2 = \beta_{C,1}^2\sigma_{F_1}^2 + \beta_{C,2}^2\sigma_{F_2}^2 + 2\beta_{C,1}\beta_{C,2}Cov(F_1,F_2) + \sigma_{\varepsilon,C}^2$$

$$(0.90)^2(0.0211) + (0.00)^2(0.0019) + 2(0.90)(0.00)(0.0015) = 0.0171$$

For market D, this is:

$$(0.80)^2(0.0211) + (0.00)^2(0.0019) + 2(0.80)(0.00)(0.0015) = 0.0135$$

Note that the variance of the markets will be higher than estimated because the analysis has not accounted for the variance of residual risk (σ_ε^2). Each market will have residual or idiosyncratic risk not explained by that market's factor sensitivities.

Discounted Cash Flow Models

A second tool for setting capital market expectations is **discounted cash flow models.** These models say that the intrinsic value of an asset is the present value of future cash flows. The advantage of these models is their correct emphasis on the future cash flows of an asset and the ability to back out a required return. Their disadvantage is that they do not account for current market conditions such as supply and demand, so these models are viewed as being more suitable for long-term valuation.

Applied to equity markets, the most common application of discounted cash flow models is the Gordon growth model or constant growth model. It is most commonly used to back out the expected return on equity, resulting in the following:

$$P_0 = \frac{\text{Div}_1}{\hat{R}_i - g} \Rightarrow \hat{R}_i = \frac{\text{Div}_1}{P_0} + g$$

where:

$\hat{R}_i$ = expected return on stock i
Div_1 = dividend next period
P_0 = current stock price
g = growth rate in dividends and long-term earnings

This formulation can be applied to entire markets as well. In this case, the growth rate is proxied by the nominal growth in GDP, which is the sum of the real growth rate in GDP plus the rate of inflation. The growth rate can be adjusted for any differences between the economy's growth rate and that of the equity index. This adjustment is referred to as the *excess corporate growth rate*. For example, the analyst may project the U.S. real growth in GDP at 2%. If the analyst thinks that the constituents of the Wilshire 5000 index will grow at a rate 1% faster than the economy as a whole, the projected growth for the Wilshire 5000 would be 3%.

Grinold and Kroner (2002)[1] take this model one step further by including a variable that adjusts for stock repurchases and changes in market valuations as represented by the price-earnings (P/E) ratio. The model states that the expected return on a stock is its dividend yield plus the inflation rate plus the real earnings growth rate minus the change in stock outstanding plus changes in the P/E ratio:

$$\hat{R}_i = \frac{D_1}{P_0} + i + g - \Delta S + \Delta\left(\frac{P}{E}\right)$$

where:

$\hat{R}_i$ = expected return on stock i; referred to as *compound annual growth rate* on a Level III exam

$\dfrac{D_1}{P_0}$ = expected dividend yield

i = expected inflation
g = real growth rate
ΔS = percentage change in shares outstanding (positive or negative)

$\Delta\left(\dfrac{P}{E}\right)$ = percentage change in the P/E ratio (repricing term)

---

1. Richard Grinold and Kenneth Kroner, "The Equity Risk Premium," *Investment Insights* (Barclay's Global Investors, July 2002).

The variables of the Grinold-Kroner model can be grouped into three components: the expected income return, the expected nominal growth in earnings, and the expected repricing return.

1. The **expected income return** is the cash flow yield for that market:

$$\text{expected income return} = \left(\frac{D_1}{P_0} - \Delta S \right)$$

D_1 / P_0 is current yield as seen in the constant growth dividend discount model. It is the expected dividend expressed as a percentage of the current price. The Grinold-Kroner model goes a step further in expressing the expected current yield by considering any repurchases or new issues of stock.

> *Professor's Note: To keep the ΔS analysis straight, just remember net stock:*
>
> - *Repurchase increases cash flow to investors and increases expected return.*
> - *Issuance decreases cash flow to investors and decreases expected return.*
>
> *The long way around to reaching these conclusions is:*
>
> - *Repurchase is a reduction in shares outstanding, and $-\Delta S$, when subtracted in GK, is $-(-\Delta S)$, which becomes $+\Delta S$ and an addition to expected return.*
> - *Issuance is an increase in shares outstanding, and $+\Delta S$, when subtracted in GK, becomes $-\Delta S$ and a reduction in expected return.*

2. The **expected nominal earnings growth** is the real growth in the stock price plus expected inflation (think of a nominal interest rate that includes the real rate plus inflation):

$$\text{expected nominal earnings growth} = (i + g)$$

3. The **repricing return** is captured by the expected change in the P/E ratio:

$$\text{expected repricing return} = \Delta \left(\frac{P}{E} \right)$$

It is helpful to view the Grinold-Kroner model as the sum of the expected income return, the expected nominal growth, and the expected repricing return.

$$\hat{R}_i = \exp(\text{income return}) + \exp(\text{nominal earnings growth}) + \exp(\text{repricing return})$$

$$\hat{R}_i = \left(\frac{D_1}{P_0} - \Delta S \right) + (i + g) + \left(\Delta \frac{P}{E} \right)$$

Suppose an analyst estimates a 2.1% dividend yield, real earnings growth of 4.0%, long-term inflation of 3.1%, a repurchase yield of –0.5%, and P/E re-pricing of 0.3%:

$$\text{expected } \textit{current yield} \text{ (income return)} = \text{dividend yield} + \text{repurchase yield}$$
$$= 2.1\% - 0.5\% = 1.6\%$$

expected *capital gains yield*

$$= \text{real growth} + \text{inflation} + \text{re-pricing}$$
$$= 4.0\% + 3.1\% + 0.3\% = 7.4\%$$

The total expected return on the stock market is 1.6% + 7.4% = 9.0%.

Estimating Fixed Income Returns

Discounted cash flow analysis of fixed income securities supports the use of YTM as an estimate of expected return. YTM is an IRR calculation and, like any IRR calculation, it will be the realized return earned if the cash flows are reinvested at the YTM and the bond is held to maturity. For zero-coupon bonds, there are no cash flows to reinvest, though the held-to-maturity assumption still applies. Alternatively, the analyst can make other reinvestment and holding period assumptions to project expected return.

Risk Premium Approach

An alternative to estimating expected return using YTM is a risk premium or buildup model. Risk premium approaches can be used for both fixed income and equity. The approach starts with a lower risk yield and then adds compensation for risks. A typical fixed income buildup might calculate expected return as:

R_B = real risk-free rate + inflation risk premium + default risk premium + illiquidity risk premium + maturity risk premium + tax premium

- The inflation premium compensates for a loss in purchasing power over time.
- The default risk premium compensates for possible non-payment.
- The illiquidity premium compensates for holding illiquid bonds.
- The maturity risk premium compensates for the greater price volatility of longer-term bonds.
- The tax premium accounts for different tax treatments of some bonds.

To calculate an expected equity return, an equity risk premium would be added to the bond yield.

Professor's Note: Equity buildup models vary in the starting point.

- *Begin with r_f. The Security Market Line starts with r_f and can be considered a variation of this approach.*
- *Other models start with a long-term default free bond.*
- *Or the corporate bond yield of the issuer.*

The point is to use the data provided.

Financial Equilibrium Models

The financial equilibrium approach assumes that supply and demand in global asset markets are in balance. In turn, financial models will value securities correctly. One such model is the International Capital Asset Pricing Model (ICAPM). The Singer and Terhaar approach begins with the ICAPM.

The equation for the ICAPM is:

$$\hat{R}_i = R_F + \beta_i \left(\hat{R}_M - R_F \right)$$

where:
$\hat{R}_i$ = expected return on asset i
R_F = risk-free rate of return
β_i = sensitivity (systematic risk) of asset i returns to the global investable market
$\hat{R}_M$ = expected return on the *global* investable market

Think of the global investable market as consisting of all investable assets, traditional and alternative.

We can manipulate this formula to solve for the risk premium on a debt or equity security using the following steps:

Step 1: The relationship between the covariance and correlation is:

$$\rho_{i,M} = \frac{Cov(i,m)}{\sigma_i \sigma_M} \Rightarrow Cov(i,m) = \rho_{i,M}\sigma_i\sigma_M$$

where:
$\rho_{i,M}$ = correlation between the returns on asset i and the global market portfolio
σ_i = standard deviation of the returns on asset i
σ_M = standard deviation of the returns on the global market portfolio

Step 2: Recall that:

$$\beta_i = \frac{Cov(i,m)}{\sigma_M^2}$$

where:
$Cov(i,m)$ = covariance of asset i with the global market portfolio
σ_M^2 = variance of the returns on the global market portfolio

Step 3: Combining the two previous equations and simplifying:

$$\beta_i = \frac{\rho_{i,M}\sigma_i\sigma_M}{\sigma_M^2} = \frac{\rho_{i,M}\sigma_i}{\sigma_M}$$

Step 4: Rearranging the ICAPM, we arrive at the expression for the risk premium for asset *i*, RP_i:

$$\hat{R}_i = R_F + \beta_i\left(\hat{R}_M - R_F\right)$$

$$\hat{R}_i - R_F = \beta_i\left(\hat{R}_M - R_F\right)$$

denoting $\hat{R}_i - R_F$ as RP_i

$$RP_i = \beta_i\left(\hat{R}_M - R_F\right); \text{ and since } \beta_i = \rho_{i,M}\frac{\sigma_i}{\sigma_M}$$

$$RP_i = \rho_{i,M}\frac{\sigma_i}{\sigma_M}\left(\hat{R}_M - R_F\right), \text{ or}$$

$$RP_i = \rho_{i,M}\sigma_i\left(\frac{\hat{R}_M - R_F}{\sigma_M}\right)$$

Note that $\left(\dfrac{\hat{R}_M - R_F}{\sigma_M}\right)$ = market Sharpe ratio

and that $\hat{R}_M - R_F$ is the market risk premium.

The final expression states that the risk premium for an asset is equal to its correlation with the global market portfolio multiplied by the standard deviation of the asset multiplied by the Sharpe ratio for the global portfolio (in parentheses). From this formula, we forecast the risk premium and expected return for a market.

Example: Calculating an equity risk premium and a debt risk premium

Given the following data, **calculate** the equity and debt risk premiums for Country X:

	Expected Standard Deviation	Correlation With Global Investable Market
Country X bonds	10%	0.40
Country X equities	15%	0.70
Market Sharpe ratio = 0.35		

$$RP_{bonds} = 10\% \times 0.40 \times 0.35 = 1.40\%$$

$$RP_{equities} = 15\% \times 0.70 \times 0.35 = 3.68\%$$

The Singer and Terhaar analysis then adjusts the ICAPM for market imperfections, such as illiquidity and segmentation. The more illiquid an asset is, the greater the liquidity risk premium should be. Liquidity is not typically a concern for developed world capital markets, but it can be a concern for assets such as direct real estate and private equity funds. In the case of private equity, an investment is usually subject to a lock-up period.

To estimate the size of the liquidity risk premium, one could estimate the *multi-period Sharpe ratio* for the investment over the time until it is liquid and compare it to the estimated multi-period Sharpe ratio for the market. The Sharpe ratio for the illiquid asset must be at least as high as that for the market. For example, suppose a venture capital investment has a lock-up period of five years and its multi-period Sharpe ratio is below that of the market's. If its expected return from the ICAPM is 16%, and the return necessary to equate its Sharpe ratio to that of the market's was 25%, then the liquidity premium would be 9%.

When markets are segmented, capital does not flow freely across borders. The opposite of segmented markets is integrated markets, where capital flows freely. Government restrictions on investing are a frequent cause of market segmentation. If markets are segmented, two assets with the same risk can have different expected returns because capital cannot flow to the higher return asset. The presence of investment barriers increases the risk premium for securities in segmented markets.

In reality, most markets are not fully segmented or integrated. For example, investors have a preference for their own country's equity markets (the *home country bias*). This prevents them from fully exploiting investment opportunities overseas. Developed world equity markets have been estimated as 80% integrated, whereas emerging market equities have been estimated as 65% integrated. In the example to follow, we will adjust for partial market segmentation by estimating an equity risk premium assuming full integration and an equity risk premium assuming full segmentation, and then taking a weighted average of the two. Under the full segmentation assumption, the relevant global portfolio is the individual market so that the correlation between the market and the global portfolio in the formula is 1. In that case, the equation for the market's risk premium reduces to:

$$\text{if } \rho_{i,M} = 1 \Rightarrow \text{ERP}_i = \sigma_i \left(\frac{\text{ERP}_M}{\sigma_M} \right)$$

In the following example, we will calculate the equity risk premium for the two markets, their expected returns, and the covariance between them. Before we start, recall from our discussion of factor models that the covariance between two markets given two factors is:

$$\text{Cov}(i,j) = \beta_{i,1}\beta_{j,1}\sigma_{F_1}^2 + \beta_{i,2}\beta_{j,2}\sigma_{F_2}^2 + \left(\beta_{i,1}\beta_{j,2} + \beta_{i,2}\beta_{j,1} \right)\text{Cov}\left(F_1, F_2 \right)$$

If there is only one factor driving returns (i.e., the global portfolio), then the equation reduces to:

$$\text{Cov}(i,j) = \beta_i \, \beta_j \, \sigma_M^2$$

Example: Using market risk premiums to calculate expected returns, betas, and covariances

Suppose an analyst is valuing two equity markets. Market A is a developed market, and Market B is an emerging market. The investor's time horizon is five years. The other pertinent facts are:

Sharpe ratio of the global investable portfolio	0.29
Standard deviation of the global investable portfolio	9%
Risk-free rate of return	5%
Degree of market integration for Market A	80%
Degree of market integration for Market B	65%
Standard deviation of Market A	17%
Standard deviation of Market B	28%
Correlation of Market A with global investable portfolio	0.82
Correlation of Market B with global investable portfolio	0.63
Estimated illiquidity premium for A	0.0%
Estimated illiquidity premium for B	2.3%

Calculate the assets' expected returns, betas, and covariance.

Answer:

First, we calculate the equity risk premium for both markets assuming full integration. Note that for the emerging market, the illiquidity risk premium is included:

$$ERP_i = \rho_{i,M}\sigma_i(\text{market Sharpe ratio})$$
$$ERP_A = (0.82)(0.17)(0.29) = 4.04\%$$
$$ERP_B = (0.63)(0.28)(0.29) + 0.0230 = 7.42\%$$

Next, we calculate the equity risk premium for both markets assuming full segmentation:

$$ERP_i = \sigma_i(\text{market Sharpe ratio})$$
$$ERP_A = (0.17)(0.29) = 4.93\%$$
$$ERP_B = (0.28)(0.29) + 0.0230 = 10.42\%$$

Note that when we calculate the risk premium under full segmentation, we use the local market as the reference market instead of the global market, so the correlation between the local market and itself is 1.0.

We then weight the integrated and segmented risk premiums by the degree of integration and segmentation in each market to arrive at the weighted average equity risk premium:

$$\text{ERP}_i = (\text{degree of integration of } i)(\text{ERP assuming full integration}) +$$
$$(\text{degree of segmentation of } i)(\text{ERP assuming full segmentation})$$
$$\text{ERP}_A = (0.80)(0.0404) + (1 - 0.80)(0.0493) = 4.22\%$$
$$\text{ERP}_B = (0.65)(0.0742) + (1 - 0.65)(0.1042) = 8.47\%$$

The expected return in each market figures in the risk-free rate:

$$\hat{R}_A = 5\% + 4.22\% = 9.22\%$$
$$\hat{R}_B = 5\% + 8.47\% = 13.47\%$$

The betas in each market, which will be needed for the covariance, are calculated as:

$$\beta_i = \frac{\rho_{i,M}\sigma_i}{\sigma_M}$$

$$\beta_A = \frac{(0.82)(17)}{9} = 1.55$$

$$\beta_B = \frac{(0.63)(28)}{9} = 1.96$$

Lastly, we calculate the covariance of the two equity markets:

$$\text{Cov}(i, j) \doteq \beta_i \, \beta_j \, \sigma_M^2$$
$$\text{Cov}(A, B) = (1.55)(1.96)(9.0)^2 = 246.08$$

*Professor's Note: Theoretically, a fully segmented market's Sharpe ratio would be independent of the world market Sharpe ratio. However, the CFA text makes the simplifying assumption to use the world market Sharpe ratio in both the segmented and integrated calculations. This is a reasonable assumption as we are valuing partially integrated/segmented markets. There is no reason to analyze the fully segmented market as outsiders **cannot**, by definition, invest in such markets.*

THE USE OF SURVEYS AND JUDGMENT FOR CAPITAL MARKET EXPECTATIONS

LOS 15.d: Explain the use of survey and panel methods and judgment in setting capital market expectations.

Capital market expectations can also be formed using **surveys**. In this method, a poll is taken of market participants, such as economists and analysts, as to what their expectations are regarding the economy or capital market. If the group polled is fairly constant over time, this method is referred to as a **panel method**. For example, the U.S. Federal Reserve Bank of Philadelphia conducts an ongoing survey regarding the U.S. consumer price index, GDP, and so forth.[2]

Judgment can also be applied to project capital market expectations. Although quantitative models provide objective numerical forecasts, there are times when an analyst must adjust those expectations using their experience and insight to improve upon those forecasts.

Economic Analysis

LOS 15.e: Discuss the inventory and business cycles, the impact of consumer and business spending, and monetary and fiscal policy on the business cycle.

The Inventory and Business Cycle

Understanding the business cycle can help the analyst identify *inflection points* (i.e., when the economy changes direction), where the risk and the opportunities for higher return may be heightened. To identify inflection points, the analyst should understand what is driving the current economy and what may cause the end of the current economy.

In general, economic growth can be partitioned into two components: (1) cyclical and (2) trend-growth components. The former is more short-term whereas the latter is more relevant for determining long-term return expectations. We will discuss the cyclical component first.

Within cyclical analysis, there are two components: (1) the inventory cycle and (2) the business cycle. The former typically lasts two to four years whereas the latter has a typical duration of nine to eleven years. These cycles vary in duration and are hard to predict because wars and other events can disrupt them.

Changes in economic activity delineate cyclical activity. The measures of economic activity are GDP, the output gap, and a recession. GDP is usually measured in real terms because true economic growth should be adjusted for inflationary components. The **output gap** is the difference between GDP based on a long-term trend line (i.e., potential GDP) and the current level of GDP. When the trend line is higher than the current GDP, the economy has slowed and inflationary pressures have weakened. When it is lower, economic activity is strong, as are inflationary pressures. This relationship is used by policy makers to form expectations regarding the appropriate level of growth and inflation. The relationship is affected by changes in technology and demographics. The third measure of economic activity, a **recession**, is defined as decreases (i.e., negative growth) in GDP over two consecutive quarters.

---

2. Accessible at *www.philadelphiafed.org;* accessed May 2016.

The **inventory cycle** is thought to be 2 to 4 years in length. It is often measured using the inventory to sales ratio. The measure increases when businesses gain confidence in the future of the economy and add to their inventories in anticipation of increasing demand for their output. As a result, employment increases with subsequent increases in economic growth. This continues until some precipitating factor, such as a tightening in the growth of the money supply, intervenes. At this point, inventories decrease and employment declines, which causes economic growth to slow.

When the inventory measure has peaked in an economy, as in the United States in 2000, subsequent periods exhibit slow growth as businesses sell out of their inventory. When it bottoms out, as in 2004, subsequent periods have higher growth as businesses restock their inventory. The long-term trend in this measure has been downward due to more effective inventory management techniques such as just-in-time inventory management.

The longer-term **business cycle** is thought to be 9 to 11 years in length. It is characterized by five phases: (1) the initial recovery, (2) early upswing, (3) late upswing, (4) slowdown, and (5) recession. We discuss the business cycle in greater detail later when we examine its effect on asset returns.

LOS 15.f: Discuss the impact that the phases of the business cycle have on short-term/long-term capital market returns.

For the Exam: Have a working knowledge of, and be able to explain, the general relationships between interest rates, inflation, stock and bond prices, inventory levels, et cetera, as you progress over the business cycle. For example, as the peak of the cycle approaches, everything is humming along. Confidence and employment are high, but inflation is starting to have an impact on markets. As inflation increases, bond yields increase and both bond and stock prices start to fall.

The Business Cycle and Asset Returns

The relationship between the business cycle and assets returns is well-documented. Assets with higher returns during business cycle lows (e.g., bonds and defensive stocks) should be favored by investors because the returns supplement their income during recessionary periods. These assets should have lower risk premiums. Assets with lower returns during recessions should have higher risk premiums. Understanding the relationship between an asset's return and the business cycle can help the analyst provide better valuations.

As mentioned before, inflation varies over the business cycle, which has five phases: (1) initial recovery, (2) early expansion, (3) late expansion, (4) slowdown, and

(5) recession. Inflation rises in the latter stages of an expansion and falls during a recession and the initial recovery. The phases have the following characteristics:

Initial Recovery

- Duration of a few months.
- Business confidence is rising.
- Government stimulation is provided by low interest rates and/or budget deficits.
- Falling inflation.
- Large output gap
- Low or falling short-term interest rates.
- Bond yields are bottoming out.
- Rising stock prices.
- Cyclical, riskier assets such as small-cap stocks and high yield bonds do well.

Early Upswing

- Duration of a year to several years.
- Increasing growth with low inflation.
- Increasing confidence.
- Increasing inventories.
- Rising short-term interest rates.
- Output gap is narrowing.
- Flat or rising bond yields.
- Rising stock prices.

Late Upswing

- Confidence and employment are high.
- Output gap eliminated and economy at risk of overheating.
- Inflation increases.
- Central bank limits the growth of the money supply.
- Rising short-term interest rates.
- Rising bond yields.
- Rising/peaking stock prices with increased risk and volatility.

Slowdown

- Duration of a few months to a year or longer.
- Declining confidence.
- Inflation is still rising.
- Falling inventory levels.
- Short-term interest rates are at a peak.
- Bond yields have peaked and may be falling, resulting in rising bond prices.
- Yield curve may invert.
- Falling stock prices.

Recession

- Duration of six months to a year.
- Large declines in inventory.
- Declining confidence and profits.

- Increase in unemployment and bankruptcies.
- Inflation tops out.
- Falling short-term interest rates.
- Falling bond yields, rising prices.
- Stock prices increase during the latter stages anticipating the end of the recession.

Inflation

Inflation means generally rising prices. For example, if the CPI index increases from 100 to 105, inflation is 5%. Inflation typically accelerates late in the business cycle (near the peak).

Disinflation means a deceleration in the rate of inflation. For example, if the CPI index then increases from 105 to 108, the rate of inflation decreases to approximately 3%. Inflation typically decelerates as the economy approaches and enters recession.

Deflation means generally falling prices. For example, if the CPI index declines from 108 to 106, the rate of inflation is approximately –2%. Deflation is a severe threat to economic activity: (1) It encourages default on debt obligations. Consider a homeowner who has a home worth $100,000 and a mortgage of $95,000; the homeowner's equity is only $5,000. A decline of more than 5% in home prices leads to negative equity and can trigger panic sales (further depressing prices), defaulting on the loan, or both. (2) Deflation limits the ability of central banks to stimulate the economy through monetary policy. Interest rates can only decline to 0%, but even zero interest provides no incentive to borrow and buy assets that are declining in price.

INFLATION AND ASSET RETURNS

LOS 15.g: Explain the relationship of inflation to the business cycle and the implications of inflation for cash, bonds, equity, and real estate returns.

The Business Cycle	Inflation	Economic Policy	Markets
Initial recovery	Initially declining inflation	Stimulative	ST rates low or declining LT rates bottoming and bond prices peaking Stock prices increasing
Early upswing	Low inflation and good economic growth	Becoming less stimulative	ST rates increasing LT rates bottoming or increasing with bond prices beginning to decline Stock prices increasing
Late upswing	Inflation rate increasing	Becoming restrictive	ST and LT rates increasing with bond prices declining Stock prices peaking and volatile

The Business Cycle	Inflation	Economic Policy	Markets
Slowdown	Inflation continues to accelerate	Becoming less restrictive	ST and LT rates peaking and then declining with bond prices starting to increase Stock prices declining
Recession	Real economic activity declining and inflation peaking	Easing	ST and LT rates declining with bond prices increasing Stock prices begin to increase later in the recession

Inflation and Relative Attractiveness of Asset Classes

Inflation at or below expectations	Cash Equivalents (CE) and Bonds: Neutral with stable or declining yields Equity: Positive with predictable economic growth Real Estate (RE): Neutral with typical rates of return
Inflation above expectations	CE: Positive with increasing yields Bonds: Negative as rates increase and prices decline Equity: Negative, though some companies may be able to pass through inflation and do well RE: Positive as real asset values increase with inflation
Deflation	CE: Negative with approximately 0% interest rates Bonds: Positive as the fixed future cash flows have greater purchasing power (assuming no default on the bonds) Equity: Negative as economic activity and business declines RE: Negative as property values generally decline

> *Professor's Note: Please note that these are generalizations that will not hold in every case. They are a good starting point for a forecaster taking a macro approach. Even if the generalizations always held, it is not easy to determine when a business cycle phase starts, how long it will last, or when it ends.*

Consumer and Business Spending

As a percentage of GDP, consumer spending is much larger than business spending. Consumer spending is usually gauged through the use of store sales data, retail sales, and consumer consumption data. The data has a seasonal pattern, with sales increasing near holidays. In turn, the primary driver of consumer spending is consumer after-tax income, which in the United States is gauged using non-farm payroll data and new unemployment claims. Employment data is important to markets because it is usually quite timely.

Given that spending is income net of savings, savings data are also important for predicting consumer spending. Saving rates are influenced by consumer confidence and changes in the investment environment. Specifically, consumer confidence increases as the economy begins to recover from a recession, and consumers begin to spend more. At the same time, stock prices start to rise and momentum begins to build. Consumers continue spending until the economy shows definite signs that it has peaked (i.e., top of the business cycle) and reversed. At this point, consumers begin saving more and more until the economy "turns the corner," and the cycle starts over.

Business spending is more volatile than consumer spending. Spending by businesses on inventory and investments is quite volatile over the business cycle. As mentioned before, the peak of inventory spending is often a bearish signal for the economy. It may indicate that businesses have overspent relative to the amount they are selling. This portends a slowdown in business spending and economic growth.

Monetary Policy

Central banks often use monetary policy as a counter-cyclical force to optimize the economy's performance. Most central banks strive to balance price stability against economic growth. The ultimate goal is to keep growth near its long-run sustainable rate, because growth faster than the long-run rate usually results in increased inflation. As discussed previously, the latter stages of an economic expansion are often characterized by increased inflation. As a result, central banks usually resort to restrictive policies towards the latter part of an expansion.

To spur growth, a central bank can take actions to reduce short-term interest rates. This results in greater consumer spending, greater business spending, higher stock prices, and higher bond prices. Lower interest rates also usually result in a lower value of the domestic currency, which is thought to increase exports. In addition to the direction of a change in interest rates being important, it is also the level of interest rates that is important. If, for example, rates are increased to 4% to combat inflation but this is still low compared to the average of 6% in a country, then this absolute rate may still be low enough to allow growth while the rise in rates may begin to dampen inflation. The equilibrium interest rate in a country (the rate at which a balance between growth and inflation is achieved) is referred to as the neutral rate. It is generally thought that the neutral rate is composed of an inflation component and a real growth component. If, for example, inflation is targeted at 3% and the economy is expected to grow by 2%, then the neutral rate would be 5%.

THE TAYLOR RULE

LOS 15.h: Demonstrate the use of the Taylor rule to predict central bank behavior.

The neutral rate is the rate that most central banks strive to achieve as they attempt to balance the risks of inflation and recession. If inflation is too high, the central bank should increase short-term interest rates. If economic growth is too low, it should cut interest rates. The **Taylor rule** embodies this concept. Thus, it is used as a prescriptive tool (i.e., it states what the central bank should do). It also is fairly accurate at predicting central bank action.

> **For the Exam:** No excuses, this is a gift. The Taylor Rule is covered at all levels of the exam.

The Taylor rule determines the target interest rate using the neutral rate, expected GDP relative to its long-term trend, and expected inflation relative to its targeted amount. It can be formalized as follows:

$$r_{target} = r_{neutral} + \left[0.5\left(GDP_{expected} - GDP_{trend}\right) + 0.5\left(i_{expected} - i_{target}\right) \right]$$

where:

r_{target} = short-term interest rate target

$r_{neutral}$ = neutral short-term interest rate

$GDP_{expected}$ = expected GDP growth rate

GDP_{trend} = long-term trend in the GDP growth rate

$i_{expected}$ = expected inflation rate

i_{target} = target inflation rate

> **Example: Calculating the short-term interest rate target**
>
> Given the following information, **calculate** the short-term interest rate target.
>
> | | |
> |---|---|
> | Neutral rate | 4% |
> | Inflation target | 3% |
> | Expected inflation | 7% |
> | GDP long-term trend | 2% |
> | Expected GDP growth | 0% |
>
> **Answer:**
>
> $$\begin{aligned} r_{target} &= 4\% + \left[0.5\left(0\% - 2\%\right) + 0.5\left(7\% - 3\%\right) \right] \\ &= 4\% + \left(-1\% + 2\%\right) = 5\% \end{aligned}$$
>
> In this example, the weak projected economic growth calls for cutting interest rates. If inflation were not a consideration, the target interest rate would be 1% lower than the neutral rate. However, the higher projected inflation overrides the growth concern because projected inflation is 4% greater than the target inflation rate. In net, the target rate is 5% because the concern over high inflation overrides the weak growth concern.

Fiscal Policy

Another tool at the government's disposal for managing the economy is fiscal policy. If the government wants to stimulate the economy, it can implement loose fiscal policy by decreasing taxes and/or increasing spending, thereby increasing the budget deficit. If they want to rein in growth, the government does the opposite to implement fiscal tightening.

There are two important aspects to fiscal policy. First, it is not the level of the budget deficit that matters—it is the change in the deficit. For example, a deficit by itself does not stimulate the economy, but increases in the deficit are required to stimulate the economy. Second, changes in the deficit that occur naturally over the course of the business cycle are not stimulative or restrictive. In an expanding economy, deficits will decline because tax receipts increase and disbursements to the unemployed decrease. The opposite occurs during a recession. Only changes in the deficit directed by government policy will influence growth.

THE YIELD CURVE

LOS 15.i: Evaluate 1) the shape of the yield curve as an economic predictor and 2) the relationship between the yield curve and fiscal and monetary policy.

The yield curve demonstrates the relationship between interest rates and the maturity of the debt security and is sensitive to actions of the federal government as well as current and expected economic conditions. When both fiscal and monetary policies are expansive, for example, the yield curve is sharply upward sloping (i.e., short-term rates are lower than long-term rates), and the economy is likely to expand in the future. When fiscal and monetary policies are restrictive, the yield curve is downward sloping (i.e., it is *inverted*, as short-term rates are higher than long-term rates), and the economy is likely to contract in the future.

Fiscal and monetary policies may reinforce or conflict each other. If the policies reinforce each other, the implications for the economy are clear. In all cases, there are likely implications for the yield curve:

- If both are stimulative, the yield curve is steep and the economy is likely to grow.
- If both are restrictive, the yield curve is inverted and the economy is likely to contract.
- If monetary is restrictive and fiscal is stimulative, the yield curve is flat and the implications for the economy are less clear.
- If monetary is stimulative and fiscal is restrictive, the yield curve is moderately steep and the implications for the economy are less clear.

ECONOMIC GROWTH TRENDS

LOS 15.j: Identify and interpret the components of economic growth trends and demonstrate the application of economic growth trend analysis to the formulation of capital market expectations.

The average growth rate over the economic cycle is limited by the long-term trend growth rate. That trend rate of growth is determined by basic economic factors:

- **Population growth and demographics** establish a limit to the growth rate of the labor force. Faster growth in population and increases in the participation rate (the percentage of population working) support faster long-term economic growth.
- **Business investment and productivity, a healthy banking system, and reasonable governmental policies** increase the growth rate of physical capital and productivity.
- Other factors or **shocks**—which are, by definition, unpredictable—may also affect the trend as well as the course of the business cycle. Examples have included war, major accounting scandals with resulting rule changes, and collapses in markets or currency value.

Overall, the trend rate of growth is relatively stable in developed economies. In emerging economies, that growth rate can be less predictable and include longer periods of rapid growth as those economies catch up with developed economies.

Longer term stability of the growth trend is related to stability in consumer spending, the largest component of both developed and emerging economies growth.

- The **wealth effect** suggests consumers spend more when wealth increases and less when it decreases. The wealth effect would contribute to swings between higher and lower spending and would amplify swings in the business cycle.
- However, the **permanent income hypothesis** asserts that consumer spending is mostly driven by long-run income expectations, not cyclical swings in wealth. This leads to countercyclical behavior, which dampens the business cycle. If income temporarily declines, consumers continue to spend (from savings) as long-term income expectations are more stable.

In summary, a basic model for forecasting trend economic growth focuses on:

- Growth in labor input based on growth in the labor force and labor participation.
- Growth in capital.
- Growth in total factor productivity.

Example: Forecasting the long-term economic growth rate

Assume that the population is expected to grow by 2% and that labor force participation is expected to grow by 0.25%. If spending on new capital inputs is projected to grow at 2.5% and total factor productivity will grow by 0.5%, what is the long-term projected growth rate?

Answer:

The sum of the components equals 2% + 0.25% + 2.5% + 0.5% = 5.25%, so the economy is projected to grow by this amount.

Professor's Note: The CFA text includes a similar example of summing factors to determine the long-term trend rate of growth. The Cobb-Douglas function later refines this as a more sophisticated weighted average calculation. If the data is available for Cobb-Douglas, that should be used; otherwise, the simple addition is all you can do.

Implications of the Growth Trend for Capital Markets

- High rates of growth in capital investment are associated with high rates of growth in the economy.
- However, these high growth rates are not necessarily linked to favorable equity returns as equity return is related to the rate of return on capital. For example, if the rate of growth of capital is faster than the rate of economic growth, return on capital and equity returns may be less attractive.

Structural (consistent, as opposed to one-time) government policies that can facilitate long-term growth are:

1. **Sound fiscal policy**. While counter-cyclical fiscal policy to dampen the business cyclical is acceptable, persistent large government budget deficits are detrimental. The government deficit is often associated with a current account deficit (caused primarily when imports exceed exports).

   The association between the government budget and current account deficits is called the **twin deficit problem**. The government deficit may be financed with excessive borrowing in the foreign markets. This borrowing in foreign (rather than domestic) markets finances the ability to import more than is exported and supports higher but unsustainable economic growth. There are several potential outcomes. The excessive borrowing can stop, leading to a substantial cutback in spending by the government and consumers. The currency can devalue when foreign investors are no longer willing to hold the debt. Alternatively, the government deficit can be financed with printing money (which leads to high inflation) or with excessive domestic borrowing by the government (which crowds out businesses borrowing to finance business investment). All of the outcomes are detrimental to continuing real growth.

2. **Minimal government interference with free markets.** Labor market rules that increase the structural level of unemployment are particularly detrimental.

3. **Facilitate competition in the private sector.** Policies to enable free trade and capital flows are particularly beneficial.

4. **Development of infrastructure and human capital**, including education and health care.

5. **Sound tax policies.** Understandable, transparent tax rules, with lower marginal tax rates applied to a broad tax base.

LOS 15.k: Explain how exogenous shocks may affect economic growth trends.

In addition to being influenced by governmental policies, trends are still subject to unexpected surprises or shocks that are exogenous to the economy, and many shocks and the degree of their impact on capital markets cannot be forecasted. For example, turmoil in the Middle East may change the long-term trend for oil prices, inflation, and economic growth in the developed world. Shocks may also arise through the banking system. An extreme example is the U.S. banking crisis of the 1930s, when a severe slowdown in bank lending paralyzed the economy.

Exogenous shocks are unanticipated events that occur outside the normal course of an economy. Since the events are unanticipated, they are not already built into current market prices, whereas normal trends in an economy, which would be considered endogenous, are built into market prices. Exogenous shocks can be caused by different factors, such as natural disasters, political events, or changes in government policies.

Although positive shocks are not unknown, exogenous shocks usually produce a negative impact on an economy and oftentimes spread to other countries in a process referred to as *contagion*. Two common shocks relate to changes in oil supplies and crises in financial markets. Oil shocks have historically involved increasing prices caused by a reduction in oil production. The increased oil prices can lead to increased inflation and a subsequent slowdown of the economy from decreased consumer spending and increased unemployment. Conversely, a decline in oil prices, as was the case in 1986 and 1999, can produce lower inflation, which boosts the economy. A significant decline in oil prices, however, can lead to an overheated economy and increasing inflation.

Financial crises are also not uncommon. Consider the Latin America debt crisis in the early 1980s, the devaluation of the Mexican peso in 1994, the Asian and Russian financial crises of the late 1990s, and most recently, the worldwide decline in property values. Banks are usually vulnerable in a financial crisis, so the central bank steps in to provide financial support by increasing the amount of money in circulation to reduce interest rates. This is difficult to do, however, in an already low inflation, low interest rate environment and especially in a deflationary environment.

Links Between Economies

LOS 15.l: Identify and interpret macroeconomic, interest rate, and exchange rate linkages between economies.

Economic links between countries have become increasingly important with globalization, especially for small countries with undiversified economies. Larger countries with diverse economies, such as the United States, are less affected but are still influenced by globalization.

Macroeconomic links can produce convergence in business cycles between two economies. International trade produces one such link, as a country's exports and economy are depressed by a slowdown in a trading partner's economy and level of imports. International capital flows produce another link if cross-border capital investing by a trading partner declines as its economy contracts.

Interest rates and **currency exchange rates** can also create linkages. A strong link is created when a smaller economy "pegs" its currency to that of a larger and more developed economy. The peg is a unilateral declaration by the pegging country to maintain the exchange rate. In general, the linkage between the business cycles of the two economies will increase, as the pegged currency country must follow the economic policies of the country to which it has pegged its currency. If not, investors will favor one currency over the other and the peg will fail.

Generally, the interest rates of the pegged currency will exceed the interest rates of the currency to which it is linked, and the interest rate differential will fluctuate with the market's confidence in the peg. If confidence is high, the rate differential can be small. If there is doubt the peg will be maintained, investors will require a larger interest rate differential as compensation for the risk of holding the pegged currency. A common problem arises if investors begin to lose confidence in the pegged currency and it begins to decline in value. The pegging country must then increase short-term interest rates to attract capital and maintain the value of the currency at the peg.

Pegs have become less common following the 1997 Asian financial crises. In the absence of pegging, the relationship of interest rate differentials and currency movement can reflect several factors:

- If a currency is substantially overvalued and expected to decline, bond interest rates are likely to be higher to compensate foreign investors for the expected decline in the currency value.
- Relative bond yields, both nominal and real, increase with strong economic activity and increasing demand for funds.
- One economic theory postulates that differences in nominal interest rates are a reflection of differences in inflation and that real interest rates are equal. However, real rates actually differ substantially, though there is a tendency for the overall level of real rates among countries to move up and down together.

Professor's Note: The relationship between currency values and interest rates is complicated. You may recall a theory from earlier levels that if real interest rates are equal and the movement of currency value consistently reflects the difference in inflation rates, then the forward exchange rate is a good predictor of what will happen in the currency market. The Level III material will not support those assumptions and does not support the use of the forward exchange rate as a predictor of what will happen. This is addressed in multiple study sessions.

EMERGING MARKET ECONOMIES

LOS 15.m: Discuss the risks faced by investors in emerging-market securities and the country risk analysis techniques used to evaluate emerging market economies.

Emerging markets offer the investor high returns at the expense of higher risk. Many emerging markets require a heavy investment in physical and human (e.g., education) infrastructure. To finance this infrastructure, many emerging countries are dependent on foreign borrowing, which can later create crisis situations in their economy, currency, and financial markets.

Many emerging countries also have unstable political and social systems. The lack of a middle class in these countries does not provide the constituency for needed structural reforms. These small economies are often heavily dependent on the sale of commodities, and their undiversified nature makes them susceptible to volatile capital flows and economic crises.

The investor must carefully analyze the risk in these countries. For the bond investor, the primary risk is credit risk—does the country have the capacity and willingness to pay back its debt? For equity investors, the focus is on growth prospects and risk. There are six questions potential investors should ask themselves before committing funds to these markets.

1. **Does the country have responsible fiscal and monetary policies?** To gauge fiscal policy, most analysts examine the deficit to GDP ratio. Ratios greater than 4% indicate substantial credit risk. Most emerging counties borrow short term and must refinance on a periodic basis. A buildup of debt increases the likelihood that the country will not be able to make its payments. Debt levels of 70 to 80% of GDP have been troublesome for developing countries.

2. **What is the expected growth?** To compensate for the higher risk in these countries, investors should expect a growth rate of at least 4%. Growth rates less than that may indicate that the economy is growing slower than the population, which can be problematic in these underdeveloped countries. The structure of an economy and government regulation is important for growth. Tariffs, tax policies, and regulation of foreign investment are all important factors for growth.

3. **Can the country maintain a stable, appropriate currency value?** Swings between over- and under-valuation are detrimental to business confidence and investment. Prolonged over-valuation promotes external borrowing, artificially stimulating the economy and imports (leading to a current account deficit and the twin deficit problem). However, the foreign debt must be serviced (interest paid and principal rolled over). A current account deficit exceeding 4% of GDP has been a warning sign of potential difficulty.

4. **Is the country too highly levered?** Although emerging countries are dependent on foreign financing for growth, too much debt can eventually lead to a financial crisis if foreign capital flees the country. These financial crises are accompanied by currency devaluations and declines in emerging market asset values. Foreign debt levels greater than 50% of GDP indicate that the country may be overlevered. Debt levels greater than 200% of the current account receipts also indicate high risk.

5. **What is the level of foreign exchange reserves relative to short-term debt?** Foreign exchange is important because many emerging country loans must be paid back in a foreign currency. The investor should be wary of countries where the foreign exchange reserves are less than the foreign debt that must be paid off within one year.

6. **What is the government's stance regarding structural reform?** If the government is supportive of structural reforms necessary for growth, then the investment environment is more hospitable. When the government is committed to responsible fiscal policies, competition, and the privatization of state-owned businesses, there are better prospects for growth.

ECONOMIC FORECASTING

LOS 15.n: Compare the major approaches to economic forecasting.

Econometric analysis uses economic theory to formulate the forecasting model. The models can be quite simple to very complex, involving several or hundreds of relationships. For example, the analyst may want to forecast GDP using current and lagged consumption and investment values. Ordinary least squares regression is most often used, but other statistical methods are also used to develop these models.

Advantages:
- Modeling can incorporate many variables.
- Once the model is specified, it can be reused.
- Output is quantified and based on a consistent set of relationships.

Disadvantages:
- Models are complex and time-consuming to construct.
- The data may be difficult to forecast and the relationships can change.

- Output may require interpretation or be unrealistic.
- Does not work well to forecast recessions.

Economic indicators are available from governments, international organizations (e.g., the Organization of Economic Cooperation and Development), and private organizations (e.g., the Conference Board in the United States).

Many analysts use a combination of publically available indicators and their own proprietary indicators. The most useful indicators are **leading indicators** that move ahead of the business cycle with a reasonable stable lead time. These can be used to predict what will happen next. The leading indicators can be used individually or as a **composite**. For example, the Conference Board provides 10 leading indicators for the United States, which can be combined into an index. Traditionally, three consecutive months of increase (decrease) for the index are expected to signal the start of an economic expansion (contraction) within a few months. A composite can also be referred to as a **diffusion index** and used to measure the number of indicators pointing towards expansion versus contraction in the economy.

There are also **coincident** and **lagging indicators** that move with and after changes in the business cycle. These can be used to confirm what is happening in the economy.

Advantages:

- Economic indicators are simple, intuitive, and easy to interpret.
- The data is often readily available from third parties.
- Indicator lists can be tailored to meet specific forecasting needs.
- Academic literature supports the approach.

Disadvantages:

- Forecasting results have been inconsistent.
- Economic indicators have given false signals.

A **checklist approach** can incorporate elements of the above but is more subjective. In this approach, an analyst considers a series of questions. For example, to forecast GDP, the analyst may consider, "What was the latest employment report? What is the central bank's next move, given the latest information released? What is the latest report on business investment?" Then, the analyst uses judgement to interpret the answers and formulate a forecast. Judgement is required both in determining what factors to consider and how to interpret them.

Advantages:

- Less complex than econometrics.
- Flexible in mixing objective statistical analysis with judgement to incorporate changing relationships.

Disadvantages:

- Subjective.
- Time–consuming.
- Complexity must be limited because it is a manual process.

ECONOMIC CONDITIONS AND ASSET CLASS RETURNS

LOS 15.o: Demonstrate the use of economic information in forecasting asset class returns.

LOS 15.p: Explain how economic and competitive factors can affect investment markets, sectors, and specific securities.

Investors ultimately use capital market expectations to form their beliefs about the attractiveness of different investments. This is one of the primary steps in top-down analysis. We next examine how economic information can be used in forecasting asset class returns. We start with cash.

Cash Instruments

Cash typically refers to short-term debt (e.g., commercial paper) with a maturity of one year or less. Cash managers adjust the maturity and creditworthiness of their cash investments depending on their forecasts for interest rates and the economy. If, for example, a manager thinks interest rates are set to rise, he will shift from 9-month cash instruments down to 3-month cash instruments. If he thinks the economy is going to improve, so that less creditworthy instruments have less chance of default, he will shift more assets into lower-rated cash instruments. Longer maturity and less creditworthy instruments have higher expected return but also more risk.

The interest rate for overnight loans among U.S. banks is the Federal Funds rate and is set by the Federal Reserve through its purchases and sales of government debt. This rate is fairly stable except during periods of unusual market volatility. In the European Union, the European Central Bank targets the repo rate.

The yield for debt securities of various maturities reflects the market's anticipation of yields over future periods. To earn excess returns, the manager must be able to forecast future rates better than other managers, and this in part requires anticipation of what the central bank will do in the future.

Credit Risk-Free Bonds

The most common type of credit risk-free bonds are those issued by governments in developed countries. The yield on these bonds is composed of a real yield and the expected inflation over the investment horizon. If, for example, the investor thinks that inflation will be 2% over the life of the bond and the investor requires a real return of 4%, then the investor would only purchase the bond if its yield were 6% or more. Based on historical data, the real yield on an ex ante basis should be roughly 2–4%.

The investor with a short time horizon will focus on cyclical changes in the economy and changes in short-term interest rates. Higher expected economic growth results in higher yields because of anticipated greater demand for loanable funds and possibly higher inflation. A change in short-term rates, however, has less predictable effects. Usually an increase in short-term rates increases the yields on medium- and long-term bonds. Medium- and long-term bond yields may actually fall, though, if the interest rate increase is gauged sufficient to slow the economy.

Over the past 40 years, the inflation premium embedded in bonds has varied quite a bit in developed countries. In the 1960s, it was quite low but rose in the late 1970s as investors became accustomed to higher inflation. More recently, it has dropped as inflation has been low.

Credit Risky Bonds

The most common type of credit risky bonds are corporate bonds. To estimate the credit risk premium assigned to individual bonds, the analyst could subtract the yield of Treasuries from that of corporate bonds of the same maturity to calculate the spread. During a recession, the credit risk premium, or spread, increases because default becomes more likely. At the same time, the credit offered by banks and the commercial paper market also dries up so that corporations have to offer higher yields to attract investors. More favorable economic conditions result in lower credit risk premiums.

Emerging Market Government Bonds

The key difference between developed country government bonds and emerging market government bonds is that most emerging debt is denominated in a non-domestic currency. Emerging market bonds are usually denominated in a hard currency (e.g., dollars, euros); thus, the emerging market government must obtain the hard currency to pay back the principal and interest. The default risk for emerging market debt is appropriately higher. To assess this risk, analysts use country risk analysis, which focuses on the economic and political environment in a country (as discussed previously for emerging markets).

Inflation-Indexed Bonds

Several governments issue bonds that adjust for inflation so that the investor is protected against it. An example is U.S. Treasury Inflation Protected Securities (TIPS). These bonds are both credit risk and inflation risk free. But they are not free of price risk. Their prices and yields still vary as economic conditions change and as the supply and demand for these instruments vary. The yield on these bonds has been correlated with three economic factors. Their yield:

- Rises (falls) as the real economy expands (contracts). This is primarily because their yield is tracking short-term interest rates, which also move with the economy.
- Falls as inflation accelerates and more investors seek to buy the inflation-index bonds. The increase in demand leads to higher prices and lower yields.
- Changes with supply and demand. These markets are somewhat small, making supply and demand changes more important.

Common Stock

To understand how economic conditions affect stock values, recall that the value of an asset is the present value of its future cash flows. For stocks, both the cash flows (earnings) and discount rate (risk-adjusted required return) are important. Earnings are commonly used to value the stock market because they should be reflected in both the cash paid out as dividends and as capital gains. Aggregate earnings depend primarily on the trended rate of growth in an economy, which in turn depends on labor force growth, new capital inputs, and total factor productivity growth.

As discussed earlier, when the government promotes competition in the marketplace, this increases the efficiency of the economy and should lead to higher long-term growth in the economy and the stock market. Of course, an investor would prefer an individual stock to have a monopolistic, noncompetitive position in their product market. This, however, would not be healthy for the growth of the overall stock market.

Shorter-term growth is affected by the business cycle. In a recession, sales and earnings decrease. Noncyclical or defensive stocks (e.g., utilities) are less affected by the business cycle and will have lower risk premiums and higher valuations than cyclical stocks (e.g., technology firms). Cyclical stocks are characterized by high business risk (sensitivity to the business cycle) and/or high fixed costs (operating leverage).

Recall that in the early expansion phase of the business cycle, stock prices are generally increasing. This is because sales are increasing, but input costs are fairly stable. For example, labor does not ask for wage increases because unemployment is still high, and idle plant and equipment can be pushed into service at little cost. Furthermore, firms usually emerge from a recession leaner because they have shed their wasteful projects and excessive spending. Later on in the expansion, earnings growth slows because input costs start to increase. As mentioned earlier, interest rates will also increase during late expansion, which is a further negative for stock valuation.

A stock's valuation in the market is reflected in its price-earnings (P/E) ratio. P/E ratios are higher in an early expansion period when interest rates are low and earnings prospects are high. They decline as earnings prospects decline. Note that for cyclical stocks, P/E ratios may be quite high in a recession, if investors are anticipating that the economy will soon recover. P/E ratios are also affected by long-term trends. For example, the 1990s was thought to be a new era of productivity, earnings growth, low inflation, and low interest rates. P/E ratios were abnormally high during this time period. Low inflation results in high P/E ratios because earnings are more *real* and less subject to interpretation.

Emerging Market Stocks

Historical returns for emerging market stocks are higher and more variable than those in the developed world and seem to be positively correlated with business cycles in the developed world. This correlation is due to trade flows and capital flows. In addition, emerging countries share many of the same sectors as those in the developed world. The analyst should have a good understanding of country and sector patterns when valuing emerging market stocks.

Real Estate

Real estate assets are affected by interest rates, inflation, the shape of the yield curve, and consumption. Interest rates affect both the supply of, and demand for, properties through mortgage financing rates. They also determine the capitalization rate (i.e., discount rate) used to value cash flows.

FORECASTING EXCHANGE RATES

LOS 15.q: Discuss the relative advantages and limitations of the major approaches to forecasting exchange rates.

The value of a currency is determined by its supply and demand, which in turn is affected by trade flows and capital flows. For example, if the United States has a trade deficit with Japan (i.e., it imports more from Japan than it exports to Japan), the value of the dollar should decline against the yen. The reason is that to obtain the foreign good, U.S. consumers are essentially selling their dollars to obtain yen.

In regard to capital flows, if U.S. Treasury bonds are in high demand due to their safety and attractive return, foreign investors will sell their currency in order to obtain dollars. The value of the foreign currency will fall while the value of the dollar will rise. Capital will flow into a country when capital restrictions are reduced, when an economy's strong growth attracts new capital, or when interest rates are attractive. Higher interest rates generally attract capital and increase the domestic currency value. At some level, though, higher interest rates will result in lower currency values because the high rates may stifle an economy and make it less attractive to invest there.

The emphasis on international diversification has increased capital flows. Capital flows can be volatile but are less so if the capital is invested in real assets through foreign direct investment. Currency values can also become volatile when a country is forced to abandon a pegged value targeted by its government.

The volatility in currency values makes them difficult to forecast but presents both risks and rewards for portfolio managers. We examine four methods of forecasting exchange rates: (1) relative purchasing power parity, (2) relative economic strength, (3) capital flows, and (4) savings and investment imbalances.

The first method is the relative form of **purchasing power parity** (PPP). PPP states that differences in inflation between two countries will be reflected in changes in the exchange rate between them. Specifically, the country with higher inflation will see its currency value decline. For example, assume Japanese inflation is projected to be a cumulative 8.2% over the next five years, while U.S. inflation is 13.2% over the same period. U.S. inflation is thus projected to be 5% higher. If the current exchange rate is ¥100/$, then the projected exchange rate is approximately ¥100/$ × (1 − 0.05) = ¥95/$ (note that the dollar has depreciated here because it buys five less yen).

PPP does not hold in the short term or medium term but holds approximately in the long term (five years or more). PPP is given attention by governments and forecasters, but its influence on exchange rates may be swamped by other factors, such as trade deficits.

The second method of forecasting currency values is the **relative economic strength approach**. The idea behind this approach is that a favorable investment climate will attract investors, which will increase the demand for the domestic currency and increase the currency's value. Investors would be attracted by strong economic growth in a country. Alternatively, high short-term interest rates may also attract investors. High short-term interest rates will attract investors who buy the currency in order to invest the currency at those high short-term rates. Interestingly, even if the general consensus is the currency is overvalued based on fundamentals, high rates may still attract attention and keep the currency overvalued or cause further appreciation in the short-run. The relative economic strength approach may be better suited to forecasting short-run changes in currency value.

The third approach to forecasting exchange rates is the **capital flows approach**. This approach focuses primarily on long-term capital flows, such as those into equity investments or foreign direct investments. For example, the strength of the U.S. dollar in the later 1990s was thought to be due to the strength of the U.S. stock market.

The flow of long-term funds complicates the relationship between short-term rates and currency values as discussed in the relative strength approach. For example, a cut in U.S. short-term rates may actually strengthen the dollar because the cut might promote U.S. growth and the attractiveness of U.S. stocks. This makes the central bank's job more difficult. If the Federal Reserve wanted to boost short-term rates to increase the value of the dollar and tame inflation, their action may actually result in a decline in the value of the dollar as investors find U.S. capital assets less attractive.

The last approach is the **savings-investment imbalances approach**. This approach is not readily implemented for forecasting but explains why currencies may diverge from equilibrium values for extended periods. This approach starts with the concept that an economy must fund investment through savings. If investment is greater than domestic savings, then capital must flow into the country from abroad to finance the investment. A savings deficit can be attributable to both the government and private sector.

In order to attract and keep the capital necessary to compensate for the savings deficit, the domestic currency must increase in value and stay strong (perhaps as a result of high interest rates or economic growth). At the same time, the country will have a current account deficit where exports are less than imports. Although a current account deficit would normally indicate that the currency will weaken, the currency must stay strong to attract foreign capital.

The aforementioned scenario typically occurs during an economic expansion when businesses are optimistic and use their savings to make investments. Eventually, though, the economy slows, investment slows, and domestic savings increase. It is at this point that the currency will decline in value.

In addition to the four approaches described previously, one could also examine government intervention to determine the future path of exchange rates. This approach is not very fruitful, though, because most observers don't think governments can exert much control over exchange rates. The reason is that government trading is too small in volume to affect the massive currency markets. Furthermore, currencies are more influenced by economic fundamentals than by periodic trading by governments.

REALLOCATING A GLOBAL PORTFOLIO

LOS 15.r: Recommend and justify changes in the component weights of a global investment portfolio based on trends and expected changes in macroeconomic factors.

For the Exam: This LOS asks you to use much of what you have learned here and apply it to portfolio management. Given that the emphasis of the Level III exam is portfolio management, you need to be able to pull all this material together.

Example: Applying capital market expectations

A portfolio manager has a global portfolio invested in several countries and is considering other countries as well. The decisions the manager faces and the economic conditions in the countries are described in the following. In each case, the portfolio manager must reallocate assets based on economic conditions.

Decision #1: Reallocation to Country A

The portfolio manager has noticed that the yield curve is downward sloping in this country. The current portfolio in this country is 60% stocks and 40% bonds. Suggest changes to the portfolio based on this information.

Decision #2: Allocation to Country B

Country B has experienced declining prices and this trend is expected to continue. The manager has no funds invested in this country yet but is considering investments in bonds, equity, and real estate. In which assets should the manager invest?

Decision #3: Allocations to Emerging Country C or Country D

The manager is considering the purchase of government bonds in either emerging Country C or D.

The countries have the following characteristics:

Characteristics of Countries C and D

	Country C	Country D
Foreign exchange/Short-term debt	147%	78%
Debt to GDP	42%	84%

Decision #4: Country, Asset, and Currency Allocations

The manager will make a long-term investment in either Country E or F, based on projections of each economy's trended growth rate. Given that decision, the manager will then decide whether to invest in stocks or bonds. Lastly, the manager will use the savings-investment imbalances approach to gauge the strength of the currencies. The countries have the following characteristics:

Characteristics of Countries E and F

	Country E	Country F
Population growth	2.5%	2.0%
Labor force participation growth	0.2%	0.9%
Growth in spending on new capital inputs	1.5%	2.2%
Growth in total factor productivity	0.4%	0.8%
Expected savings relative to investment	Surplus	Deficit

Answers:

Decision #1: Reallocation to Country A

The downward sloping yield curve indicates that the economy is likely to contract in the future. In recessions, bonds outperform stocks because inflation and interest rates decrease and economic growth is slow. Assuming the accuracy of the yield curve forecast and that interest rates will fall further, the portfolio manager should consider reallocating from stocks into bonds.

Decision #2: Allocation to Country B

The manager should invest in bonds. In periods of declining prices or deflation, bonds perform well because there is no inflation and interest rates are declining. Stocks usually perform poorly during deflationary periods because economic growth is slowing. Real estate also performs poorly during deflationary times, particularly when the investment is financed with debt.

Decision #3: Allocations to Emerging Country C or Country D

The manager should purchase the bonds of Country C. Many emerging market bonds are denominated in a hard currency, so less risky countries have greater foreign currency reserves. Low levels of leverage are also preferred. One measure of leverage is the debt to GDP ratio.

Decision #4: Country, Asset, and Currency Allocations

To forecast the long-term economic growth rate, we sum population growth, labor force participation growth, growth in spending on new capital inputs, and growth in total factor productivity.

In Country E, it is 2.5% + 0.2% + 1.5% + 0.4% = 4.6%.

In Country F, it is 2.0% + 0.9% + 2.2% + 0.8% = 5.9%.

Country F has the higher trended growth rate, so the manager should invest there. The growth rate of 5.9% is quite attractive, and given that the manager is investing for the long term, the investment should be made in equities because equities will benefit the most from this high growth rate. Bond returns are based more on expectations of interest rates and inflation. A high growth economy may experience higher inflation and interest rates at some point that would be negative for bonds.

In the absence of other information, we would surmise from the savings-investment imbalances approach that Country E's currency will depreciate because the country has a savings surplus. Foreign capital will not be needed and, hence, Country E does not require a high currency value. Country F's currency will appreciate because the savings deficit will require a strong currency to attract foreign capital.

For the Exam: In sum, you need to be able to determine the relevant inputs to economic forecasts and what the forecasted economic conditions mean for asset values. Also, be ready to use the forecasting tools discussed earlier and identify problems in forecasting.

KEY CONCEPTS

LOS 15.a

Capital market expectations (macro expectations) help in formulating the strategic asset allocation. They can also assist in detecting short-term asset mispricing exploitable through tactical asset allocation. Formulating capital market expectations is referred to as beta research because it is related to systematic risk.

To formulate capital market expectations, use the following process:
- Determine the relevant capital market expectations given the investor's tax status, allowable asset classes, and time horizon.
- Investigate assets' historical performance as well as the determinants of their performance.
- Identify the valuation model used and its requirements.
- Collect the best data possible.
- Use experience and judgment to interpret current investment conditions.
- Formulate capital market expectations.
- Monitor performance and use it to refine the process.

LOS 15.b

Limitations in the use of economic data for forecasting include the following:
- Data is reported with a lag, subject to revision, and defined inconsistently in different countries.
- Data is subject to biases and errors such as transcription errors, survivorship bias, and smoothed (appraised) data estimates.
- Using historical data is less appropriate when economic conditions change (regime change and nonstationary issues).
- Ex post risk generally understates ex ante risk, as surviving the past does not guarantee the future cannot be worse.
- Analyst bias in selective data mining or selection of time periods to examine.
- Failure to condition information for the likely state of the economy.
- Misinterpreting correlation with causation. Does A cause B, does B cause A, or are both just associated with some other factor C?
- Psychological traps related to cognitive errors and emotional biases.
- Errors in selecting the wrong model or inputs.

LOS 15.c

Statistical tools include:
- Using historical data to develop descriptive statistics.
- Applying shrinkage estimates to weight historically based estimates with model-based estimates.
- Using time series models to estimate variance.
- Using a single data set and multifactor models to generate internally consistent estimates of return, risk, and covariances between asset classes.

Discounted cash flow models include:
- Grinold-Kroner to estimate equity market return.
- YTM for bond return.

Buildup models of "risk-free" plus risk premiums for bond and equity return.

Financial equilibrium models (Singer-Terhaar) based on the world market Sharpe ratio, the individual market's standard deviation, and degree of integration; plus any non-systematic risk premiums.

LOS 15.d
Capital market expectations can also be formed using surveys. In this method, a poll is taken of market participants (e.g., economists and analysts) to determine what their expectations are regarding the economy or capital market. If the group polled is constant over time, this method is referred to as a panel method.

Surveys have been taken regarding the equity risk premium, with investors expecting a premium in the range of 2% to 3.9%. Other studies have found that the expectations of practitioners are consistently more optimistic than that of academics.

Judgment can also be applied to project capital market expectations. Although quantitative models provide objective numerical forecasts, there are times when an analyst must adjust those expectations using her experience and insight to improve upon those forecasts.

LOS 15.e
Understanding the business cycle can help the analyst identify inflection points where the risk and opportunities for higher return may be heightened. To identify inflection points, the analyst should understand what is driving the current economy and what may cause the end of the current economy.

The inventory cycle is often measured using the inventory to sales ratio. The measure increases when businesses gain confidence in the future of the economy and add to their inventories in anticipation of increasing demand for their output. As a result, employment increases with subsequent increases in economic growth. This continues until some precipitating factor, such as a tightening in the growth of the money supply, intervenes. At this point, inventories decrease, employment declines, and economic growth slows.

LOS 15.f
The relationship between the business cycle and assets returns is well documented. Assets with higher returns during business cycle lows (e.g., bonds and defensive stocks) should be favored by investors because the return supplements their income during recessionary periods—these assets should have lower risk premiums. Assets with lower returns during recessions should have higher risk premiums. Understanding the relationship between an asset's return and the business cycle can help the analyst provide better valuations.

LOS 15.g
Inflation varies over the business cycle, rising in the latter stages of an expansion and falling during a recession and the initial recovery.

Deflation reduces the value of investments financed with debt (e.g., real estate) because leverage magnifies losses.

Bond prices will rise during a recession when inflation and interest rates are declining. In a strong expansion, bonds tend to decline in price as inflationary expectations and interest rates rise.

Equities provide an inflation hedge when inflation is moderate. High inflation can be problematic because slow growth may result from central bank action. Declining inflation or deflation is harmful because this can result in declining economic growth.

Increasing inflation is positive for cash instruments because the returns on cash instruments increase as inflation increases. Deflation is negative for cash because the return falls to zero.

LOS 15.h
The Taylor rule:

$$r_{target} = r_{neutral} + \left[0.5 \left(GDP_{expected} - GDP_{trend} \right) + 0.5 \left(i_{expected} - i_{target} \right) \right]$$

- A central bank can use the Taylor rule to determine the appropriate level for short-term interest rates.
- An investment strategist who expects unanticipated changes in the inputs to the Taylor rule can use the rule to anticipate changes in short-term interest rates by the central bank.

LOS 15.i
The yield curve demonstrates the relationship between interest rates and the maturity of the debt security and is sensitive to actions of the federal government as well as current and expected economic conditions. For example, when both fiscal and monetary policies are expansive, the yield curve is sharply upward sloping, which indicates that the economy is likely to expand in the future. When fiscal and monetary policies are restrictive, the yield curve is downward sloping, indicating that the economy is likely to contract in the future.

When fiscal and monetary policies are in disagreement, the shape of the yield curve is less definitively shaped. Recall that monetary policy controls primarily short-term interest rates. If monetary policy is expansive while fiscal policy is restrictive, the yield curve will be upward sloping, though it will be less steep than when both policies are expansive. If monetary policy is restrictive while fiscal policy is expansive, the yield curve will be more or less flat.

LOS 15.j
In forecasting a country's long-term economic growth trend, the trend growth rate can be decomposed into two main components and their respective subcomponents:
1. Changes in employment levels.
   - Population growth.
   - Rate of labor force participation.

2. Changes in productivity.
   - Spending on new capital inputs.
   - Total factor productivity growth.

LOS 15.k

Exogenous shocks are unanticipated events that occur outside the normal course of an economy and have a negative impact upon it. They can be caused by different factors, such as natural disasters, political events, or changes in government policies. Typically, two types of shocks have occurred, which are oil shocks and financial crises. Oil shocks are usually caused by crises in the Middle East followed by decreased oil production, leading to increasing prices, inflation, reduced consumer spending, higher unemployment, and a slowed economy. The opposite shock would be a decline in oil prices, leading to lower inflation and boosting the economy. Financial crises have occurred when countries can't meet their debt payments, currencies are devalued, and property values have declined. In a financial crisis, banks usually become vulnerable, forcing the central bank to provide stability to the economy by reducing interest rates, which is difficult to do in an already low interest rate environment.

LOS 15.l

Macroeconomic links refer to similarities in business cycles across countries. Economies are linked by both international trade and capital flows so that a recession in one country dampens exports and investment in a second country, thereby creating a slowdown in the second country.

Exchange rate links are found when countries peg their currency to others. The benefit of a peg is that currency volatility is reduced and inflation can be brought under control. Interest rates between the countries will often reflect a risk premium, with the weaker country having higher interest rates.

Interest rate differentials between countries can also reflect differences in economic growth, monetary policy, and fiscal policy.

LOS 15.m

Emerging market risks stem from unstable political and social systems and heavy infrastructure investments financed by foreign borrowing. Investors should answer six questions before investing in these markets:

1. Does the country have responsible fiscal and monetary policies? This is determined by examining the deficit to GDP ratio.

2. What is the expected growth? Should be at least 4%.

3. Does the country have reasonable currency values and current account deficits? A volatile currency discourages needed foreign investment, and an overvalued currency encourages excessive government borrowing.

4. Is the country too highly levered? Too much debt can lead to a financial crisis if foreign capital flees the country.

5. What is the level of foreign exchange reserves relative to short-term debt? Many emerging country loans must be paid back in a foreign currency.

6. What is the government's stance regarding structural reform? A supportive government makes the investment environment more hospitable.

LOS 15.n

Econometric analysis utilizes economic theory to formulate the forecasting model. The models range from being quite simple to very complex, involving several data items of various time period lags to predict the future.

Economic indicators attempt to characterize an economy's phase in the business cycle and are separated into lagging indicators, coincident indicators, and leading indicators. Analysts prefer leading indicators because they help predict the future path of the economy.

In a checklist approach, the analyst checks off a list of questions that should indicate the future growth of the economy. Given the answers to these questions, the analyst can then use his judgment to formulate a forecast or derive a more formal model using statistics.

LOS 15.o

Investors ultimately use capital market expectations to form their beliefs about the attractiveness of different investments. Following are examples of how specific information can be used to forecast asset class returns.

- If a cash manager thought that interest rates were set to rise, she would shift to short-term cash instruments.
- A change in short-term rates has unpredictable effects for the yields on long-term bonds.
- During a recession, the risk premium on credit risky bonds increases.
- Most emerging market debt is denominated in a non-domestic currency, which increases its default risk.
- The yields for inflation-indexed bonds will fall if inflation increases.
- In the early expansion phase of the business cycle, stock prices are increasing. Later in the expansion, earnings growth and stock returns slow.
- The returns for emerging market stocks are affected by business cycles in the developed world.
- Interest rates affect real estate returns through both the supply and demand as well as the capitalization rate used to discount cash flows.

LOS 15.p

When the government promotes competition in the marketplace, the efficiency of the economy increases, likely leading to higher long-term growth in the economy and the stock market.

Shorter-term growth is affected by the business cycle. In a recession, sales and earnings decrease. Non-cyclical or defensive stocks are less affected by the business cycle and thus will have lower risk premiums and higher valuations than cyclical stocks. Cyclical stocks are characterized by high business risk and/or high fixed costs.

LOS 15.q

- The relative form of purchasing power parity (PPP) states that differences in inflation between two countries will be reflected in changes in the exchange rate between them. Specifically, the country with higher inflation will see its currency value decline.
- The relative economic strength approach: The idea behind this approach is that a favorable investment climate will attract investors, which will increase the demand for the domestic currency, therefore increasing its value.
- The capital flows approach focuses primarily on long-term capital flows such as those into equity investments or foreign direct investments.
- The savings-investment imbalances approach starts with the concept that an economy must fund investment through savings. If investment is greater than domestic savings, then capital must flow into the country from abroad to finance the investment.

LOS 15.r

Be able to discuss how the relationships covered in the previous LOS can be used in assessing relative attractiveness of asset classes (i.e., using historically based estimates of expected return and risk, Singer-Terhar, phases of the business cycle, and the Taylor rule).

CONCEPT CHECKERS

1.   An analyst uses a variety of valuation approaches for different asset classes and collects the necessary data from multiple sources. The analyst does not make any effort to systematically compare the data used. As a result, the analyst uses relatively low discount rates for equity analysis (overestimating theoretical value) and high discount rates for fixed income (underestimating theoretical value). **Discuss** the likely effect on the analyst's asset allocation recommendations.

2.   An analyst would like to forecast U.S. equity returns. She is considering using either the last 3 years of historical annual returns or the last 50 years of historical annual returns. **Provide** an argument for and against each selection of data length.

3.   An analyst realizes that the variance for an exchange rate tends to persist over a period of time, where high volatility is followed by more high volatility. What statistical tool would the analyst *most likely* use to forecast the variance of the exchange rate?

4. Suppose an analyst is valuing two markets, A and B. What is the equity risk premium for the two markets, their expected returns, and the covariance between them, given the following?

Sharpe ratio of the global portfolio	0.29
Standard deviation of the global portfolio	8.0%
Risk-free rate of return	4.5%
Degree of market integration for Market A	80%
Degree of market integration for Market B	65%
Standard deviation of Market A	18%
Standard deviation of Market B	26%
Correlation of Market A with global portfolio	0.87
Correlation of Market B with global portfolio	0.63
Estimated illiquidity premium for Market A	0.0%
Estimated illiquidity premium for Market B	2.4%

5. Are there any attractive investments during deflationary periods?

6. During an economic expansion, an analyst notices that the budget deficit has been declining. She concludes that the government's fiscal policy has shifted to a more restrictive posture. **Comment** on her conclusion.

©2016 Kaplan, Inc.

7.   **Calculate** the short-term interest rate target given the following information.

Neutral rate	5%
Inflation target	3%
Expected Inflation	6%
GDP long-term trend	3%
Expected GDP	5%

8.   A forecaster notes that the yield curve is steeply upwardly sloping. **Comment** on the likely monetary and fiscal policies in effect and the future of the economy.

9.   An analyst would like to project the long-term growth of the economy. Which of the following would you recommend he focus on: changes in consumer spending or potential changes in tax policy due to a new government coming into office?

10.   An analyst is evaluating an emerging market for potential investment. She notices that the country's current account deficit has been growing. Is this a sign of increasing risk? If so, **explain** why.

11.   An analyst is evaluating two countries. Maldavia has a GDP of $60 billion and has an economy that is dominated by the mining industry. Oceania has a GDP of $1.2 trillion and has an economy that sells a variety of items. He is predicting a global economic slowdown. Which country is at greater risk?

12.   An analyst believes that GDP is best forecast using a system of equations that can capture the fact that GDP is a function of many variables, both current and lagged values. Which economic forecasting method is she *most likely* to use?

13.   At a conference, Larry Timmons states that a pegged exchange rate allows a less developed country to achieve greater currency and economic stability, as well as relatively lower and more stable interest rates, and to pursue the fiscal and economic policies to maximize the country's real economic growth. **Explain** what is correct and incorrect in Timmons's statement.

14.   At the beginning of the fiscal year, Tel-Pal, Inc., stock sells for $75 per share. There are 2,000,000 shares outstanding. An analyst predicts that the annual dividend to be paid in one year will be $3 per share. The expected inflation rate is 3.5%. The firm plans to issue 40,000 new shares over the year. The price-to-earnings ratio is expected to stay the same, and nominal earnings will increase by 6.8%. Based upon these figures, what is the expected return on a share of Tel-Pal, Inc., stock in the next year?

15.   An analyst forecasts the historical covariance of the returns between Tel-Pal, Inc., stock and Int-Pal, Inc., stock to be 1,024. A newly forecasted covariance matrix predicts the covariance will be 784. The analyst weights the historical covariance at 30% and the forecast at 70%. **Calculate** the shrinkage estimate of the covariance.

16. **Explain** why smoothed data may be used for some types of alternative investments and the consequences for the expected return, risk, and correlation to other assets from using such data.

17. An analyst notices that the growth of the national inventory-to-sales ratio has slowed after increasing for several years. **Identify** what this implies for stage of the business cycle and for economic growth. **Explain** how a recent phenomenon has affected the ratio, independent of the business cycle.

18. The phase of the business cycle where we *most likely* expect to observe rising short-term interest rates and flat bond yields is:
    A. late expansion.
    B. initial recovery.
    C. early expansion.

For more questions related to this topic review, log in to your Schweser online account and launch SchweserPro™ QBank; and for video instruction covering each LOS in this topic review, log in to your Schweser online account and launch the OnDemand video lectures, if you have purchased these products.

ANSWERS – CONCEPT CHECKERS

1. The analyst has not been systematic and has used inconsistent assumptions. In this case, the result is overstating the attractiveness of equity and understating the attractiveness of fixed income. The result would be allocating too much to equity.

2. Pro: The recent three-year period is more likely to reflect the current economic and political environment.

   Con: The recent shorter period does not reflect the full course of a business cycle or a variety of possible economic conditions.

   Pro: The longer period is more likely to reflect various economic conditions that can occur.

   Con: The longer period is more likely to be subject to regime change, be nonstationary, and reflect conditions that are no longer relevant.

3. The analyst would most likely forecast the variance using time series analysis. In time series analysis, forecasts are generated using previous values of a variable and previous values of other variables. If an exchange rate exhibits volatility clustering, then its variance will persist for periods of time and can be forecasted using a time series model.

4. First, we calculate the equity risk premium for both markets assuming full integration. Note that for Market B, the illiquidity risk premium is added in:

$$\text{ERP}_i = \rho_{i,M}\sigma_i\left(\frac{\text{ERP}_M}{\sigma_M}\right)$$

$$\text{ERP}_A = 0.87(0.18)0.29 = 4.54\%$$
$$\text{ERP}_B = 0.63(0.26)0.29 + 0.0240 = 7.15\%$$

The equity risk premium for both markets assuming full segmentation is:

$$\text{ERP}_i = \sigma_i\left(\frac{\text{ERP}_M}{\sigma_M}\right)$$

$$\text{ERP}_A = (0.18)0.29 = 5.22\%$$
$$\text{ERP}_B = (0.26)0.29 + 0.0240 = 9.94\%$$

Weighting the integrated and segmented risk premiums by the degree of integration and segmentation in each market:

$$\text{ERP}_A = (0.80 \times 0.0454) + \left[(1-0.80) \times 0.0522\right] = 4.68\%$$
$$\text{ERP}_B = (0.65 \times 0.0715) + \left[(1-0.65) \times 0.0994\right] = 8.13\%$$

The expected return in each market is then:

$$\hat{R}_A = 4.5\% + 4.68\% = 9.18\%$$
$$\hat{R}_B = 4.5\% + 8.13\% = 12.63\%$$

The betas in each market are:

$$\beta_i = \rho_{i,M} \sigma_i / \sigma_M$$

$$\beta_A = (0.87)(18) / 8 = 1.96$$

$$\beta_B = (0.63)(26) / 8 = 2.05$$

The covariance is then:

$$\text{cov}_{i,j} = \beta_i \beta_j \sigma_M^2$$

$$\text{cov}_{A,B} = (1.96)(2.05)(8.0)^2 = 257.15$$

5. Bonds actually perform well during periods of falling inflation or deflation because interest rates are declining. This holds true as long as credit risk does not increase. Equities do poorly in periods of declining inflation or deflation due to declining economic growth and asset prices. Deflation also reduces the value of investments financed with debt, such as real estate, because leverage magnifies losses. Deflation is negative for cash because the return on cash declines to near zero.

6. Her conclusion may not be warranted. In an economic expansion, the budget deficit will decline naturally because tax receipts increase and disbursements to the unemployed decrease. The changes she is observing may be independent of the government's fiscal policy.

   Note that only government-directed changes in fiscal policy influence the growth of the economy. Changes in the deficit that occur naturally over the course of the business cycle are not stimulative or restrictive.

7. $r_{target} = 5.0\% + [0.5 \times (5\% - 3\%) + 0.5 \times (6\% - 3\%)]$

   $\qquad = 5.0\% + [1.0\% + 1.5\%] = 7.5\%$

   In this example, the higher than targeted growth rate and higher than targeted inflation rate argue for a targeted interest rate of 7.5%. This rate hike is intended to slow down the economy and inflation.

8. If the yield curve is steeply upwardly sloping, then it is likely that both fiscal and monetary policies are expansive. The economy is likely to expand in the future.

9. Although consumer spending is the largest component of GDP, it is fairly stable over the business cycle as consumers primarily base spending decisions on more stable, permanent income rather than more volatile, immediate income. Thus, it is likely that the analyst should focus on the potential changes in tax policy. This governmental structural policy has a potentially large impact on the long-run growth rate of an economy.

10. When exports are less than imports, a current account deficit usually results. This can be problematic because the deficit must be financed through external borrowing. If the emerging country becomes overlevered, it may not be able to pay back its foreign debt. A financial crisis may ensue where foreign investors quickly withdraw their capital. These financial crises are accompanied by currency devaluations and declines in emerging market asset values.

11. A global economic slowdown would affect smaller countries with undiversified economies more because economic links are more important for these types of countries. Larger countries with diverse economies are less affected by events in other countries.

12. Econometric analysis would be the best approach to use. It can model the complexities of reality using both current and lagged values. Ordinary least squares regression is most often used, but other statistical methods are also available.

13. Greater currency and economic stability: True. The peg is likely to create a more stable currency that provides confidence for investors and business, both of which promote economic stability. Maintaining the peg prevents excessive money creation, which holds down inflation and also promotes economic stability. The peg is a commitment to follow the policies needed to maintain the value of the currency.

    Relatively lower and more stable interest rates: Partially true (or partially false). Interest rates will be related to but higher than the country to which the currency is pegged. The interest rate premium will reflect the investor's perception of the country's commitment and ability to maintain the peg. If that comes into question, the country will likely have to increase interest rates in order to maintain the currency value. The goal of the peg is lower and more stable rates, but if the peg fails, the opposite can occur.

    Pursue the fiscal and economic policies to maximize the country's real economic growth: False. The country must largely follow the economic policies of the country to which it is pegged. These may or may not be optimal for the country's growth.

14. The equation for expected return on Tel-Pal, Inc., using these inputs is:

$$\hat{R}_T = \frac{Div_1}{P_0} + \text{inflation} + \text{real growth in earnings} - \%\Delta \text{ shares} + \Delta\left(\frac{P}{E}\right)$$

$$\hat{R}_T = \left(\frac{\$3}{\$75} \times 100\right) + 3.5\% + 3.3\% - 2\% + 0$$

$$\hat{R}_T = 8.8\%$$

    The expected return is 8.8%. The expected dividend return is 4%, and the expected percentage increase in the number of shares is 2%. Expected inflation is 3.5%, which should be subtracted from the nominal earnings forecast to get the forecast of real earnings growth.

15. The shrinkage estimate is simply the weighted average of the historical value and the forecasted value. The shrinkage estimate is:

    $856 = 30\% \times 1{,}024 + 70\% \times 784$

16. Some types of alternative investments are not regularly traded, and only infrequent prices (smoothed data) are available.

    This has no systematic effect on the estimated returns, but it makes the calculated standard deviation lower because there are no actual periodic changes in value (there are no prices to examine). The smoothed return data also appears to be less correlated with the more erratic pricing of other asset classes that have and report actual trading prices. The correlation will appear closer to zero.

17. A slowing in the growth of the aggregate inventory-to-sales ratio in an economy is associated with later stages of the business cycle, perhaps late upswing or slowdown. It is likely caused by less business optimism with reductions in production and employment, hence a lower rate of economic growth.

    Business has adopted just-in-time inventory approaches and generally reduced the amount of inventory they hold. As a result, inventory-to-sales ratios have declined in general and are independent of the stage of the business cycle.

18. **C** *Early Expansion*: In this period of the business cycle, we expect to observe rising short-term interest rates and flat or rising bond yields.

    The expectations of short-term and long-term yields for the other phases are listed as follows:

    Late Expansion: Both short-term and long-term rates increasing.

    Initial Recovery: Low or falling short-term rates, and bond yields have bottomed out.

The following is a review of the Economic Concepts for Asset Valuation in Portfolio Management principles designed to address the learning outcome statements set forth by CFA Institute. Cross-Reference to CFA Institute Assigned Reading #16.

EQUITY MARKET VALUATION[1]

EXAM FOCUS

Any of the calculations and approaches in this Topic Assignment are fair game for the exam. Some may be familiar from other levels of the exam and some will be new. The focus will be on formulating capital market expectations for the equity asset class and not on individual security valuation. Also be prepared for conceptual questions regarding implications or drawing conclusions when there is insufficient data for a calculation but sufficient data for a directional conclusion.

COBB-DOUGLAS PRODUCTION FUNCTION

LOS 16.a: Explain the terms of the Cobb-Douglas production function and demonstrate how the function can be used to model growth in real output under the assumption of constant returns to scale.

The **Cobb-Douglas production function (CD)** is used in the neoclassical approach to estimate a country's production function. CD uses the country's labor input and capital stock to estimate the total real economic output. The general form of the function is:

$$Y = AK^{\alpha} L^{\beta}$$

where:
Y = total real economic output
A = total factor productivity (TFP)
K = capital stock
L = labor input
α = output elasticity of K ($0 < \alpha < 1$)
β = output elasticity of L ($\alpha + \beta = 1$)

However, it is more useful in security analysis to rearrange the equation to estimate future economic growth. Applying natural logs, assuming that $\beta = (1 - \alpha)$, and making a few other assumptions, we see the form of the CD that is used to estimate *expected*

---

1. Terminology used throughout this topic review is industry convention as presented in Reading 16 of the 2017 Level III CFA exam curriculum.

changes in real economic output. Each of the inputs, as well as the output, is now stated in terms of growth (i.e., percentage change), a simple linear equation:

$$\frac{\Delta Y}{Y} \cong \frac{\Delta A}{A} + \alpha \frac{\Delta K}{K} + (1-\alpha)\frac{\Delta L}{L}$$

where:

$$\frac{\Delta Y}{Y} = \% \text{ change in real output } (\%\Delta Y)$$

$$\frac{\Delta A}{A} = \% \text{ change in total factor productivity } (\%\Delta TFP)$$

$$\frac{\Delta K}{K} = \% \text{ change in capital stock } (\%\Delta K)$$

$$\frac{\Delta L}{L} = \% \text{ change in labor } (\%\Delta L)$$

Empirical studies also suggest it is reasonable to assume *constant returns to scale*, any given change in capital or labor (for example, from 2% to 3% or 5% to 6%) has a linear effect on output. Constant returns to scale also means TFP can be assumed to be a constant. This is an elaborate way of saying the linear version of Cobb-Douglas produces reasonable results.

Assume both capital and labor increase by 4%, and TFP is 2%. The resulting expected change in real GDP is 6%.

$$\%\Delta Y = \%\Delta TFP + \alpha(\%\Delta K) + (1 - \alpha)\%\Delta L$$
$$= 2\% + \alpha(4\%) + (1 - \alpha)4\% = 6\%$$

More realistic assumptions might have capital and labor grow by different rates. Suppose TFP, capital, and labor increase by 1.7%, –0.5%, and 2.1% respectively, with $\alpha = 0.35$:

$$\%\Delta Y = 1.7\% + 0.35(-0.5\%) + 0.65(2.1\%)$$
$$= 1.7\% + -0.175\% + 1.365\% = 2.89\%$$

Estimating TFP (the Solow Residual)

Percentage changes in capital and labor can be obtained from national accounts, and α and β, the output elasticities of capital and labor, vary from country to country. The change in TFP (i.e., $\%\Delta A$) is the **Solow residual** and can be determined by rearranging the equation:

$$\text{Solow residual} = \%\Delta TFP = \%\Delta Y - \alpha(\%\Delta K) - (1-\alpha)\%\Delta L$$

An economy's TFP can change over time due to the following:

- Changing technology.
- Changing restrictions on capital flows and labor mobility.

- Changing trade restrictions.
- Changing laws.
- Changing division of labor.
- Depleting/discovering natural resources.

Essentially, TFP is the rate of managerial and technological innovation, measuring the ability of an economy to produce more real output for the same inputs of labor and capital.

LOS 16.b: Evaluate the relative importance of growth in total factor productivity, in capital stock, and in labor input given relevant historical data.

Estimating the inputs for CD typically starts with historical data to estimate past values. It is important to select past time periods that are expected to be similar to the future period or otherwise adjust past data to better reflect expected future conditions.

Example: Effects of changing factors on economic growth

Factor	Direction of Factor Change	Consequences for Economic Growth
Savings rate	Increase	Increase as a greater supply of financial capital lowers real interest rates and increases the growth rate of physical capital.
Population growth rate	Increase	Increase as the labor force growth rate increases.
Labor force participation rate	Increase	Increase as the rate of growth in labor can increase independent of the underlying population growth rate.
Environmental, pollution controls, and regulation	Increase	Associated with a one-time decrease in growth and TFP.
Reform measures	Increase	Associated with a one-time increase in growth and TFP.

Miscellaneous other factors can also affect TFP and growth. Those factors include production processes, literacy, and skills of the workforce.

Example: Estimating the change in economic output

While performing an analysis of three economies, an analyst compiled the growth and elasticity data in the following table.

10-Year Forecast (Growth Figures Are Annual Averages)

Country	% Growth in Total Factor Productivity	% Growth in Capital Stock	% Growth in Labor Input	Output Elasticity of Capital (α)
A	1.0	2.0	1.0	0.5
B	2.0	2.5	4.5	0.3
C	3.0	8.0	2.5	0.7

i.   For each economy, **determine** the expected 10-year average annual GDP growth rate.

ii. **Comment** on the three economies.

Answer:

i.   Expected growth in GDP:

$$\%\Delta Y \cong \%\Delta A + \alpha(\%\Delta K) + (1-\alpha)(\%\Delta L)$$

A: $\%\Delta Y = 1.0 + 0.5(2.0) + 0.5(1.0) = 2.50\%$
B: $\%\Delta Y = 2.0 + 0.3(2.5) + 0.7(4.5) = 5.90\%$
C: $\%\Delta Y = 3.0 + 0.7(8.0) + 0.3(2.5) = 9.35\%$

ii. Over the next ten years, economies A, B, and C are expected to experience average annual GDP growth rates of 2.50%, 5.90%, and 9.35%, respectively. The population of Economy A would appear to be close to equilibrium, as it is expected to grow at an average annual rate of only 1%. Together, the lower growth rates in capital, labor, TFP, and output for Economy A suggest it is a large, developed economy.

The workforce growth rate of 4.5% for Country B is relatively high, and Country B gains significantly from growth in the workforce. Increases in the capital stock, on the other hand, have less of an effect on output. The impressive workforce growth rate combined with a modest expected growth in capital stock could indicate a relatively small economy in the early stages of development.

Growth in the workforce of Economy C has slowed. Capital stock, however, is expected to increase significantly over the next ten years. Relative to Economy B, rapidly growing capital stock combined with an ability to translate capital growth into increased economic output (i.e., $\alpha = 0.7$) indicates an economy that is larger, more developed, and faster growing.

LOS 16.c: Demonstrate the use of the Cobb-Douglas production function in obtaining a discounted dividend model estimate of the intrinsic value of an equity market.

LOS 16.d: Critique the use of discounted dividend models and macroeconomic forecasts to estimate the intrinsic value of an equity market.

Cobb-Douglas provides a macroeconomic forecast of the growth rate for the underlying economy and this is the base for estimating cash flow and dividend growth rates for dividend discount models (DDM). There are likely to be significant differences and challenges in applying DDM to developed markets versus less developed and emerging markets.

For **developed markets**, the corporate share of aggregate economic activity and dividend payouts are likely to be relatively stable. Therefore, both dividend and economic growth rates will be closely tied. In addition, long-term trend growth is more stable making the Gordon Growth (single stage) DDM model appropriate. Finally, risk should be more predictable and stable, making the appropriate discount rate more predictable.

For **less developed economies**, the challenges are greater and they make the H-model (two stage growth) DDM a more reasonable approach to valuing such markets. The challenges include:

- Economic data is less available and less reliable.
- The link between economic and corporate cash flow/dividend growth is less direct.
  - Structural and governmental changes can lead to long periods when the growth rates of the two diverge.
- Periods of dramatic change in inflation can disrupt valuation input estimates. As a result:
  - Growth rates can diverges dramatically from historical rates.
  - Estimating suitable discount rates to reflect risk is substantially more difficult.
  - Economies are likely to show more dramatic fluctuation in annual growth.

Gordon Growth Model (GGM) for Mature Economies

$$V_0 = \frac{D_1}{r - \bar{g}} = \frac{D_0(1 + \bar{g})}{r - \bar{g}}$$

H-Model for Emerging Economies

$$V_0 = \frac{D_0}{r - g_L}\left[(1 + g_L) + \frac{N}{2}(g_S - g_L)\right]$$

where:
V_0 = the theoretical fair (intrinsic) value for the market
D_0 = current dividend

r   = the real discount rate

$\bar{g}$ = the real single stage growth rate

g_L = the real long term sustainable (lower) growth rate

g_S = the real shorter term (higher) growth rate

N   = the number of years over which g_S converges in linear fashion to g_L

The preference is to use real (before inflation) rather than nominal values in the models when estimating intrinsic value for markets because:

- Cobb-Douglas is commonly used to estimate the real growth rate.
- Inflation rates fluctuate over time and vary between countries making it easier to compare real data.
- With inflation excluded, real inputs tend to be more stable and thus easier to estimate.

Variations on the DDM approaches:

- To facilitate comparison of results over time and between countries, a common approach is to divide V_0 by E_1 to calculate a justified P/E ratio.
- The GGM can be easily used to solve for either the implied growth rate or r by inserting the actual price of the market (P_0) into the formula and solving for the desired item.
  - If the analyst believes growth will be higher/lower than implied growth, the market is under-/overvalued.
  - When implied r is calculated, it becomes the long-term estimated return that will be earned based on initial market price (if the market is reasonably valued initially). If the analyst believes implied r is higher/lower than appropriate, then the market is under-/overvalued.

Example: Estimating the intrinsic value and justified P/E ratio of a developing equity market

To estimate the intrinsic value of a developing market index using the H-Model, we need the real required return (r = 10%), the current dividend (D_0 = 12), the supernormal rate of growth (g_s = 10.5%), the long-term sustainable rate of growth (g_L = 3%), and the period of time (N = 30) over which the growth rate will decline linearly. Forecasted EPS are 20.30.

Answer:

Justified P/E is based on forecasted EPS:

$$V_0 = \frac{D_0}{r - g_L}\left[(1 + g_L) + \frac{N}{2}(g_S - g_L)\right]$$

$$= \frac{12}{0.10 - 0.03}\left[(1.03) + \frac{30}{2}(0.105 - 0.03)\right] = 369.43$$

$$\frac{P}{E}(\text{justified}) = \frac{369.43}{20.30} = 18.199 = 18.20$$

Example: Estimating the sustainable rate of growth, required return, and intrinsic value of a developed equity market

An analyst has gathered the data in the following table for a large, mature developed market index. The current level of the index is 3,250, and the current dividend is $150.

Long-Term Economic Growth Factors

% Growth in Total Factor Productivity	% Growth in Capital Stock	% Growth in Labor Input	Output Elasticity of Capital (α)	Output Elasticity of Labor ($1 - \alpha$)
1.5	1.5	0.5	0.6	0.4

i.   **Determine** the implied sustainable rate of growth in GDP.
ii. Using the growth rate calculated in *i*, **calculate** the required market return.
iii. The analyst believes a required return of 7.0% is appropriate for this market. Based on the analyst's required return, **calculate** the intrinsic value of the index.

Answer:

i.   Based on the expected long-term rates of change in capital, labor, and total factor productivity, the long-term sustainable growth in GDP is estimated at 2.6%:

$$\%\Delta Y \cong \%\Delta A + \alpha(\%\Delta K) + (1-\alpha)(\%\Delta L) = 1.5 + 0.6(1.5) + 0.4(0.5) = 2.6\%$$

ii. Because this is a mature, developed market, we can use the constant growth dividend discount model, rearranged to solve for *r*, to estimate the market required return:

$$P_0 = \frac{D_1}{r-g} = \frac{D_0(1+g)}{r-g} \Rightarrow r = \frac{D_0(1+g)}{P_0} + g$$

$$r = \frac{150(1+0.026)}{3,250} + 0.026 = \frac{153.90}{3,250} + 0.026 = 0.07335 = 7.3\%$$

iii. Using the current dividend of $150, the long-term sustainable rate of growth of 2.6%, and the analyst's required return of 7.0%, the analyst would estimate the intrinsic value of the index at 3,498:

$$P_0 = \frac{D_1}{r-g} \Rightarrow \frac{153.90}{0.07 - 0.026} \cong 3,498$$

Based on the analyst's estimated required return, the index is undervalued by 3,498 – 3,250 = 248 points or 7.1% below fair value.

LOS 16.e: Contrast top-down and bottom-up approaches to forecasting the earnings per share of an equity market index.

In a **top-down forecast**, the analyst utilizes macroeconomic factors (e.g., interest rate expectations, expected growth in GDP) to estimate the performance of market-wide indicators, such as the S&P 500. Successive steps include identifying sectors in the market that will perform best, given market expectations.

The analyst could start by comparing the relative values of various market composites to their historical patterns to identify any that appear to be under- or over-priced. Next, the analyst could attempt to identify any momentum in the indices. In the final macro-analysis, the analyst compares the expected performance of the indices to general asset classes, such as equities, bonds, and alternatives to identify which class of assets will be expected to under- or out-perform. After selecting asset classes to over- or under-weight, the analyst could move down to sector and security selection if desired.

In a **bottom-up forecast**, the analyst first takes a microeconomic perspective by focusing on the fundamentals of individual firms. The analyst starts the bottom-up analysis by looking at an individual firm's product or service development relative to the rest of the industry. The analyst should assess the firm's management and its willingness and ability to adopt the technology necessary to grow or even maintain its standing in the industry. Given the analyst's expectations for the firm, the analyst uses some form of cash flow analysis to determine the firm's investment potential (i.e., expected return). If desired, the individual security analysis could be aggregated up into sector and asset class returns that could be compared to the top-down estimates.

Which to Use

The method used depends on the analyst's strategy, as well as any portfolio constraints. For example, a manager who focuses on a long-short, market-neutral strategy would probably pursue a purely bottom-up analysis. The manager has little need for aggregating the forecasts for individual securities into industry or market forecasts. Another manager's strategy could focus on allocating among markets or industries. In these cases, there is little need for the top-down manager to go any lower, or the bottom-up manager to go any higher, than the first step.

For the Exam: To determine which approach is better for the manager, you will have to determine the manager's focus. For example, if you encounter a macro hedge fund manager who focuses on optimal allocations of global markets or currencies, a purely top-down approach would be indicated. An active manager who buys and sells individual securities to capture short-term pricing inefficiency should utilize a bottom-up approach.

Estimating Market Earnings Per Share (EPS)

Analysts are sometimes encouraged to confirm market EPS estimates by using both the top-down and bottom-up methods. If the methods yield significantly different estimates, the analyst should analyze both estimates to determine the source(s) of discrepancy. There are two primary reasons why forecasting earnings per share with the two methods can yield different results:

1. *The models used in a top-down analysis.* Econometric models use historical values and variables adjusted to varying degrees by the user, and they suffer from the same weaknesses as all such models. For example, they may be slow in capturing structural changes (i.e., changes in the sensitivities of the individual factors). The model might have worked well in the past, but recent structural changes might have altered the relationships between the independent and dependent variables.

   The models can also be specified incorrectly. Variables in the model that explained behavioral and financial relationships in the past might no longer be appropriate, and/or other variables might be more appropriate.

2. *Manager bias.* A bottom-up analysis is usually based, to a degree, on manager expectations. Because most managers expect their firms to out-perform the industry average, aggregating individual manager expectations can lead to significantly over-estimated industry expectations.

   Also, believing they can hold on longer than other firms as the economy sinks into a recession, individual managers tend to be more optimistic than would be warranted by a top-down model. On the other hand, they will tend to be more pessimistic as the market begins to recover. The potential for these biases must be assessed when the economy is entering or leaving a recession. If there is evidence of significant manager bias, the top-down method might be more appropriate.

> **For the Exam:** The bottom line is that both top-down analysis and bottom-up analysis have strengths and weaknesses. Top-down analysis doesn't incorporate the input of individual managers, while individual managers tend to be overly optimistic about their firm's future. Be able to recognize the deficiencies of each method and discuss the implications.

RELATIVE EQUITY MARKET VALUATION

LOS 16.f: Discuss the strengths and limitations of relative valuation models.

LOS 16.g: Judge whether an equity market is under-, fairly, or over-valued using a relative equity valuation model.

Relative value models use the relative values of assets and markets to identify investment opportunities. In the following material, we will discuss three relative value models: (1) the Fed model, (2) the Yardeni model, and (3) the 10-year Moving Average Price/

Earnings model. These models are used to assess the relative attractiveness of stocks versus bonds.

The **Fed model** assumes that the expected operating earnings yield on the S&P 500 (i.e., expected aggregate operating earnings divided by the current index level) should be the same as the yield on long-term U.S. Treasuries:

$$\text{Fed model ratio} = \frac{\text{S\&P earnings yield}}{\text{10-year Treasury yield}}$$

If the S&P 500 earnings yield is higher than the Treasury yield, the interpretation is that the index value is too low relative to earnings. Equities are undervalued and should increase in value. Likewise, if the earnings yield is lower than the Treasury yield, the index is considered too high for the level of earnings. Equities are over-valued and should fall.

There are three basic criticisms of the Fed model, based on implied assumptions regarding risk, growth, and inflation.

The Fed model does the following:

1. *Ignores the equity risk premium.* Assuming the yield on treasuries is the same as the earnings yield on the S&P ignores the inherent risk of equities.

2. *Ignores earnings growth.* Growth expectations affect earnings, but Treasury yields have no growth components. By assuming the yield on a Treasury should be the same as corporate earnings yield, the model implicitly assumes zero growth in earnings.

3. *Compares a real variable to a nominal variable.* Earnings yield is considered a real variable because the future level of earnings is not fixed and in the long run tends to adjust upward with inflation. A stock investor tends to benefit from rising future inflation compared to a bond investor. In contrast, the Treasury yield is a nominal rate. The build up model of interest rates decomposes the stated nominal yield into a real rate and expected future inflation. From the investor's perspective, once a bond is purchased the cash flows are fixed and do not adjust for the actual future course of inflation.

Although flawed, the Fed model is used by analysts in a type of spread analysis. Rather than assume the two yields should be equal, as in the model, analysts watch the *ratio* of the earnings and Treasury yields. When the ratio is above its long-term average, the difference between the earnings yield and Treasury yield (the spread) is historically high. Equity prices would be expected to increase, lowering the earnings yield and, thus, the ratio of the two yields (i.e., the yield spread would narrow).

> **For the Exam:** If asked to list criticisms of the Fed model, mention that it:
> *   Does not consider the equity risk premium.
> *   Ignores growth in earnings.
> *   Compares a real variable (index level) to a nominal variable (Treasury yield).

The Yardeni Model

The **Yardeni model** for estimating the equilibrium earnings yield (i.e., the fair earnings yield) is based on a variation of the constant growth dividend discount model (CGM), in which investors value total earnings rather than dividends:

$$P_0 = \frac{E_1}{r-g}$$

We can restate the CGM to show that the earnings yield must be the difference between the required return on equity and expected long-term growth. This is logical, because we assume the total return on equity, r, must be the sum of the earnings yield, E_1 / P_0, and growth (i.e., capital gains), g:

$$P_0 = \frac{E_1}{r-g} \;\Rightarrow\; r = \frac{E_1}{P_0}+g \;\Rightarrow\; \frac{E_1}{P_0} = r-g$$

Yardeni incorporates risk into his model by using the yield on A-rated corporate bonds, Y_B, as the required return on equity, r. The difference between the yields on A-rated corporates and risk-free treasuries serves as a proxy, although most likely understated, for the equity risk premium. Also, instead of the long-term growth assumed in the CGM, Yardeni uses a 5-year growth forecast, LTEG,[2] for the S&P 500. The model becomes:

$$\frac{E_1}{P_0} = Y_B - d(LTEG)$$

where:

$\dfrac{E_1}{P_0}$　　　　　= expected market (e.g., S&P) earnings yield

Y_B　　　　　= yield on A-rated corporate bonds

d　　　　　= weighting factor for the importance of earnings growth; historically around 0.10

$Y_B - d(LTEG)$ = Yardeni earnings yield

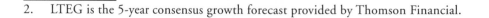

Professor's Note: Yardeni uses the yield on A-rated corporates. Viewed from the perspective of a build up model, this would include the risk-free rate plus a default premium. Effectively, the default premium is approximating the equity risk premium. Then, to account for the fact that the earnings yield on the left-hand side of the equation ignores growth, he subtracts a growth factor.

The terms P_0 and V_0 are not used consistently in this reading. Whenever one of the models discussed is used to solve for P_0 or P/E or E/P, the model is solving for the theoretical fair value of that item.

2.　LTEG is the 5-year consensus growth forecast provided by Thomson Financial.

The earnings yield from the Yardeni model is compared to the market earnings yield. If the market yield is high compared to the Yardeni earnings yield, equities are under-priced. Equities would be expected to rise in value, reducing the market earnings yield.

$$\text{if } \frac{E_1}{P_0} - \left[Y_B - d(LTEG)\right] > 0 \Rightarrow \text{market is undervalued}$$

$$\text{if } \frac{E_1}{P_0} - \left[Y_B - d(LTEG)\right] < 0 \Rightarrow \text{market is overvalued}$$

Like the Fed model, the Yardeni model can be applied as a ratio:

$$\text{if } \frac{E_1}{P_0} - \left[Y_B - d(LTEG)\right] > 0 \Rightarrow \frac{\text{earnings yield}}{Y_B - d(LTEG)} > 1.0 \Rightarrow \text{market is undervalued}$$

$$\text{if } \frac{E_1}{P_0} - \left[Y_B - d(LTEG)\right] < 0 \Rightarrow \frac{\text{earnings yield}}{Y_B - d(LTEG)} < 1.0 \Rightarrow \text{market is overvalued}$$

The Yardeni model can also be used to estimate a fair value for the equity market. If we rearrange the model to solve for P_0, it starts to look like the traditional CGM with Y_B in place of the required return and $d(LTEG)$ in place of g:

$$\frac{E_1}{P_0} = Y_B - d(LTEG) \Rightarrow V_0 = \frac{E_1}{Y_B - d(LTEG)}$$

Example: Using the Yardeni Model

i.   Assume the long-term (5-year) growth forecast is 9.85% and d = 0.10. If A-rated corporate bonds yield 6%, **determine** the fair earnings yield.

ii. If the current earnings yield implied by the equity index and projected forward earnings is 5.5%, **determine** whether equities are over- or undervalued.

iii. Using the Yardeni model, **calculate** a fair value of the market P/E ratio.

Answer:

i.
$$\frac{E_1}{P_0} = Y_B - d(LTEG)$$
$$= 0.06 - 0.10(0.0985) = 0.05015 = 5.015\%$$

ii. The fair earnings yield predicted by the Yardeni model is about 5%. If the current market earnings yield is 5.5%, this would imply that the value of the index is too low compared to projected earnings. According to the Yardeni model the market is *undervalued*.

iii. The Yardeni model calculates the fair earnings ratio, which is the ratio of earnings to price. To convert the earnings ratio to a P/E ratio, we simply invert it:

$$\frac{E_1}{P_0} = 0.05015 \ \Rightarrow \ \frac{P_0}{E_1} = \frac{1}{0.05015} = 19.94$$

For the Exam: When answering questions about the Yardeni model, important considerations include the following:

• It incorporates a proxy for the equity market risk premium (the yield on A-rated corporate debt).
• The risk premium used is actually a measure of default risk, not a true measure of equity risk.
• It relies on an estimate of the value investors place on earnings growth (*d*), which is assumed to be constant over time.
• The growth rate used in the model (LTEG) might not be an accurate estimate of long-term sustainable growth.

10-Year Moving Average Price/Earnings Ratio, P/10-Year MA(E)

The numerator of the **P/10-year MA(E)** is the market price of the S&P 500 price index, and the denominator is the average of the previous ten years' reported real earnings. Both the numerator and denominator are adjusted for inflation using the consumer price index. Similar to a trailing P/E ratio, the P/10-year MA(E) compares the inflation adjusted price of the market at a point in time to the market's average real earnings over the previous ten years.

To use the P/10-year MA(E) the analyst compares its current value to its historical average to determine whether the market is over- or underpriced. If the ratio currently stands at 18.0, and the historical average is 16.0, for example, the current price (i.e., level of the index) is high relative to earnings. The index would be considered over-priced and would be expected to revert to its historical mean of 16.

Professor's Note: Real simply means restating the price or earnings in today's dollars. For example, you could restate earnings from past years in real terms by multiplying the earnings figure by the ratio of today's CPI to the relevant year CPI. Assume earnings per share for 2008 were $3.00, and you wish to restate them as of June 2010 (i.e., restate them in June 2010 dollars). You would multiply December 2008 EPS by the ratio of 217.965 to 210.228, the CPIs for June 2010 and December 2008, respectively.

$$restated\ 2008\ earnings = nominal\ 2008\ earnings \times inflation\ adjustment\ factor$$

$$= nominal\ 2008\ earnings \times \left(\frac{CPI_{6/2010}}{CPI_{12/2008}} \right)$$

$$= \$3.00 \times \left(\frac{217.965}{210.228} \right) = \$3.00 \times 1.036803 = \$3.11$$

When you restate values at a later date (bring them forward in time), the ratio of CPIs will be greater than 1.0 so that the value increases. To restate them in a previous year (take them back in time), the ratio of the CPIs will be less than 1.0, and the value decreases, assuming a positive inflation rate.

For the Exam: When answering questions about the P/10-year MA(E), important considerations include:

- By restating earnings and prices according to CPI, it considers the effects of inflation.
- By using 10-year average earnings, it captures the effects of business cycles, but by its nature it is backward-looking—current or expected earnings could provide more useful information.
- It does not consider the effects of changes in accounting rules or methods.
- Empirical studies have found that very high or low P/10-year MA(E) ratios have persisted, limiting its usefulness in forming short-run expectations.

Asset-Based Models

Tobin's q compares the current market value of a company to the replacement cost of its assets. The theoretical value of Tobin's q is 1.0. If the current Tobin's q is above (below) 1.0 the firm's stock is presumed to be overpriced (underpriced).

The **equity q** focuses directly on equity values. It compares the aggregate market value of the firm's equity to the replacement value of the firm's net worth (i.e., net assets). Again, the neutral value of the ratio is 1.0.

Both ratios are considered *mean-reverting*. A q value for either above 1.0 would be expected to fall as the overvalued stock price declines. Using the opposite argument, a value less than 1.0 suggests the undervalued stock should rise.

$$\text{Tobin's q} = \frac{\text{asset market value}}{\text{asset replacement cost}} = \frac{\text{market value of debt + equity}}{\text{asset replacement cost}}$$

$$\text{equity q} = \frac{\text{market value of equity}}{\text{replacement value of net worth}} = \frac{\text{\# outstanding shares} \times \text{price per share}}{\text{replacement value of assets} - \text{liabilities}}$$

Both ratios have some long term value as indicators. However, it is difficult to estimate replacement values and high or low q ratios can persist for long periods of time; in other words, the expected stock price correction may not quickly occur.

KEY CONCEPTS

LOS 16.a

The Cobb-Douglas function (CD) relates real economic output to capital stock and labor as well as factor productivity:

$$Y = AK^\alpha L^\beta$$

By applying natural logs and making other assumptions, it can be restated to predict changes in output:

$$\frac{\Delta Y}{Y} \cong \frac{\Delta A}{A} + \alpha \frac{\Delta K}{K} + (1 - \alpha)\frac{\Delta L}{L}$$

$$\text{Solow residual} = \Delta TFP = \frac{\Delta A}{A} \cong \frac{\Delta Y}{Y} - \alpha \frac{\Delta K}{K} - (1 - \alpha)\frac{\Delta L}{L}$$

where:
A = total factor productivity (TFP)
K = capital stock
L = labor input
α = output elasticity of K; the change in Y for a 1-unit change in K ($0 < \alpha < 1$)
β = output elasticity of L; the change in Y for a 1-unit change in L ($\alpha + \beta = 1$)

LOS 16.b

Once we have estimated the growth equation, $\%\Delta Y = \%\Delta A + \alpha\ \%\Delta K + (1 - \alpha)\ \%\Delta L$, we can use the historical growth of capital and labor, along with the estimates of output elasticities for labor and capital, to decompose the growth of GDP in order to evaluate the relative effects of labor growth, capital accumulation, and increases in factor productivity on economic growth.

LOS 16.c,d

We assume the growth rate in corporate earnings and dividends is the same as the growth rate in gross domestic product (GDP). If an economy is expected to grow at a particularly high rate of growth for a number of years and then revert to a sustainable growth rate, we apply the H-model:

$$V_0 = \frac{D_0}{r - g_L}\left[(1 + g_L) + \frac{N}{2}(g_S - g_L)\right]$$

When growth is assumed constant, we can use the constant growth dividend discount model:

$$V_0 = \frac{D_1}{r - \bar{g}} = \frac{D_0(1 + \bar{g})}{r - \bar{g}}$$

LOS 16.e

In a top-down forecast, the analyst utilizes macroeconomic factors to estimate the performance of market-wide indicators. Successive steps include identifying sectors in the market and then individual securities that will perform best, given market expectations.

In a bottom-up forecast, the analyst first takes a microeconomic perspective by focusing on the fundamentals of individual firms. For a macro forecast, the analyst can then aggregate the expected performance of individual securities.

To determine which to use, determine the manager's focus. For example, a macro hedge fund manager who focuses on optimal allocations of global markets or currencies would use a purely top-down approach. An active manager who buys and sells individual securities to capture short-term pricing inefficiency would utilize a bottom-up approach.

LOS 16.f,g

The Fed model assumes the yield on long-term U.S. Treasuries should be the same as the expected operating earnings yield on the S&P 500. When the S&P 500 earnings yield is higher (lower) than the Treasury yield, the interpretation is that the index is too low (high).

The Fed model:
- Does not consider the equity risk premium.
- Ignores growth in earnings.
- Compares a real variable (index level) to a nominal variable (Treasury yield).

The Yardeni model assumes investors value total earnings rather than dividends:

$$P_0 = \frac{E_1}{r - g} \Rightarrow \frac{E_1}{P_0} = Y_B - d(LTEG)$$

Important considerations include:
- It uses the yield on A-rated corporate debt as the equity risk premium.
- The risk premium used is actually a measure of default risk, not a true measure of equity risk.
- It relies on an estimate of the value investors place on earnings growth (*d*), which is assumed to be constant over time.
- The growth rate used in the model (LTEG) might not be a fair estimate of long-term sustainable growth.

P/10-year MA(E): The numerator is the value of the price index, and the denominator is the average of the previous ten years' reported earnings. Both are adjusted for inflation using the consumer price index.

Important considerations include:
- It considers the effects of inflation.
- It captures the effects of business cycles.
- Current or expected earnings could provide more useful information.
- It does not consider the effects of changes in accounting rules or methods.
- Very high or low P/10-year MA(E) ratios can persist, limiting its usefulness in forming short-run expectations.

$$\text{Tobin's q} = \frac{\text{market value of debt } + \text{ equity}}{\text{asset replacement cost}}$$

$$\text{equity q} = \frac{\text{market value of equity}}{\text{replacement value of assets} - \text{liabilities}}$$

Important considerations include:
- Both ratios are mean-reverting.
- Both have demonstrated a negative relationship with equity returns.
- Replacement costs can be difficult to estimate.
- Very high or low ratios can persist, limiting their usefulness in forming short-run expectations.

CONCEPT CHECKERS

1. While analyzing potential global investments, Gretchen Fenledder, CFA, gathered the data in Table A on emerging Equity Market Index Y:

    Table A: Economic Data for Index Y*

Last dividend (D_0)	150
Forecast earnings per share	600
Current and sustainable long-term growth rate	2.5%
Required return	8.5%
Forward operating yield (E/P)	6.0%

    * Yield on 10-year government bond = 6%

    Based on the data in Table A:
    a. **Determine** the intrinsic price level of the index.
    b. **Determine** whether the market is over- or under-valued using the Fed model.

2. Fenledder also gathered data for Equity Market Index Z as shown in Table B:

    Table B: Economic Data for Equity Market Index Z

Expected growth in total factor productivity	1.5%
Expected growth in labor	3.0%
Expected growth in capital stock, $\alpha = 0.6$	2.2%

    a. **Explain** each of the terms in the Cobb-Douglas production function (CD) as it is used to forecast economic growth.
    b. **Calculate** the implied growth (percentage change) for Market Z using the data in Table B.
    c. **Explain** the Solow residual and **state** three factors that would likely produce a long-term change in its value.

3. **Describe** top-down and bottom-up economic analysis. **Explain** the situations that would imply either a top-down or a bottom-up analysis would be more appropriate and when the use of both would be justified.

4. **Compare** Tobin's q and the equity q for market valuation. **Provide** and **explain** one strength and one weakness of each.

5. **Explain** three weaknesses of the Fed model.

6. **Describe** the Yardeni model. Referring to specific variables in each, **explain** how the Yardeni and Fed models could arrive at different conclusions about the relative value of an equity market.

7. In the template provided, **indicate** and **explain** the effect on the growth of an economy, given the indicated change in the following growth factors:
    i.   Slowing growth of the population.
    ii. Decrease in the government-mandated retirement age.
    iii. Relaxation of import duties and other trade restrictions.
    iv. Tax relief to encourage technological innovation.

Template for Question 7:

Factor	Effect on Economic Growth (circle one)	Explanation
i. Slowing growth of the population.	Increase Decrease	
ii. Decrease in the government-mandated retirement age.	Increase Decrease	
iii. Relaxation of import duties and other trade restrictions.	Increase Decrease	
iv. Corporate tax relief to encourage technological innovation.	Increase Decrease	

8.   In the template provided, **determine** whether a top-down or bottom-up forecast would be better indicated for each scenario. **Justify** your selection.

Template for Question 8:

Scenario	Top-Down or Bottom-Up (circle one)	Justification
A global macro-hedge fund takes large positions in foreign currencies.	Top-down Bottom-up	
Portfolio manager Active A employs a market neutral strategy and adds market exposure with equity futures.	Top-down Bottom-up	
Active Investors, LLP, advertises that they earn alpha through stock selection.	Top-down Bottom-up	

For more questions related to this topic review, log in to your Schweser online account and launch SchweserPro™ QBank; and for video instruction covering each LOS in this topic review, log in to your Schweser online account and launch the OnDemand video lectures, if you have purchased these products.

ANSWERS – CONCEPT CHECKERS

1.

Last dividend (D_0)	150
Current and sustainable long-term growth rate	2.5%
Required return	8.5%
Forward operating yield (E/P)	6.0%

* Yield on 10-year government bond = 6%

a.   We are provided with the long-term sustainable growth rate, the required return, and the current dividend, so we know to use the constant growth dividend discount model to determine the intrinsic value of the index:

$$P_0 = \frac{D_1}{r-g} = \frac{D_0(1+g)}{r-g} = \frac{150(1.025)}{0.085-0.025} = \frac{153.75}{0.06} = 2,562.50$$

b.   The Fed model compares the operating yield on the index to the yield in the intermediate-term government bond:

Fed model ratio = earnings yield / government yield = 0.06 / 0.06 = 1.0

Based on expected earnings, the market appears to be correctly priced.

If the Fed model produces a ratio greater than 1.0, the earnings yield is considered too high (earnings are high relative to prices), indicating that the market is currently under-valued and would be expected to rise. If the ratio is less than 1.0, the earnings yield is too low, and the market is deemed to be over-valued.

2.   a.

$$\frac{\Delta Y}{Y} \cong \frac{\Delta A}{A} + \alpha \frac{\Delta K}{K} + (1-\alpha)\frac{\Delta L}{L}$$

$\frac{\Delta Y}{Y}$ = % change in real output ($\%\Delta Y$): growth in GDP

$\frac{\Delta A}{A}$ = % change in total factor productivity ($\%\Delta TFP$)

$\frac{\Delta K}{K}$ = % change in capital stock ($\%\Delta K$)

$\frac{\Delta L}{L}$ = % change in labor ($\%\Delta L$)

α and $(1 - \alpha)$ are the weights for capital and labor in the economy.

b.

Expected growth in total factor productivity	1.5%
Expected growth in labor	3.0%
Expected growth in capital stock, $\alpha = 0.6$	2.2%

$$\frac{\Delta Y}{Y} \cong \frac{\Delta A}{A} + \alpha \frac{\Delta K}{K} + (1-\alpha)\frac{\Delta L}{L}$$

$$\frac{\Delta Y}{Y} \cong 1.5\% + 0.6(2.2\%) + 0.4(3.0\%) = 4.02\%$$

c.   The Solow residual refers to using Cobb-Douglas and historical or estimated change in the real economic output, expected changes in labor and capital, and the economy's elasticities of capital and labor to then solve for TFP. It is useful because it is difficult to otherwise estimate TFP.

An economy's TFP can change over time due to the following factors:
1.   Better technology improves TFP.
2.   More restrictions on capital flows and labor mobility reduce TFP.
3.   More trade restrictions reduce TFP.
4.   Changing laws that impose costs or increase uncertainty reduce TFP.
5.   Ineffient division of labor reduces TFP.
6.   Depleting/discovering natural resources reduces/increases TFP.

3.   In a top-down forecast, the analyst utilizes macroeconomic factors to estimate the performance of market-wide indicators, such as the S&P 500. Successive steps include identifying sectors in the market that will perform best given market expectations.

The analyst starts by comparing the relative values of various market composites to their historical patterns to identify any that appear to be under- or over-priced. Next, the analyst attempts to identify any momentum in the indices. In the final macro-analysis, the analyst compares the expected performance of the indices to general asset classes, such as equities, bonds, and alternatives to identify which class of assets will be expected to under- or out-perform.

In a bottom-up forecast, the analyst takes a microeconomic perspective by focusing on the fundamentals of individual firms. The analyst starts the bottom-up analysis by looking at an individual firm's product or service development relative to the rest of the industry. The analyst should assess the firm's management and its willingness and ability to adopt the technology necessary to grow or even maintain its standing in the industry. Given the analyst's expectations for the firm, the analyst uses some form of cash flow analysis to determine the firm's investment potential (i.e., expected return).

The method used depends on the analyst's strategy. A manager who utilizes a long-short, market neutral strategy would probably pursue a purely bottom-up analysis. Another manager's strategy could focus on allocating among markets or industries. In these cases, there is little need for the top-down manager to go any lower or the bottom-up manager to go any higher than the first step.

When approaching or leaving recessions, manager expectations can be biased. It would be wise in these situations for the bottom-up analyst to also utilize a top-down approach to confirm earnings estimates.

4.   Tobin's q compares the current market value of a company to the replacement cost of its assets. The theoretical value of Tobin's q is 1.0. If the current Tobin's q is above (below) 1.0, the firm's stock is presumed to be overpriced (underpriced).

The equity q compares the current market value of the firm's equity to the replacement value of the firm's net worth (i.e., net assets). Again, the expected value of the ratio is 1.0.

Both ratios are considered *mean-reverting*. With a q value above 1.0, stock price should fall and below 1.0, stock price should rise.

$$\text{Tobin's q} = \frac{\text{asset market value}}{\text{asset replacement cost}} = \frac{\text{market value of debt} + \text{equity}}{\text{asset replacement cost}}$$

$$\text{equity q} = \frac{\text{market value of equity}}{\text{replacement value of net worth}} = \frac{\text{\# outstanding shares} \times \text{price per share}}{\text{replacement value of assets} - \text{liabilities}}$$

Strengths of both models include:
- Both are mean-reverting, so they are easy to use.
- Both have usefulness as demonstrated by a negative relationship with equity returns. Higher (lower) ratios have forecasted lower (higher) equity returns.

Weaknesses include:
- Replacement costs can be difficult to estimate.
- Empirical studies have found that very high or low ratios have persisted for both, limiting their usefulness in forming short-run expectations.

5.   The Fed model does not consider the equity risk premium, it ignores growth in earnings, and it compares a real variable (index level) to a nominal variable (Treasury yield).

Ignores growth in earnings: It compares the earnings yield on the market index (only a portion of the total return on the index) to the total expected return on the Treasury security. It does not include the growth portion of the expected index return.

Real and nominal variables: The yield on the Treasury security includes an inflation premium while earnings are considered a real variable.

6.   The Yardeni model is based on the constant growth dividend discount model (CGM), stated in terms of earnings rather than dividends:

$$P_0 = \frac{E_1}{r - g}$$

The earnings yield must be the difference between the required return on equity and expected long-term growth:

$$P_0 = \frac{E_1}{r - g} \;\Rightarrow\; r = \frac{E_1}{P_0} + g \;\Rightarrow\; \frac{E_1}{P_0} = r - g$$

The model uses the yield on A-rated corporate bonds as the required return on equity. Instead of the long-term growth assumed in the CGM, Yardeni uses a 5-year growth forecast for the S&P 500.

$$\frac{E_1}{P_0} = Y_B - d(LTEG)$$

where:
Y_B = yield on A-rated corporate bonds
d = a weighting factor for the importance of earnings growth; historically around 0.10

If the current market earnings yield is high compared to the Yardeni earnings yield, equities are under-priced. Equities would be expected to rise in value:

$$\text{if } \frac{E_1}{P_0} - \left[Y_B - d(LTEG)\right] > 0 \Rightarrow \text{market is under-valued}$$

$$\text{if } \frac{E_1}{P_0} - \left[Y_B - d(LTEG)\right] < 0 \Rightarrow \text{market is over-valued}$$

The Fed model assumes the expected operating earnings yield on the S&P 500 should be same as the yield on long-term U.S. Treasuries:

$$\text{Fed model ratio} = \frac{\text{S\&P earnings yield}}{\text{Treasury yield}}$$

If the S&P 500 earnings yield is higher than the Treasury yield, the index value is low relative to earnings, and the market should increase in value. If the S&P 500 earnings yield is lower than the Treasury yield, the index value is high relative to earnings, and the market should drop in value.

In order to discuss circumstances where the two could yield different conclusions about market valuation, we reproduce them as ratios and see that both contain the expected S&P earnings yield in the numerator:

$$\text{Fed model ratio} = \frac{\text{S\&P earnings yield}}{\text{Treasury yield}}$$

$$\text{Yardeni ratio} = \frac{\text{S\&P earnings yield}}{Y_B - d(LTEG)}$$

In situations where $[Y_B - d(LTEG)]$ is dramatically different from the Treasury yield, the two ratios can yield conflicting conclusions. For example, Y_B might be historically high while interest rates are historically low (i.e., interest rates are low but risk aversion is high, making the risk premium on A-rated bonds high). In that case, the resulting Yardeni ratio could be less than 1.0 (indicating the market is over-valued) while the Fed model is greater than 1.0 (indicating the market is under-valued).

7.

Factor	Effect on Economic Growth (circle one)	Explanation
i. Slowing growth of the population.	Decrease	Increase in labor input slowing.
ii. Decrease in the government-mandated retirement age.	Decrease	Assuming it induces individuals to retire earlier, reduction in labor input.
iii. Relaxation of import duties and other trade restrictions.	Increase	Increased international competition; falling prices.
iv. Corporate tax relief to encourage technological innovation.	Increase	Short-term depression on growth with increased costs and retooling but increased in long-run due to technological improvements.

8.

Scenario	Top-Down or Bottom-Up (circle one)	Justification
A global macro-hedge fund takes large positions in foreign currencies.	Top-down	With their focus on the relative values of global currencies, there is no need for the hedge fund to focus on individual firms.
Portfolio manager Active A employs a market neutral strategy and adds market exposure with equity futures.	Bottom-up	Active A's primary strategy is market neutral. They generate alpha by going long and short in individual stocks expected to out- or under-perform in weights that will drive the ultimate market exposure (systematic risk) to zero. The selection of equity futures is a passive approach to adding market exposure.
Active Investors, LLP, advertises that they earn alpha through stock selection.	Bottom-up	Stock selection represents the stereotypical bottom-up approach. Because they generate alpha through stock selection, the focus is on the valuation of individual stocks, not macro-wide indices or factors.

You have now finished the Economic Analysis topic area. To get immediate feedback on how effective your study has been for this material, log in to your Schweser online account and take the self-test for this topic area. Questions are more exam-like than typical Concept Checkers or QBank questions; a score of less than 70% indicates that your study likely needs improvement. These tests are timed and allow three minutes per question.

ASSET ALLOCATION

EXAM FOCUS

This assignment returns to the earlier topic of strategic asset allocation (SAA) and explores six approaches to SAA. Some of the approaches are highly mathematical and discussed in concept only. In other cases, the math is illustrated and testable. Before moving into the discussion of the approaches to strategic asset allocation, a variety of related and often previously covered topics are discussed. The section on what constitutes an asset class, when an asset class will add value to the portfolio, and issues associated with international investments deserve some attention.

The mean-variance approach to SAA has been taught at Levels I and II; be familiar with it. The basics are reviewed again and the practical use of corner portfolios is added as a realistic way to simplify the math and construct a close approximation of the efficient frontier (EF). Know the math for corner portfolios. The last approach to SAA covered is the experience-based approach, which is just another name for the process of elimination covered in earlier sessions on the IPS. The assignment concludes with an introductory discussion of tactical asset allocation (TAA). TAA will be covered in more detail in later sessions.

Grasp the basics and the concept of the six approaches to SAA, how they differ, and the pros and cons, plus any math for mean-variance and corner portfolios. The experience-based approach has been frequently tested as part of an IPS question. Be prepared.

Note: The assigned material is quite explicit that the computer-based approaches are available through commercially available software packages. Do not try and learn details that are not covered in the material. If you want to pursue some of these for personal interest after the exam, a Google search is a good starting point.

STRATEGIC ASSET ALLOCATION

LOS 17.a: Explain the function of strategic asset allocation in portfolio management and discuss its role in relation to specifying and controlling the investor's exposures to systematic risk.

Strategic asset allocation combines capital market expectations (expected return, standard deviation, and correlation) with the investor's risk, return, and investment constraints (from the IPS). Strategic asset allocation is long term in nature, and the weights are called *targets* and the portfolio represented by the strategic asset allocation is a *policy portfolio*, or *target portfolio* or *benchmark*.

Each asset class has its own quantifiable systematic risk, and strategic asset allocation is a conscious effort to gain the desired exposure to systematic risk via specific weights to individual asset classes. Each asset class represents relatively similar investments (e.g., long-term corporate bonds) with similar systematic risk factors. Exposure to specific asset classes in specific proportions enables portfolio managers to effectively monitor and control their systematic risk exposure. In other words, strategic asset allocation reflects the investor's desired systematic risk exposure.

TACTICAL ASSET ALLOCATION

LOS 17.b: Compare strategic and tactical asset allocation.

Tactical asset allocation is the result of active management wherein managers deviate from the strategic asset allocation to take advantage of any perceived *short-term* opportunities in the market. Hence, tactical asset allocation introduces additional risk, which should be justified by additional return, often called alpha.

LOS 17.c: Discuss the importance of asset allocation for portfolio performance.

Asset allocation is performed as two distinct processes: (1) strategic and (2) tactical asset allocation. The first, strategic allocation, responds to the interaction of the investor's long-term strategic (policy) needs and long-run capital market expectations. The allocation itself is typically specified in a range of percentages (e.g., a strategic allocation for domestic equity of 30% to 40%), and if the actual percentage wanders outside that range, the portfolio is rebalanced.

SAA is generally the prime determinate of performance. One empirical study showed that 94% of the variability of total portfolio returns is explained by the strategic asset allocation.[1] Other studies show similar results. In contrast, TAA is a small increment in return. Beyond its empirical importance, SAA benefits the client and manager with a clearly defined allocation based upon systematic risk factors consistent with the client's objectives and constraints.

LOS 17.d: Contrast the asset-only and asset/liability management (ALM) approaches to asset allocation and discuss the investor circumstances in which they are commonly used.

ALM strategic asset allocation is determined in conjunction with modeling the liabilities of the investor. For investors with specific liabilities (e.g., defined benefit pension

---

1. Brinson, Gary P., L. Randolph Hood, and Gilbert L. Beebower. 1986. "Determinants of Portfolio Performance." *Financial Analysts Journal*, vol. 42, no. 4 (July/August).

plans or insurance companies), asset allocation is tailored to meet liabilities and to maximize the surplus given an acceptable level of risk. This usually results in a relatively high allocation to fixed-income assets. Strategic asset allocation involves specifically modeling liabilities and determining the asset allocation appropriate to fund them. Even for those investors who don't have specific (contractual) liabilities, future obligations (e.g., retirement living expenses for an individual investor) can be modeled as liabilities, and an ALM approach to strategic asset allocation can be applied.

In *asset-only* strategic asset allocation, the focus is on earning the highest level of return for a given (acceptable) level of risk without any consideration for liability modeling. The liability (explicit or implied from future expected cash outflows) is indirectly taken into consideration through the required rate of return. Because the asset-only approach does not specifically model liabilities, the risk of not funding liabilities is not accurately controlled.

DYNAMIC AND STATIC ASSET ALLOCATION

LOS 17.e: Explain the advantage of dynamic over static asset allocation and discuss the trade-offs of complexity and cost.

Dynamic asset allocation takes a multi-period view of the investment horizon. In other words, it recognizes that asset (and liability) performance in one period affects the required rate of return and acceptable level of risk for subsequent periods. *Static asset allocation* ignores the link between optimal asset allocations across different time periods. For example, the manager using a static approach might estimate the necessary mean-variance inputs at a point in time and then construct the long-term portfolio accordingly. The manager using dynamic allocation allows for changing parameters over time using such techniques as Monte Carlo simulation. This allows the manager to build in expected changes to inputs as well as model unanticipated changes in macroeconomic factors.

Dynamic asset allocation is difficult and costly to implement. However, investors who have significant liabilities, especially those with uncertain timing and/or amount (e.g., non-life insurance companies), find the costs acceptable. Investors who undertake an asset-liability approach to strategic asset allocation typically prefer dynamic asset allocation to static asset allocation.

LOS 17.f: Explain how loss aversion, mental accounting, and fear of regret may influence asset allocation policy.

Recall that **loss aversion** makes investors focus on gains and losses rather than risk and return as prescribed by modern portfolio theory. Loss aversion can lead an investor to take increasingly greater risk in an attempt to recover from a loss. This *risk-seeking behavior* in turn can lead to highly concentrated or otherwise riskier portfolios.

Mental accounting is the tendency for individuals to identify and immunize individual goals rather than use a diversified portfolio to meet all goals considered together. This can be thought of as a pyramiding approach. The base of the pyramid represents the largest and most critical goals, such as retirement living expenses and children's educations. The investor focuses on immunizing these goals with very low risk investments, such as Treasuries and high-grade corporate bonds. Once the most important goals are met, the investor looks at the goals that are secondary in importance and uses somewhat riskier investments to meet them. In this fashion, the individual moves in a step-wise manner, identifying and immunizing goals of continually decreasing importance.

Regret is the feeling of disappointment or shame that investors feel from having to admit making a poor investment decision. A feeling of regret can be avoided if the investor does not have to actually recognize a loss. For example, an investor will hold an investment, even though it has fallen in value, in hopes that it will return to its previous, higher level. If the investor instead sold the investment at a loss, the investor would feel the resulting stigma of having made a bad investment.

Fear of regret can make investors avoid taking actions that could lead to regret. For example, the investor holding the losing investment will continue holding the asset rather than sell it. The result could obviously be an even greater loss. From the opposite perspective, an investor fearing regret will tend to hold a winner too long. Fearing selling a rising stock too soon and losing out on even higher returns, the investor will continue holding the stock, possibly until it begins to fall in value. Thus, fear of regret leads investors to hold both losing and winning investments too long.

Fear of regret can also lead to investing only in "comfortable" investments, such as domestic stocks and bonds. By deliberately excluding some asset classes, such as foreign investments, the investor avoids the possibility of making uninformed and possibly poor investment decisions he could later regret. Thus, fearing making a poor decision, the investor fails to hold investments that could improve the return/risk characteristics of the portfolio.

SPECIFYING RISK AND RETURN OBJECTIVES

LOS 17.g: Evaluate return and risk objectives in relation to strategic asset allocation.

Professor's Note: Return and risk objectives are determined in accordance with the investor's constraints. This section and the process of elimination SAA are better covered in the earlier study sessions devoted to those topics. Ultimately the SAA must blend the client's O&C with reasonable capital market expectations.

This reading includes another discussion of combining a distribution rate and future inflation rate to determine the required rate of return for a portfolio. It slightly favors the compounding over the arithmetic approach. To illustrate, suppose a portfolio has a current value of 100 units. Last year, five units was the needed distribution amount. Inflation was and is expected to continue to be 6%.

Step 1: Calculate the needed amount for distribution in the coming period to account for inflation over the past year:

$$5 \text{ units} \times 1.06 = 5.30 \text{ units}$$

Step 2: Calculate the distribution rate:

$$5.30 \text{ units} / 100 \text{ units} = 5.30\%$$

Step 3: Calculate the required rate of return needed to meet the distribution and maintain the real value of the portfolio after the effects of inflation in the future (i.e., calculate the required nominal rate of return):

Compounded: $(1.053)(1.06) - 1 = 11.62\%$

Additive: $5.30 + 6 = 11.3\%$

This reading points out the following:

- *Compounded produces a higher return target.*
- *Compounded is preferable in multiperiod settings and when there are path dependency issues (such as a distribution amount that increases with inflation and is likely to be associated with a lower portfolio market value).*
- *The difference in the methods is smaller at lower rates of return.*

Unless given other information in the case, exam answers have shown a preference for, and we recommend, additive for individuals and compounded for foundations and endowments. Answers have frequently shown the other method as an acceptable alternate answer (i.e., compounded for individuals and additive for foundations and endowments).

The investor's **risk objective** should be specified in light of the investor's risk aversion. Investors can be placed into numerical categories using answers to questionnaires. One possible numerical rating scheme might be to score investors from 1 to 8 based upon their tolerance for risk. Those with below-average risk tolerance (highly risk-averse investors) are given a score of 6 to 8, while those who are highly tolerant of risk (low risk aversion) are given a score of 1 to 2.

Then, using a well-accepted quantitative relationship, we can determine the *utility-adjusted* return the investor will realize from the portfolio:

$$U_P = \hat{R}_P - 0.005(A)\left(\sigma_P^2\right)$$

where:
U_P = the investor's utility from investing in the portfolio
　　　(i.e., the investor's utility-adjusted return)
$\hat{R}_P$ = the portfolio expected return
A = the investor's risk aversion score
σ_P^2 = the portfolio variance

Suppose an investor requires before-tax return of 8%, his risk aversion score is 7, and he can invest in one of two portfolio allocations, A or B, which meet his required return and risk (standard deviation) objectives:

- Allocation A (Portfolio A) has an expected return of 8.5% and a standard deviation of 9%.
- Allocation B (Portfolio B) has an expected return of 8.8% and a standard deviation of 10%.

The investor would be better off with Allocation A. Even though it has a somewhat lower expected return, its risk-adjusted return is actually higher:

$$U_A = \hat{R}_A - 0.005(A)\left(\sigma_A^2\right) = 8.5\% - 0.005(7)(9\%)^2 = 5.67\%$$
$$U_B = \hat{R}_B - 0.005(A)\left(\sigma_B^2\right) = 8.8\% - 0.005(7)(10\%)^2 = 5.30\%$$

> *Professor's Note: Be able to make the calculation if asked.* **This formula is also used in the CFA text with 0.5 instead of 0.005 as a multiplier. 0.5 can be used but the inputs of expected return and risk must be entered in decimal fashion and the output will be in decimal expression.** *The result will be the same. For example, for Portfolio A and B:*
>
> $$U_A = \hat{R}_A - 0.5(A)\left(\sigma_A^2\right) = 0.085 - 0.5(7)(0.09)^2 = 0.0567 = 5.67\%$$
> $$U_B = \hat{R}_B - 0.5(A)\left(\sigma_B^2\right) = 0.088 - 0.5(7)(0.10)^2 = 0.0530 = 5.30\%$$

Suppose the investor's risk aversion score was 2:

$$U_A = \hat{R}_A - 0.005(A)\left(\sigma_A^2\right) = 8.5\% - 0.005(2)(9\%)^2 = 7.69\%$$
$$U_B = \hat{R}_B - 0.005(A)\left(\sigma_B^2\right) = 8.8\% - 0.005(2)(10\%)^2 = 7.80\%$$

Now Allocation B is preferred. There are at least two implications of these results:

1. When choosing from a set of efficient portfolios such as Portfolio B versus A where Portfolio B has both a higher expected return and higher standard deviation than A, the choice is driven by the investor's risk aversion.

2. As risk aversion increases (denoted with a higher risk aversion score), the deduction for (adjustment for) risk increases.

Roy's Safety-First Measure

In addition to standard deviation as a measure of risk (volatility), the acceptable level of risk can be stated in terms of *downside risk* measures such as shortfall risk, semivariance, and target semivariance. **Shortfall risk** is the risk of exceeding a maximum acceptable dollar loss. **Semivariance** is the *bottom half* of the variance (i.e., the variance calculated using only the returns below the expected return). **Target semivariance** is the semivariance using some target minimum return, such as zero.

Roy's Safety-First Measure is one of the oldest and most cited measures of downside risk. The measure is stated as a ratio of *excess return* to risk:

$$RSF = \frac{\hat{R}_P - R_{MAR}}{\sigma_P}$$

where:

$\hat{R}_P$ = portfolio expected return
R_{MAR} = the investor's minimum acceptable return
σ_P = portfolio standard deviation

The *excess return* in Roy's measure is the expected return in excess of the investor's minimum acceptable return. Dividing excess return by the portfolio standard deviation tells us how many standard deviations the minimum acceptable return lies below the portfolio expected return.

For example, we will assume our investor in the previous example also requires that the portfolio not lose any money (i.e., the minimum acceptable return is 0). Applying Roy's Safety-First Measure to Allocations A and B, we determine that Allocation A is preferred:

$$RSF_A = \frac{\hat{R}_P - R_{MAR}}{\sigma_P} = \frac{8.5 - 0}{9} = 0.94$$

$$RSF_B = \frac{\hat{R}_P - R_{MAR}}{\sigma_P} = \frac{8.8 - 0}{10} = 0.88$$

For the Exam: Notice that the two measures, utility-adjusted return and Roy's Safety-First Measure, chose the same allocation for the first investor (aversion score of 7) but not the second investor (aversion score of 2). All risk-adjusted measures do not produce the same rankings. On the exam follow directions carefully as to what measure is specified.

SPECIFYING ASSET CLASSES

LOS 17.h: Evaluate whether an asset class or set of asset classes has been appropriately specified.

Throughout our discussion of strategic and tactical asset allocation, we have assumed that asset classes are correctly identified. We assumed that the manager has appropriately placed assets into groups according to their descriptions and characteristics such as risk and return. For example, including emerging markets equities and domestic equities in a single class labeled *equities* would be appropriate only from a general description standpoint; their risk and return characteristics are obviously significantly different. A primary factor to consider in determining whether asset classes are properly defined is whether the classes held together will produce the desired diversification.

In addition to their descriptions and characteristics, we should ensure that the classes are not highly correlated. A high correlation between classes would indicate that the classes are related from a risk and return standpoint and would defeat the purpose of holding separate classes in an allocation (lack of diversification).

Individual assets should be defined clearly within a single classification. If it can be legitimately argued that assets can be placed in more than one class, the descriptions of the classes are too vague (have not been correctly specified). Again, this defeats the purpose of placing assets into classes for allocation purposes.

In addition to the desired diversification effect, the asset classes should define the majority of all possible investable assets. This not only increases the set of investable assets, but also pushes up the efficient frontier (i.e., increases return at all levels of risk). Remember that the domestic efficient frontier for equities is shifted upward with the inclusion of international equities and that the frontier is pushed even farther up with the inclusion of other asset classes.

Depending upon the strategy employed, the manager will want to rebalance the portfolio to the original strategic allocation, whether the allocation has varied due to performance or tactical allocation. This implies that the asset classes should have sufficient liquidity.

To sum up, asset classes have been appropriately specified if:

1. Assets in the class are similar from a descriptive as well as a statistical perspective.

2. They are not highly correlated so they provide the desired diversification.

3. Individual assets cannot be classified into more than one class.

4. They cover the majority of all possible investable assets.

5. They contain a sufficiently large percentage of liquid assets.

Some well-accepted asset classes include domestic equity, domestic fixed income, global equity, global fixed income, cash and equivalents, and alternative investments, which may be further divided into classes, such as real estate, private equity, et cetera.

 Professor's Note: LOS 17.i is discussed later with LOS 17.r.

Inflation-Adjusted Securities, Global Securities, and Alternative Investments

LOS 17.j: Evaluate the theoretical and practical effects of including additional asset classes in an asset allocation.

The goal in selecting asset classes for strategic asset allocation is to improve the long-term portfolio risk and return. Asset classes that meet the five criteria of a well-specified asset class and accomplish this goal should be included in the SAA. On a short-term basis, asset classes that improve risk and return could be included in a tactical asset allocation.

Theoretical effects would include the effect on overall portfolio risk and return. This effect will depend on the asset class's return, stand-alone risk (standard deviation), and correlation with other portfolio assets. Practical effects would include issues such as liquidity, legal, tax, political, currency, and other factors that vary by asset class.

Inflation-protected "bond-like" securities such as Treasury Inflation Protected Securities (TIPS) are an example of a recently developed asset class that provides theoretical and practical benefits. They provide a fixed real coupon rate, but the principal and coupon payments adjust upward (or downward) with inflation (or deflation). The coupon payment on any payment date is the fixed real rate times the adjusted principal. Final principal payment is also in adjusted principal. TIPS meet the criteria of an appropriate asset class because:

1. TIPS of varying maturity are strongly correlated with each other.

2. Their correlation with traditional, nominal bonds and equities are low.

3. They respond to different economic variables than do nominal bonds. Nominal bond volatility responds to the volatility of nominal interest rates, while TIPS volatility responds to the volatility of real interest rates.

4. TIPS provide inflation protection not found in traditional fixed or floating bonds.

International investments and alternative investments (such as real estate, private equity, and hedge funds) also exhibit the characteristics of distinct asset classes and provide benefits warranting inclusion in the asset allocation process. Inclusion would mean they should be considered as an asset class for asset allocation. Their use for a specific client would also depend on that client's objectives and constraints.

Determining Whether to Add an Investment to the Portfolio

LOS 17.k: Demonstrate the application of mean–variance analysis to decide whether to include an additional asset class in an existing portfolio.

Mean-variance analysis assumes asset classes can be analyzed and described by expected return, standard deviation, and correlation. If the asset class considered for inclusion is constrained to a positive weight (no short selling), a relatively simple decision rule can be used to determine if it will be beneficial to add the asset class to the portfolio. A decision rule based on the new investment's Sharpe ratio, the current portfolio Sharpe ratio, and the correlation of the returns on the two is used.[2] If the Sharpe ratio of the new investment is greater than the current portfolio Sharpe ratio multiplied by the correlation of the new investment's returns with the portfolio's returns, adding the investment to the portfolio will improve the portfolio Sharpe ratio:

if $S_i > S_p \times \rho_{i,p}$ adding the investment will improve the portfolio Sharpe ratio

where:
S_i = Sharpe ratio of proposed investment
S_p = current portfolio Sharpe ratio
$\rho_{i,p}$ = correlation of the returns on the proposed investment with the portfolio returns

Sharpe Ratio is the: (expected return of the asset less the risk free rate) divided by the standard deviation of the asset.

---

2. This methodology can be applied to individual assets or asset classes.

Example 1: Will adding the asset improve the portfolio Sharpe ratio?

A manager is considering adding an investment to his diversified portfolio, but he is unsure of the correlation of the new investment with his portfolio. **Determine** the maximum correlation between the new investment and his portfolio that would make the new investment acceptable (risk-free rate = 3%).

	Portfolio	New Investment[1]
Expected return	12%	12%
Standard deviation	18%	30%
Sharpe ratio	(12 – 3) / 18 = 0.50	(12 – 3) / 30 = 0.30

1. Remember, the proposed investment could have been an asset class. For example, a manager might be considering adding a class of foreign investments to a domestic portfolio.

Answer 1: Calculate the correlation coefficient that makes the equation an identity.

$$S_i = S_p \times \rho_{i,p}$$

$$0.30 = 0.50 \times \rho_{i,p} \Rightarrow \rho_{i,p} = \frac{0.30}{0.50} = 0.60$$

- If the correlation of the new investment with the portfolio is 0.60, then $S_i = S_p \times \rho_{i,p}$, and adding the new investment will leave the portfolio Sharpe ratio unchanged.
- If the correlation is less than 0.60, then $S_i > S_p \times \rho_{i,p}$, and adding the investment will *increase* the portfolio Sharpe ratio.
- If the correlation is greater than 0.60, then $S_i < S_p \times \rho_{i,p}$, and adding the investment will *decrease* the portfolio Sharpe ratio.

Example 2: Selecting an asset for the portfolio

A portfolio manager is considering three investments, only one of which he will add to his portfolio. Data on the investments and his portfolio are provided in the table. Based on the data provided, determine which investment the manager should select.

	Portfolio	Investment 1	Investment 2	Investment 3
Sharpe ratio[1]	0.41	0.30	0.31	0.19
Correlation with current portfolio, ρ		0.77	0.80	0.40

1. $S_i = \dfrac{\hat{R}_i - R_F}{\sigma_i}$

Answer 2: Follow these steps:

1. If Sharpe ratios are not presented, you would be provided with expected returns, standard deviations, and the risk-free rate.

2. Multiply the portfolio Sharpe ratio by the correlation of each asset with the portfolio.

3. If the Sharpe ratio of an investment is greater than the respective product in #2, the investment is acceptable.

$$\text{if } S_i > S_p \times \rho_{i,p} \Rightarrow \text{ the investment will increase the portfolio Sharpe ratio}$$
$$S_1 = 0.30; \quad S_p \times \rho_{1,p} = 0.41 \times 0.77 = 0.316; \quad S_1 < S_p \times \rho_{i,p}$$
$$S_2 = 0.31; \quad S_p \times \rho_{2,p} = 0.41 \times 0.80 = 0.328; \quad S_2 < S_p \times \rho_{i,p}$$
$$S_3 = 0.19; \quad S_p \times \rho_{3,p} = 0.41 \times 0.40 = 0.164; \quad S_3 > S_p \times \rho_{i,p}$$

We see from the calculations that only Investment 3 would increase the portfolio Sharpe ratio. Even though it has the lowest Sharpe ratio of the three investments, it also has the lowest correlation with the portfolio.

RISK IN INTERNATIONAL ASSETS

LOS 17.l: Describe risk, cost, and opportunities associated with nondomestic equities and bonds.

The additional risks to consider are currency risk, political risk, and home country bias.

Currency risk: Investing in a foreign-denominated security exposes the investor to changes in value of foreign asset and changes in value of the foreign currency. This has implications for the return of the asset and for its volatility.

Professor's Note: For example, a German investor could buy a U.K. stock or bond denominated in GBP. If income and price change of the asset in GBP is 5%, the total return for an investor who values her portfolio in GBP is 5%. I'll refer to this as the local market return (LMR). However the German investor is also affected by the change in value of the GBP, the foreign currency from the investor's perspective. If the GBP declines 2%, the total return for the German investor is approximately 5% – 2% = 3%. Referring to the change in value of the foreign currency (–2%) as the local currency return (LCR), the total return on the investment is approximately LMR + LCR. If the LMR and LCR are consistently either both positive or both negative, this positive correlation amplifies return volatility for the foreign investor. On the other hand, if LMR and LCR have negative correlation, this will reduce return volatility for the foreign investor.

These concepts should sound familiar from earlier levels of the CFA material. The math will be discussed further in other readings and study sessions. The rest of this section is a non-math discussion of theoretical and practical issues in adding international investments to the portfolio. Mathematical discussions of this material are found in other parts of the curriculum.

Currency should generally be a smaller concern than some naive investors may fear.

The correlation of LMR and LCR is generally less than +1.0. Therefore, the volatility of the investor's position will be less than the sum of the volatility of the LMR and LCR. The more the correlation of LMR and LCR approach –1.0, the lower the volatility of the investment for the investor. For example, suppose every time LCR is negative, LMR is positive and vice versa; total return to the investor can be quite stable.

In a global portfolio exposed to multiple currencies, some will likely have positive LCR while others have negative LCR. The correlations across all currencies would likely be less than +1.0, again creating a diversification effect. In addition, over time, a currency is unlikely to continually appreciate or depreciate; it will more likely show mean reversion. Over time currency risk tends to become a smaller consideration.

Empirical evidence suggests that the standard deviation of currency is only about half the standard deviation of stock prices. It is the less important determinant of risk. (In the bond market, the currency volatility is generally higher than bond volatility, reflecting bonds are generally less volatile than stocks, making it a more important consideration for bond investors).

Political risk: Exists when a country has (1) irresponsible fiscal and/or monetary policy, and/or (2) lacks reasonable legal and regulatory rules to support but not stifle financial markets. It could arise if a government confiscates property without compensation, unduly restricts foreign investment or suspends capital and currency movement, manipulates the currency or taxes foreign investors unfairly, is unstable or defaults on its debt, and allows or requires companies to be managed for goals inconsistent with those of the shareholders.

Home country bias: Refers to the observation that investors tend to overweigh investments in their own country, creating a suboptimal portfolio allocation. It could reflect lack of familiarity with foreign investments, financial reporting, and language. It can also reflect lack of liquidity and higher political risk in foreign markets or a need to match domestic liabilities with domestic assets.

Costs in International Assets

- Transaction costs can be higher and liquidity can be lower. Market impact transaction costs (a buy order that drives up the market price or a sell order that drives down the market price before order completion) are more significant than explicit transaction costs such as commissions or bid asked spread. Market impact cost is highest in emerging markets.
- Withholding taxes on foreign investors may not be fully offset by tax treaties. For tax exempt investors, they are a pure cost as the investor has no tax return in their own country on which to claim an offset.
- Free-float can be an issue. The stated market capitalization may include shares held by the government or other investors who will not sell.
- Inefficient market infrastructure can result in high costs for security registration, settlement, custody, management, or information.

Opportunities in International Assets

The theoretical argument for international investment is potentially higher return and lower risk with low correlation resulting in enhanced Sharpe ratios. Empirical evidence does not always support this expectation because it appears correlations of financial markets rise during financial crises. When diversification is most needed, all markets go down together. Another argument against diversification is that if an investor resides in a country with high returns, international diversification will lower the return.

The rise in correlation during financial crises can be explained by:

- Markets becoming less segmented and more integrated. In a segmented market, the economy of that country should determine return and risk characteristics. As a country integrates, its economy is more correlated with other economies, and its expected markets would become more correlated.
- Industry factors becoming more important than country factors in determining a company's risk and return. In integrated economies, companies can diversify their operations internationally, making company results more dependent on the economies where the company operates and less dependent on the economy of its home country.

The empirical evidence on country risk varies. It supports that currency and industry risk factors dominate developed market equity returns, while country factors remain important for emerging markets. Despite this, diversification across countries remains important because:

- The importance of country or industry factors is not consistent but varies by the specific industry in the specific country. Investors need to consider both factors.
- In small economies investors have few investment opportunities and must consider international investment to gain reasonable diversification.

- Investment opportunity can be better outside the investor's country.
- Currency matters and may itself provide diversification (if the LMR and LCR returns have low correlation).

In conclusion, the benefits of international diversification are:

1. Foreign markets could be undervalued and, thus, offer better expected return.

2. While the investor's home market may have had the best returns in the past, that is not a reliable indicator of future returns.

3. Even if correlations rise in the short run during crises, the long-run benefits of diversification can remain.

4. Correlations among bond markets tend to be lower than among equity markets. Adding international bonds to domestic-only portfolios can be particularly beneficial in reducing risk for risk averse investors.

Global index funds can be used to gain diversification at lower cost and without home country bias.

LOS 17.m: Explain the importance of conditional return correlations in evaluating the diversification benefits of nondomestic investments.

The previously discussed approach to determining whether a new asset class will benefit the portfolio compares the Sharpe ratio of the new asset class to the existing portfolio Sharpe times correlation of the new asset class to existing portfolio. This is a mean-variance based approach that assumes correlations and standard deviations are stable over time. The observation that correlations increase during financial crises is inconsistent with this assumption and indicates **conditional return correlations** (i.e., correlations that depend on market volatility and conditions). Diversification benefits fail when they are most needed.

Part (but not all) of the rising correlation can be explained away by technical issues in the way correlation is calculated; the mathematics of calculating correlation bias the statistic upward as standard deviations rise. Alternative methods exist to calculate correlation conditioned on the level of return. A portfolio could be optimized both assuming normal conditions and assuming crisis conditions.

A simpler method to determine what is happening to correlation is to plot rolling correlations between markets over time. The plot reveals:

- Correlations have been rising over time, and potential diversification benefits have decreased as markets integrate.
- Correlations did rise during crises periods and then fell back after the crises, within a generally rising upward trend.

Emerging Markets

Emerging markets are economies early in the integration process. Brazil, Russia, India, China, and other smaller markets are often classified as emerging. Emerging markets could be 25% of world equity value and a rising portion of government and corporate bond value as more debt is issued in such markets. The traditional thinking is they offer higher return and stand-alone risk but low correlation with other markets. As these economies mature, their return characteristics are converging with developed markets. However, as they attract more capital, their asset and currency values can appreciate. The special considerations of emerging market investing include:

- Investability. Liquidity and free-float can be limited with adverse market impact, which drives up the price paid to execute purchase orders. Governments of emerging market economies may impose capital and currency restrictions or discriminatory taxes.
- Non-normal return distributions inconsistent with mean-variance assumptions. Returns can be leptokurtic (fat tails with extreme high and low returns occurring more often than consistent with a normal distribution). The return patterns show periods of both positive and negative skew in the returns. Daily returns can be extreme and make up most of the annual return.
- Strong economic growth may not benefit existing shareholders. New share issuance increases equity market cap but dilutes existing shareholder value. Strong growth could already be priced into the stock price. Growth opportunities could be unfairly allocated by the government and not be available to publicly owned companies or disproportionately benefit labor with higher compensation. Corporate governance to protect shareholders can be weak.
- Contagion has been exhibited when a crisis in one emerging market or in developed markets spreads to other emerging markets (essentially just another example or rising correlation during crisis).
- Currency devaluations as emerging market governments devalue their currency (creating a negative LCR) or restrict the ability of an investor to repatriate the funds back to their own market. A currency crisis in one emerging market has been observed to lead to contagion (the crisis in one emerging market leads investors to flee other emerging markets, causing the crisis to spread). Despite these crises, the evidence suggests declines in emerging market currency value can be offset by rising stock prices over time.
- Inefficient markets may allow better informed and capitalized institutional investors or those with local presence to earn excess returns.

LOS 17.n: Explain expected effects on share prices, expected returns, and return volatility as a segmented market becomes integrated with global markets.

As markets integrate and move through emerging market status to developed market status, the general progression is:

- Equity share prices rise as (1) capital can now flow into the formerly uninvestable market, and (2) to reflect declining stand-alone risk.

- Expected returns increase as capital flows into the market but then declines after the initial inflow to be consistent with the now higher stock prices and lower risk going forward.
- Long-run return volatility should decline as prices reflect information that is more freely available and political risk declines.
- Diversification benefits can decline despite the fall in stand-alone risk as correlation and covariance with world markets increases.
- Market microstructure and efficiency improve as transaction costs fall, liquidity increases, and prices are more informationally efficient.
- Capital costs fall with higher stock prices and lower risk. Lower capital costs finance higher economic growth.

STEPS IN ASSET ALLOCATION

LOS 17.o: Explain the major steps involved in establishing an appropriate asset allocation.

The asset allocation process is basically the portfolio management process we have identified throughout the CFA curriculum (i.e., construct the portfolio, monitor its progress, and revise the portfolio as necessary).

As we saw in Study Sessions 4 and 5, the asset allocation process starts with determining the investor's return requirement and risk tolerance, subject to the investor's current wealth and constraints. The manager formulates long-term capital market expectations and their potential effects on the various asset classes. The job is then to determine the mix of assets (allocation) that best meets the objectives defined in the IPS, subject to any other limitations specified by the investor. For example, an investor might strictly forbid investment in cigarette companies or companies that do business with certain countries.

Once the strategic allocation has been implemented, it should be monitored regularly as specified in the IPS. The monitoring process should contain a feedback loop so that changes in long-term market factors can be incorporated back into the "model" and an assessment made to determine whether adjustments to the strategic allocation are justified. If the market changes are only short term in nature, the manager should consider implementing tactical allocation measures, which have been approved in the IPS.

APPROACHES TO ASSET ALLOCATION

LOS 17.p: Discuss the strengths and limitations of the following approaches to asset allocation: mean–variance, resampled efficient frontier, Black–Litterman, Monte Carlo simulation, ALM, and experience based.

The Mean-Variance Optimization (MVO) Approach

The mean-variance approach to strategic asset allocation is a static approach (versus a multi-period dynamic approach). The mean-variance frontier is the *outer edge* of a graphical plot of all possible combinations of risky assets. The efficient frontier is the portion of the mean-variance frontier that contains portfolios (combinations) with the highest expected return at each level of risk. Figure 1 shows an example of a mean-variance frontier and the efficient frontier.

The horizontal axis represents risk as measured by standard deviation. The vertical axis represents portfolio-expected return. All portfolios below the efficient frontier, even those on the mean-variance frontier but below the global minimum variance portfolio, are sub-optimal. This is because there is a portfolio (on the efficient frontier) that has a higher expected return for the same amount of risk.

Figure 1: Mean-Variance (Efficient) Frontier

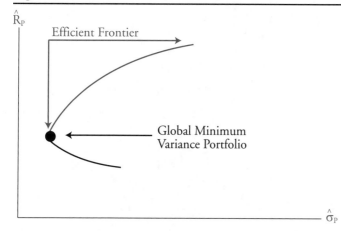

Efficient portfolios are essentially portfolios with varying allocations to the available asset classes. To determine an efficient portfolio with an expected return of *k* and given that there are *j* asset classes, we find the allocation that has the lowest standard deviation, such that:

$$\hat{R}_P = \sum w_i \left(\hat{R}_i \right) = k \ \text{ for } i = 1 \text{ through } j$$

where:
$\hat{R}_P$ = expected return on the portfolio
w_i = weight of class i and $\sum w_i = 1$
$\hat{R}_i$ = expected return for class i

MVO identifies at each level of return the portfolio with the lowest standard deviation and the asset allocation for that portfolio. The efficient frontier then starts with the portfolio with the lowest standard deviation and rises to the right. MVO and the EF can be constructed on either a constrained or unconstrained basis. Unconstrained allows short selling of asset classes, in other words negative asset weights, while constrained does not. In both cases the weights of the portfolio must total 100% (1.00). For the unconstrained version Black (1972) proposed a 2-fund theorem that the asset class weights of any minimum-variance portfolio can be found as a weighted average of the asset class weights of a pair of minimum-variance portfolios.

Professor's Note: This concept will be important later in this session as the basis of the corner portfolio theorem. Both here and later the correlation between the pair is ignored, which is equivalent to making it 1.0 so no diversification benefit occurs.

This simplification is reasonable when the pair is a set of corner portfolios, but not when it is any random pair as implied in 2-portfolio theorem. The 2-portfolio theorem will not be discussed again in the CFA curriculum but the same calculations will be used with corner portfolios. Know them by exam day. It is just a weighted average calculation.

Example: Efficient frontier

Assume only four asset classes combined into Portfolio A ($w_1 = 0.25$, $w_2 = 0.15$, $w_3 = 0.20$, $w_4 = 0.40$) and Portfolio B ($w_1 = 0.30$, $w_2 = 0.20$, $w_3 = 0.35$, $w_4 = 0.15$), which lie on the efficient frontier. Portfolio A has an expected return of 10%, and Portfolio B has an expected return of 15%. **Calculate** the asset class weightings (combination of Portfolios A and B) for the efficient portfolio with an expected return of 11%.

Answer:

We solve for w in the following equation:

$$\hat{R}_P = w_A\hat{R}_A + w_B\hat{R}_B \Rightarrow \text{letting } w_B = (1 - w_A)$$
$$0.11 = w_A(0.10) + (1 - w_A)(0.15)$$
$$w_A = 0.80, \text{ so } w_B = 0.20$$

Thus, the weights of the individual asset classes in the resulting efficient portfolio allocation with an expected return of 11% are:

Asset class 1: $(0.80 \times 0.25) + (0.20 \times 0.30) = 0.26$
Asset class 2: $(0.80 \times 0.15) + (0.20 \times 0.20) = 0.16$
Asset class 3: $(0.80 \times 0.20) + (0.20 \times 0.35) = 0.23$
Asset class 4: $(0.80 \times 0.40) + (0.20 \times 0.15) = \underline{0.35}$
$$\sum = 1.00$$

Cash Equivalents: Is There a Risk-Free Asset?

MVO is a 1-period model (generally one year) and essentially assumes the inputs will remain constant over time. Over a single, discrete time period it is generally possible to identify a risk-free asset with a known return, zero standard deviation, and correlation to other asset returns of zero. A discount government security normally approximates the requirements of risk free. When such an asset exists it leads to the concept of CALs and the CML. A CAL is a line between the risk-free asset and a portfolio of risky assets while the CML is the line between the risk-free asset and the market portfolio of risky assets. It is important because if an investor can borrow and lend at the risk-free asset rate the investor can construct any portfolio on the CML and these optimal portfolios on the CML then dominate (are superior to) the otherwise optimal portfolios on the EF of risky assets. The market portfolio is the only portfolio common to the CML and EF.

While correct as stated, there are conceptual and practical problems with using the CML to construct an SAA:

- For the multiple and often ongoing time periods of a typical portfolio there is no risk-free asset that meets the required definition of known return with zero standard deviation and correlation. The single-period government security will have a changing return over time and a standard deviation of return. The typical MVO may or may not include a cash equivalent asset class. If included it would be a risky asset with an expected return, standard deviation, and correlation. It will be treated as any other asset class to construct an EF but not a CML.

- Even if a risk-free asset existed for a client concerned with only a single period, there could be practical problems. Consider a client seeking a return higher than the market; the CML would require borrowing on an ongoing basis to take a leveraged position in the market. Generally borrowing creates risk and imposes obligations to the lender that are unacceptable to most investors as a long-term strategy. Even the low-risk client who on the CML would invest in the market and a risk-free asset may have issues as a long-term strategy with paying active management fees for this approach.

> *Professor's Note: Be well familiar with the concepts of the EF, CALs, and CML, plus borrowing and lending at the risk-free rate to construct efficient portfolios on the CML. This is well covered at all CFA levels. Be prepared to articulate and explain any of these issues in a constructed response question. Be able to give a short answer or a longer answer with additional details and maybe an illustration to meet the minutes and point value of the question.*
>
> *Levels I and II have briefly discussed the limitations of the CML concept. At Level III, assume the CML approach is not relevant for SAA and portfolios should be selected from the EF unless the question clearly directs borrowing and lending at the risk free rate is acceptable or the question directly asks for a CML solution.*

Resampled Efficient Frontier (REF)

A significant drawback to generating an efficient frontier through traditional mean-variance optimization methods is the *sensitivity* of the frontier to changes in the inputs. Because the inputs themselves (e.g., expected returns, covariances) are estimates, reliance on an efficient frontier developed through a traditional, single mean-variance optimization is questionable.

In response, Michaud[3] developed a simulation approach utilizing historical means, variances, and covariances of asset classes, which, combined with capital market forecasts, assumes they are fair representations of their expectations. His *resampling*

3. Michaud, Richard, 1989. "The Markowitz Optimization Enigma: Is Optimized Optimal?" *Financial Analysts Journal*, January.

technique is based on a Monte Carlo simulation that draws from the distributions to develop a simulated efficient frontier. Because the simulation is run thousands of times, the efficient portfolio at each return level, and hence the resulting efficient frontier, is the result of an averaging process.

Rather than a single, sharp curve, the resampled efficient frontier is a blur. At each level of return is a simulated efficient portfolio at the center with a distribution of portfolios above and below it. Think of the portfolio in the middle as being at the center of a normal distribution. The asset mix at any point on the resampled efficient frontier is an average of many portfolios that might have been constructed to meet that return. It is not possible to know the single exact portfolio that is optimal and like any average, the average is more stable than any single portfolio that might be generated by a single MVO calculation.

By utilizing this resampling technique, a portfolio manager is able to judge the need for rebalancing. For example, if the manager's portfolio is within a 90% confidence interval of the most efficient portfolio, it could be considered *statistically equivalent*. That is, rebalancing to the most optimal weights would not produce a statistically significant change in its risk-return profile.

Resampling has *advantages* over traditional MVO:

- It utilizes an averaging process and generates an efficient frontier that is more stable than a traditional mean-variance efficient frontier. Small changes in the input variables result in only minor changes in the REF.
- Portfolios generated through this process tend to be better diversified.
- By comparing any asset mix of an existing portfolio to the range of asset mixes across the multiple portfolios on the REF that could have generated the required return, it is possible to see if the current mix is within the boundaries of what is acceptable. This is likely to lead to less portfolio turnover and lower transaction costs.

A *disadvantage* of resampling is its lack of a sound theoretical basis. There is no theoretical reasoning to support the contention that a portfolio constructed through resampling should be superior relative to another constructed through traditional mean-variance analysis. In addition and like MVO, the inputs are often based on historical data that could lack current relevance.

Black-Litterman

With the same motivations as Michaud (resampling), Black and Litterman developed two models for dealing with the problems associated with estimation error, especially expected return: (1) the unconstrained Black-Litterman model (UBL) and (2) the Black-Litterman model (BL). Hint: The assigned reading focuses primarily on BL (i.e., constrained for no short selling).

The **unconstrained Black-Litterman model** (UBL) starts with the weights of asset classes from a global index. Applying a Bayesian process, the manager increases or decreases the weights based upon her views of expected asset class returns and the strengths of those views with no constraint against short sales (negative weights are allowed). The UBL is intuitive in that the manager starts with market weightings and directly increases or decreases those weights based on the manager's opinion of what will outperform or underperform. If the manager has a strong opinion domestic equity will underperform, the manager can shift significant assets out of domestic equity to a specific asset class expected to outperform or broadly across all other classes if the manager has no specific views on what will outperform.

UBL does not define how to make these adjustments to weights, but in practice most managers select relatively diversified portfolios without negative weights.

The **Black-Litterman (constrained) model** (BL) allows no negative asset weights, also produces well-diversified portfolios that incorporate the manager's views on asset class returns, and is a more defined process. It is a rigorous mathematical process starting with reverse optimization. BL can be used to both calculate the market's consensus expectations of returns by asset class and then construct an MVO portfolio adjusted for the manager's views of those returns. The BL model requires several steps:

- Select a relevant, global market index. Input the market weights for the asset classes in that index and a covariance matrix for those classes.
- Use reverse optimization to back-solve for the implied, expected returns of those asset classes. Having started with a market index and the market's weightings, these will be consensus returns expectations.
- The manager then reviews the implied returns and expresses any opinions regarding the returns and the strength of those opinions.
- The manager then resets any implied returns up or down to reflect the manager's opinions and conviction level. For example suppose the back-solving implies Spanish equities have an expected return of 12% while the manager expects 14% but with low confidence. This could be expressed as a 14% expected return but with a high standard deviation.
- A new MVO is run using the adjusted returns where the manager had an opinion and the market consensus return where the manager has no opinion. The new MVO produces the recommended asset mix.

Like UBL, the manager's opinions and level of conviction are incorporated, but BL then uses MVO to also factor in asset volatility and correlations in a disciplined process to find the optimal mix. BL tends to be less sensitive to changes in inputs and less likely to produce the under diversification common in traditional MVO.

Example: Asset allocation using BL

A portfolio manager has asked the quantitative department of his firm to reverse engineer the expected returns of a global index. The quant department has provided the following data:

Table A: Global Asset Class Weights

Assets	Class 1	Class 2	Class 3	Class 4	Class 5	Class 6	Class 7
E(R)	9.5%	4.5%	5.1%	4.7%	6.2%	5.6%	6.9%
% weights	10%	15%	5%	25%	20%	10%	15%

a. Assuming the manager has no market views and the client has *average risk tolerance*, **determine** the optimal portfolio asset class allocations.

(2 minutes)

b. Now, assume the manager expects asset class 1 and 3 to have equal returns of 8%, while class 5 outperforms class 2 by 1%. **Describe** the most likely affect of the manager's views on the weightings of the classes where the manager has a view and the next steps the manager would take if using the Black-Litterman model for asset allocation.

(9 minutes)

Answer:

a. If the manager has no particular expectations or is otherwise uncomfortable adjusting asset class expected returns and the risk tolerance of the client is average, the market portfolio would be held. She would weight the asset classes in the portfolio the same as their global weights shown in Table A.

b. The market-implied returns of 1 and 3 are 9.5% and 5.1%, respectively. The view adjusted return is 8% for both. Running a new MVO with a lower 8% return for #1 would likely lower its weight. A higher 8% return for #3 would produce a higher weight.

The market-implied returns for 5 and 2 are 6.2% and 4.5%, respectively, a difference of 1.7%. The view adjusted is only a 1% difference so the relative return of #5 will shift down for a lower weight and #2's relative return shifts up for a higher weight.

The next steps would be to quantify the return levels for #5 and #2 consistent with a 1% difference and indicate confidence in the views. Then run a new MVO using the manager-adjusted returns to establish the new optimal portfolio weights.

Monte Carlo Simulation (MCS)

MCS is a statistical modeling tool often used to complement MVO or other asset allocation tools. For example a manager could begin by selecting several optimal portfolios using MVO that have acceptable risk and return for the client and then use MCS to generate multiple simulated paths displaying how these portfolios would perform over time. The MCS can consider path dependency effects on the portfolio, such as a constant nominal or real amount of funds withdrawn periodically or taxes paid on the returns. The MCS paths could be ranked in order of value to facilitate answering such questions as: Will the portfolio be exhausted? When? How bad or good could it be?

> *Professor's Note: This is another nice discussion of MCS to complement the earlier discussions. Remember that in SAA, MCS does not replace MVO and the other techniques. MCS further analyzes the SAA output of the other models for path dependency issues and further statistical analysis.*

Surplus Asset Liability Management

The allocation methodologies discussed thus far attempt to identify the strategic allocation that achieves the best long-run results (i.e., the best asset-only allocation). Asset liability management (ALM), on the other hand, considers the allocation of assets with respect to a given liability or set of liabilities. The ALM approach searches for the set of allocations, which maximize the *difference* (the *surplus*) between assets and liabilities at each level of risk (much like the efficient frontier represents the maximum return at each level of risk).

Figure 2 shows an example of an ALM efficient frontier[4] for a generic defined benefit pension plan.

Figure 2: The Asset Liability Management (ALM) Efficient Frontier

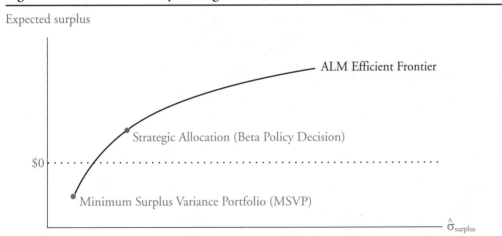

The vertical axis in Figure 2 is the value of the expected surplus (assets minus liabilities), and the horizontal axis represents the associated risk, measured by standard deviation of surplus. As with any *efficient* frontier, there is a minimum-variance portfolio, which

---

4. The ALM efficient frontier is sometimes referred to as the *surplus* efficient frontier.

in this case is the minimum variability of surplus. With the lowest risk it will also generate the minimum expected surplus. As you move to the right on the frontier, both the expected surplus and the risk increase. There is no assurance the MSVP will have a positive surplus. In this case the MSVP has a negative surplus.

The choice of any portfolio on the frontier is a client and manager decision; they accept more and more risk as they move out on the frontier. In Figure 2, management has selected the allocation labeled Strategic Allocation. Because it is a risker decision than selecting the MSVP it could be called a beta policy decision. Because the MSVP is negative, the client and manager could choose to be somewhat more aggressive and move up and out the frontier (a beta decision) or the client could increase funding to increase the assets and the surplus.

The ALM efficient frontier could also be presented in terms of the funding ratio (i.e., the value of plan assets divided by the value of plan liabilities). In that case, the ratio is presented along the vertical axis, as either a percentage or a ratio, and risk is plotted along the horizontal axis. Other than the way the vertical axis is labeled, the analysis is the same.

As with other optimization procedures, ALM requires estimations of all associated mean-variance parameters and thus suffers from the same estimation biases. Of course this now also includes estimating the liabilities as well. To help avoid these inherent limitations of MVO, the manager can utilize a resampling technique or the Black-Litterman approach for ALM. Monte Carlo simulation could then be added as a compliment to examine path dependency and gain statistical probability insight to the behavior of the surplus over time.

Example: Surplus ALM with simulation as a complement

A pension plan or any other portfolio with definable and quantifiable liabilities (future payouts) can benefit from ALM and further benefit from MCS analysis.

Step 1: Run a surplus MVO and select several portfolios from the surplus EF that provide acceptable risk and return combinations.

Proposed SAA	E(R) of Surplus	Standard Deviation of Surplus
A	1.0%	0.0%
B	1.5%	3.1%
C	2.0%	6.4%
Current Portfolio	1.6%	5.3%

It should be clear the current portfolio is inefficient. A better combination of risk and return could be achieved with a linear combination of B and C. 80% invested in portfolio B plus 20% in C will have a weighted average return of 1.6% and a lower weighted average standard deviation. The current portfolio will plot on the interior of the efficient frontier.

Step 2: Use Monte Carlo simulation to examine the future performance of the assets, liabilities, and resulting surplus of the selected portfolios over time. Each curved line on the graph represents the max value of the surplus at some probability as time passes. For example, the 90% line indicates that 90% of the time the surplus will be at or below the line and 10% of the time the surplus could be higher.

$

Portfolio A

Current surplus

90%, 50%, and 10%

0

Years   30

$

Portfolio B

Current surplus

90%
50%
10%

0

Years   30

$

Portfolio C

Current surplus

90%
50%

0   10%

Years   30

> *Step 3:* Examine the output and determine the next steps. The manager determines the current portfolio is unacceptable and rejects C as too risky for the client because at the 10% probability it would be exhausted prior to the 30-year horizon and require additional funding by the client. The manager decides A, which is the MSVP and has a zero standard deviation of surplus, is too conservative and recommends B as the appropriate portfolio.
>
> It is reasonable to conclude A has a 0.0 standard deviation of surplus because the surplus has no variability at 90, 50, and 10% probability. Because 0.0 is the lowest standard deviation, A must be the MSVP.

Experience-Based Techniques (EBTs)

> **For the Exam:** EBT is just the process of elimination, which is covered in more detail in the earlier study sessions. It is commonly tested. Know it well. The EBT approach is more typically used with individuals who lack the background to understand the more mathematical approaches. This is less of an issue than it might appear because the experience-based rules of the process of elimination are in fact generally well supported by the more mathematically based approaches.
>
> Common EBT rules include the following:
>
> - A 60/40 mix of equity and fixed income is a good starting point for the average risk investor. More aggressive (less aggressive) investors should increase (decrease) the equity allocation and make the corresponding adjust the fixed income allocation. A longer time horizon is generally consistent with more equity.
> - 100 – investor's age is sometimes used as the starting equity allocation. (Hint: I would not put much reliance on this last one as it has not been used very much in past answers. The concept is fine but other factors have to be considered as well.)

Summary of the Six Approaches

Figure 3: Strengths and Limitations of Asset Allocation Approaches

Asset Allocation Approach	Strengths	Limitations
Mean-variance optimization (MVO)	• Optimization programs used to generate the efficient frontier are inexpensive and readily available. • Identifies portfolios with the highest expected return at each level of risk and the associated asset allocation. • It is typically sign constrained to prevent negative weights (short selling). • Cash equivalents are modeled as a risky asset class if included. • Widely understood and accepted. • Easily adapted to model risk as downside risk or tracking error, return as excess return over some minimum threshold return, constrain the deviations of asset weights versus some relevant benchmark, model the correlation to change over time and converge during periods of stress (high volatility). • The modeling of the EF can be simplified with the use of corner portfolios. • Commercially available software.	• The number and nature of estimates required (e.g., expected returns, variances, covariances) can be overwhelming as the number of asset classes increases • Expected returns are subject to estimation bias. • Static (1-period) approach. • Can yield under-diversified (concentrated) portfolios unless constrained. • MVO output can be very sensitive to the inputs, making the resulting output unstable.
Resampled efficient frontier	• EF is more stable than traditional MV. • Small changes in inputs produce only minor changes in SAA. • Portfolios tend to be better diversified than traditional MVO. • Commercially available software.	• No theoretical basis for the approach. • Inputs often based on historical data.
Black-Litterman	• Theoretically justified way to address the sensitivity of inputs problem and incorporate manager views. • Typically generates more stable SAA and better diversification. • Can be constrained or unconstrained though constrained is the more useful and rigorous approach. • BL (constrained) quantifies and begins with market consensus expected returns and allows the manager to systematically diverge from this starting point. • Commercially available software.	• Often the inputs are based on historical data. • Complicated.

Figure 3: Strengths and Limitations of Asset Allocation Approaches (Cont.)

Asset Allocation Approach	Strengths	Limitations
Monte Carlo simulation	• Statistical analysis tool to further analyze the SAA output of the other approaches. • Models path dependency issues. • Generates statistical probabilities of meeting or not meeting return objectives. • Can also model liabilities and surplus. • Used to complement the other approaches. • Commercially available software.	• Can be complex to implement. • Can generate false confidence; the output is only as accurate as the inputs.
ALM	• Considers the allocation of assets with respect to liabilities. • Can generate a surplus frontier that shows the combinations of risk and return. • Otherwise similar to MVO. • Commercially available software.	• Same issues as MVO.
Experience based	• Incorporates decades of asset allocation experience. • Easy to understand and consistent with the more complex approaches. • Inexpensive to implement. • Useful on the exam.	• Allocation rules may be too simple for some investors. • Experience-based rules can be contradictory in some applied settings.

CONSTRAINTS AGAINST SHORT SALES

LOS 17.q: Discuss the structure of the minimum-variance frontier with a constraint against short sales.

When short selling is constrained (prohibited) all asset class weights will be positive or zero and must of course sum to 1.00. In the constrained situation the earlier 2-portfolio theorem leads to the much more useful corner portfolio theorem. This allows the EF to be closely approximated by linear combinations of a small number of corner portfolios. The global minimum-variance portfolio is by definition a corner portfolio and is the left-most point of the EF. All other "corners" are set when the weight of an asset class changes from zero to positive or from positive to zero for a portfolio on the EF. In addition whichever corner has the highest Sharpe ratio can be modeled as being the market portfolio.

Professor's Note: MVO modeling is still needed to initially identify the corner portfolios. Note as well that two factors can define a corner portfolio. There could be a change in asset class weight from + to 0 or 0 to +. But, by definition, the GMVP is always a CP. This has implications for the data you can see. The lowest return corner portfolio will always be the GMVP. Starting from that lowest return GMVP and moving to the next lowest return CP, there may or may not be the + to 0 or 0 to + asset weight change. Then, moving up one more step in return, there will always be the + to 0 or 0 to + change in asset classes weight. You will come across examples of both situations.

Figure 4 shows an example of an efficient frontier with six corner portfolios and one additional portfolio (L). Portfolio A is the global minimum-variance (GMV) portfolio, which is always included as one of the corner portfolios. To approximate any portfolio on the efficient frontier, we only need the two *adjacent* corner portfolios. For example, Portfolio L is a weighted average of Portfolios B and C.

Figure 4: Efficient Frontier with Corner Portfolios

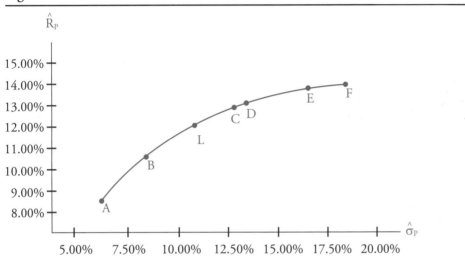

Corner Portfolios and Interpolating Points Between

Mathematically, calculating the standard deviation of an efficient portfolio, given the adjacent corner portfolios' standard deviations, is identical to the calculations we use when we calculate the weights of a portfolio necessary to achieve an expected return.

Example: Standard deviation using corner portfolios

An analyst has selected the two adjacent corner portfolios A and B. Their expected returns are 10% and 15% respectively, while their standard deviations are 12% and 16%. Calculate the weights of A and B to construct a portfolio with an 11% expected return. Calculate this new portfolio's standard deviation.

Answer:

First calculate the required weight of Portfolio A is 0.80 and the weight of Portfolio B is 0.20. Without knowing the correlation of A and B, the standard deviation of the weighted portfolio is closely approximated by a weighted average of A's and B's standard deviations:

$$\hat{R}_P = w_A \hat{R}_A + w_B \hat{R}_B \Rightarrow \text{letting } w_B = (1 - w_A)$$
$$0.11 = w_A(0.10) + (1 - w_A)(0.15)$$
$$w_A = 0.80, \text{ so } w_B = 0.20$$
$$\sigma_P = 0.80(\sigma_A) + 0.20(\sigma_B)$$
$$\sigma_P = 0.80(0.12) + 0.20(0.16) = 0.128 = 12.8\%$$

Professor's Note: Mathematically this is the same result as if we used the more complex portfolio variance formula but with all correlations of 1.0—in other words, we allowed for no diversification between the corners. The corners themselves do consider diversification and correlation, making the final results quite accurate. By calculating a simple weighted average of standard deviation the risk will be slightly overstated, not by much, and a slight overstatement is much better than understating risk.

Hint: Always use the closest bracketing pair of corners. In the previous example that was A and B. The calculations could be done with other combinations but the estimations of standard deviation will be higher, less accurate, and therefore wrong.

LOS 17.i: Select and justify an appropriate set of asset classes for an investor.

LOS 17.r: Formulate and justify a strategic asset allocation, given an investment policy statement and capital market expectations.

Professor's Note: The following example looks intimidating. Take the time to go through it a step at a time. Taking it one step at a time it is not so bad.

Example: Strategic asset allocation

Jim Sheehan is the portfolio manager for the $200 million Brent Industries defined benefit pension fund. Jim is planning on making a presentation to the trustees of the pension plan. His firm has come up with the long-term capital market expectations as shown in the following figure.

Capital Market Expectation

Asset Class	Expected Return	Expected Std. Dev.	Correlations				
			1	2	3	4	5
U.S. equity	12.00%	16.00%	1.00				
U.S. bonds	8.25%	6.50%	0.32	1.00			
Int'l equities	14.00%	18.00%	0.46	0.22	1.00		
Int'l bonds	9.25%	12.25%	0.23	0.56	0.32	1.00	
Alternative inv.	11.50%	21.00%	0.25	0.11	0.08	0.06	1.00

Using the capital market expectations, Jim identifies an efficient frontier with the six corner portfolios (see the following graphic) with the characteristics shown in the following table.

Corner Portfolio	Expected Return	Expected Std. Dev.	Sharpe Ratio	Asset Class Weights				
				U.S. Equity	U.S. Bonds	Int'l Equities	Int'l Bonds	Alt. Inv
1	14.00%	18.00%	0.639	0.00%	0.00%	100.00%	0.00%	0.00%
2	13.66%	16.03%	0.696	0.00%	0.00%	85.36%	0.00%	14.64%
3	13.02%	13.58%	0.775	21.69%	0.00%	56.56%	0.00%	21.75%
4	12.79%	13.00%	0.792	21.48%	0.00%	52.01%	5.24%	21.27%
5	10.54%	8.14%	0.988	9.40%	51.30%	26.55%	0.00%	12.76%
6	8.70%	6.32%	0.981	0.00%	89.65%	4.67%	0.00%	5.68%

Efficient Frontier for Brent Industries Pension Fund

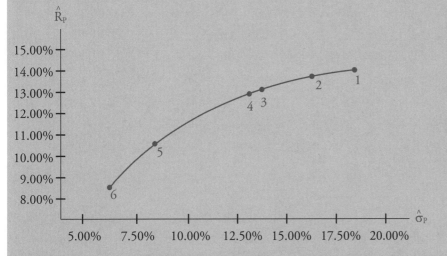

The following additional information is available about the pension fund:

- The trustees have established a spending rate of 8.50%. Inflation is expected to be 2% per year, and the cost of managing the fund is expected to be 0.40%. The trustees would like to preserve the purchasing power of the fund and are concerned with multi-period compounding issues.
- The majority of plan participants are young, so additional liquidity needs are minimal.
- The trustees would like to limit risk (as defined by standard deviation) to no more than 10% per year.

A.   **Calculate** the fund's required rate of return and **determine** the appropriate strategic asset allocation.

(10 minutes)

B.   **Calculate** the Sharpe ratio of the market and the risk-free rate.

(4 minutes)

C.   **Discuss** whether a risk-free asset should have been included as an asset.

(4 minutes)

Answer:

A.   The required return is 11.11% [= (1.085)(1.02)(1.004) – 1], which lies between Corner Portfolios 4 and 5 with their expected returns of 12.79% and 10.54%. We solve for w in the following equation:

$$0.1111 = w_4(0.1279) + (1 - w_4)(0.1054)$$

$$w_4 = 0.25 \Rightarrow w_5 = 0.75$$

In other words, the efficient portfolio with an expected return of 11.11% has 25% weight of Corner Portfolio 4 and 75% weight of Corner Portfolio 5. With respect to asset classes, the weights are then derived as follows:

U.S. equity = (0.25)(0.2148) + (0.75)(0.0940) = 0.1242 = 12.42%

U.S. bonds = (0.25)(0.0000) + (0.75)(0.5130) = 0.3848 = 38.48%

Int'l equity = (0.25)(0.5201) + (0.75)(0.2655) = 0.3292 = 32.92%

Int'l bonds = (0.25)(0.0524) + (0.75)(0.0000) = 0.0131 = 1.31%

Alt. invest. = (0.25)(0.2127) + (0.75)(0.1276) = 0.1489 = 14.89%

Additional comments, not for the answer on exam day:

- Adding the return components is incorrect given the trustee's statements.
- In the above computation for U.S. equity, 0.25 (the weight of Corner Portfolio 4) is multiplied by 21.48% (the proportion of U.S. equity in Corner Portfolio 4). Similarly, 0.75 (the weight of Corner Portfolio 5) is multiplied by 9.40% (the proportion of U.S. equity in Corner Portfolio 5). We then add these together to arrive at 12.42% as the weight of U.S. equity in the efficient portfolio with an expected return of 11.11%. We repeat the same process for each asset class.

1. Sum of weights should be 100%:

0.1242 + 0.3848 + 0.3292 + 0.0131 + 0.1489 = 1.00 = 100%

2. Also, check that the sum of the weights of each asset class multiplied by their expected returns adds up to 11.11%:

$$\hat{R}_P = (0.1242)(0.12) + (0.3848)(0.0825) + (0.3292)(0.14)$$
$$+ (0.0131)(0.0925) + (0.1489)(0.1150)$$
$$= 0.1111 = 11.11\%$$

Also note that the standard deviation of this portfolio is (approximately) the weighted average of the standard deviations of Corner Portfolios 4 and 5, which satisfies the risk requirement of the fund:

$$\sigma_P = (0.25)(0.13) + (0.75)(0.0814) = 0.09355 = 9.36\%$$

B. The corner portfolio with the highest Sharpe ratio will approximate the market portfolio. That is Corner Portfolio 5 in the table. Therefore the Sharpe of the market is 0.988. No other data is provided for calculating the market Sharpe directly.

This can be used to derive the risk-free rate as we know Corner Portfolio 5 (the market) has a Sharpe of 0.988, expected return of 10.54% and standard deviation of 8.14%. Therefore:

Sharpe of market = MRP / standard deviation of market = MRP / 8.14 = 0.988

MRP = 8.04%

MRP = return of market – risk-free return = 8.04 = 10.54 – risk-free return

risk-free return = 2.50%

C. Over the multi periods of a pension plan there is no effective risk-free asset with known return over all periods. It would be possible to model cash equivalents as a risky asset class with an estimate return and standard deviation but it is not essential. A wide range of global equity and fixed income and alternatives is already being considered.

Special Considerations

The IPS may specify near-term liquidity needs. For example, an individual investor may consider providing for retirement her primary investment goal. However, she may have a secondary goal of taking a vacation in six months and wants to have a specific dollar amount available toward that planned expense. In such a situation, the present value of the projected cash flow should be invested in cash equivalents. The remainder of the portfolio is allocated according to the weights previously established.

Example: Planned cash outflow

Suppose a question stated $20,000,000 is required as a liquidity reserve to fund retiree pension buyouts planned in the next year. **Determine** the appropriate strategic asset allocation for the fund.

Answer:

Determine the appropriate SAA using any of the tools available. Then set aside the necessary cash equivalents of $20,000,000 before applying the SAA to the remaining funds.

For the Exam: This is a frequent situation on the exam. Now suppose the question states the expenditure will be in one year and the one-year interest rate is 5%. Set aside the PV at 5% of $20,000,000.

The Capital Allocation Line

The capital allocation line (CAL) is the straight line drawn from the risk-free rate to the **tangency portfolio** on the efficient frontier, where *the tangency portfolio is the corner portfolio with the highest Sharpe ratio.* If the investor's required rate of return is lower than the expected return on the tangency portfolio, the investor will invest a portion of the funds in a risk-free asset and the remainder in the tangency portfolio. If, on the other hand, the investor's required rate of return is higher than the tangency portfolio's expected rate of return, the investor will use margin (borrow at the risk-free rate) to leverage the return. If the IPS specifically prohibits borrowing, then we select different corner portfolios above the tangency portfolio. The new corner portfolios will be the ones that bracket the investor's required rate of return.

Example: Determining the tangency portfolio

Continuing the previous example (the figure from the previous example is reproduced for your convenience).

Corner Portfolio	Expected Return	Expected Std. Dev.	Sharpe Ratio	Asset Class Weights				
				U.S. Equity	U.S. Bonds	Int'l Equities	Int'l Bonds	Alt. Inv
1	14.00%	18.00%	0.639	0.00%	0.00%	100%	0.00%	0.00%
2	13.66%	16.03%	0.696	0.00%	0.00%	85.36%	0.00%	14.64%
3	13.02%	13.58%	0.775	21.69%	0.00%	56.56%	0.00%	21.75%
4	12.79%	13.00%	0.792	21.48%	0.00%	52.01%	5.24%	21.27%
5	10.54%	8.14%	0.988	9.40%	51.30%	26.55%	0.00%	12.76%
6	8.70%	6.32%	0.981	0.00%	89.65%	4.67%	0.00%	5.68%

1. **Determine** which portfolio is the most suitable candidate for the tangency portfolio.

2. Assuming no constraint against leverage and a risk-free rate of 2.5%, **determine** the asset allocation for the pension fund if management chooses an available corner portfolio.

3. Assume you are not allowed to leverage. **Determine** the asset allocation if management chooses an available corner portfolio.

Answers:

1. Corner Portfolio 5 with an expected return of 10.54%, has the highest Sharpe ratio (0.988) and would be the most suitable candidate for the tangency portfolio. Because it has the highest Sharpe ratio, Portfolio 5 is the tangency portfolio for the capital allocation line. If allowed to borrow and lend at the risk-free rate, the investor will combine Portfolio 5 with the risk-free asset to attain the desired expected return.

2. The fund's required rate of return is 11.11%, the risk-free rate is 2.50%, and the expected return of the tangency portfolio is 10.54%. Let w_{RF} denote the weight of the risk-free asset and $(1 - w_{RF})$ denote the weight of the tangency portfolio:

$$0.1111 = (w_{RF})0.0250 + (1 - w_{RF})0.1054$$
$$0.1111 = 0.0250w_{RF} + 0.1054 - 0.1054w_{RF}$$
$$0.0804w_{RF} = -0.0057$$
$$w_{RF} = -0.07; (1 - w_{RF}) = 1.07$$

Therefore, we borrow 7% and invest 107% in the tangency portfolio.

3. In the situation where using margin is not allowed (i.e., cannot borrow at the risk-free rate), the investor will combine the two corner portfolios adjacent to the required return. We will assume the investor has a required return of 11.11% and no borrowing is allowed. In this situation, Corner Portfolios 4 and 5 (expected returns of 12.79% and 10.54%, respectively) will be combined.

Let w_4 be the weight of Corner Portfolio 4 in the combination of 4 and 5:

$$11.11 = w_4(12.79) + (1 - w_4)(10.54)$$
$$11.11 = 12.79w_4 + 10.54 - 10.54w_4$$
$$0.57 = 2.25w_4$$
$$w_4 \approx 0.25$$
$$w_5 \approx 0.75$$

Investing 25% of our funds in Corner Portfolio 4 and 75% in Corner Portfolio 5, the asset class weights in the final portfolio are:

Asset class weight	$= (w_4)$(wt in 4)	$+ (w_5)$(wt in 5)	
U.S. equity	$= (0.25)(21.48)$	$+ (0.75)(9.40)$	$= 12.42\%$
U.S. bonds	$= (0.25)(0.00)$	$+ (0.75)(51.30)$	$= 38.48\%$
International equity	$= (0.25)(52.01)$	$+ (0.75)(26.55)$	$= 32.91\%$
International bonds	$= (0.25)(5.24)$	$+ (0.75)(0.00)$	$= 1.31\%$
Alternative investments	$= (0.25)(21.27)$	$+ (0.75)(12.76)$	$= 14.89\%$

STRATEGIC ASSET ALLOCATION ISSUES

LOS 17.s: Compare the considerations that affect asset allocation for individual investors versus institutional investors and critique a proposed asset allocation in light of those considerations.

For the Exam: The CFA® text for this section is long. Treat it as a cursory review of important topics: IPS, SAA, and human capital covered earlier and in more detail.

We are intentionally keeping this section brief in order to utilize candidate time effectively. I recommend reading the next few pages, verify it is familiar, and review the earlier write-ups as needed. Do review the section on TAA, as it is a nice preview of material that will come in later study sessions.

Individuals. Individuals' goals include meeting living expenses, funding children's educational expenses, funding retirement, setting up trusts, et cetera. In other words, the individual typically looks primarily at wealth accumulation to meet required as well as *desired* expenditures. This does not preclude applying the concepts of ALM if the goals can be numerically quantified and treated as quasi-liabilities.

Another primary difference between an individual investor and an institutional investor is the patterns of income generation and wealth accumulation. Unlike the institutional investor, the typical individual's wealth is accumulated over many years, while the ability to generate income reaches a peak and falls to zero at retirement. The individual's *human capital* (the total present value of future employment income), therefore, is greatest at an early age, while his financial capital (accumulated wealth) increases over time and reaches a maximum at retirement.

The individual's human capital can be a major component of her total assets and must be considered in determining an appropriate strategic asset allocation. Think of the individual's human capital as an allocation to bonds (i.e., return comes in the form of income and isn't as risky as equities). As the young professional starts out, her earnings potential (human capital) is considerable and more than likely comprises the vast majority of her total portfolio (human capital plus financial capital).

At younger ages, then, she has a considerable allocation to *bonds* (her human capital) and the allocation of her financial assets should be toward riskier, higher-return assets like equities. As she ages and accumulates financial capital, her human capital becomes a smaller and smaller component of her total portfolio, and the financial assets require more protection (i.e., an allocation to safer assets).

Another factor that separates individuals from institutions is **longevity risk**. This is the possibility of living longer than planned. For example, the individual might do a very good job of planning for a 25-year retirement at the age of 60 and then live to be older than 100. In this situation, the accumulated wealth is probably not going to be sufficient to fund the extra years. The inverse (sort of) of longevity risk is **mortality risk**; the risk of dying younger than expected. Mortality risk is usually mitigated by purchasing life insurance. Note that the individual bears at least part of the longevity risk, but the individual's spouse and other heirs bear the mortality risk.

Figure 5 presents hypothetical asset allocations for an individual according to age. The client has a changing mix of human capital (HC) and financial capital (FC) as she ages. Her goal is to maintain a SAA of total wealth (TW) at 50/50 between equity and bonds. The table shows how the allocation of equity/bond within FC will change over time to maintain TW at her goal of 50/50. It shows she retires at age 60.

Figure 5: Mix of Human and Financial Capital and Financial Asset Allocation by Age

Age	Proportions of TW	Characteristic of HC	Allocation of FC for Desired 50/50 Allocation of TW	Allocation of TW Achieved
30	10% FC & 90% HC	100% bond like	100% equity	10% equity & 90% bond
50	60% FC & 40% HC	100% bond like	83.33% equity & 16.67% bond	50% equity & 50% bond
60	100% FC	n.a.	50% equity & 50% bond	50% equity & 50% bond

The table shows that her goal of 50/50 for SAA in the early years is not possible. Her 90% of TW in HC that is bond-like only allows her to achieve a 10% allocation of TW to equity even with 100% of FC in equity. As her HC proportion declines, it is possible to allocate the FC to achieve her SAA of 50/50. The table illustrates that there are limits to achieving her SAA goal when HC is taken into account. There is no particular reason her HC had to be viewed as 100% bond-like or that her SAA goal had to be 50/50 or could not change over time. These are simply assumptions that can be changed.

Institutional investors. Institutional investors may be concerned with meeting liabilities, increasing wealth, or both. An insurance company must fund liabilities and grow surplus. Banks must meet reserve requirements, make loans, and manage the investment portfolio to correct the imbalance between loans and deposits with respect to duration, credit quality, and liquidity; while seeking a return. Entities with definable, measurable liabilities should evaluate portfolios from an ALM perspective.

Defined benefit pension plans. Defined benefit pension plans are concerned foremost with meeting pension obligations, so an ALM process is generally employed. The pension fund manager estimates the minimum acceptable (inflation-adjusted) return and then searches for the appropriate strategic allocation. Any future changes to the strategic allocation for the pension fund are based on several factors.

- The proposed allocation must meet the plan's risk and return objectives. Potential allocations are often compared on a risk-adjusted basis using the Sharpe ratio.
- The volatility of the plan surplus must be maintained within established bounds.
- The allocation must meet liquidity requirements.

Models, such as Monte Carlo simulation, can be employed to determine the long-term effects of the proposed allocation.

Endowments. The primary goal of an endowment is meeting spending requirements while protecting the fund principal. Note that the relevant rate of inflation for an endowment is the rate that affects its institutional beneficiary. For example, a university's costs typically rise at a higher rate than the overall economy, so its endowment fund must incorporate this higher rate into return calculations. Risk is a very important concern for an endowment because its funding is usually critical to the beneficiary.

Because bonds, especially Treasuries, are incapable of meeting their long-term return requirements, endowments usually allocate to a mix of debt for income and stability and equity for long-term returns and growth.

 Professor's Note: When you think about a successful university endowment, you realize that the endowment must (1) meet a portion of the university's current spending needs, (2) keep up with inflation to protect the fund's principal, and (3) meet increased future needs caused by enrollment increases.

Foundations. Although not usually tied to a single beneficiary, foundations are formed to provide grants to individuals, communities, and/or organizations. Depending upon their legal status, foundations are required to make minimum annual payouts based on a percentage of fund assets. The primary goal is to cover the spending requirement while protecting the fund's principal. From a strategic asset allocation standpoint, foundations and endowments are very similar. On the exam, be sure to select an allocation that meets the spending requirements, covers expected inflation, and provides for sufficient growth to fund anticipated growth.

Insurance companies. A characteristic that distinguishes insurance companies from most other institutional investors is the need to *segment* their portfolio. The portfolio is segmented along product lines, as each line has risk and return objectives related to its specific constraints.

Portfolio constraints can differ significantly across segments. For example, if the segment funds fixed-annuity products, the fund should be allocated in fixed-income securities. A segment that funds variable annuities and variable life products indexed to equity markets should be allocated to equities. Of course, as we discussed in Study Session 5, the surplus portfolio is usually invested heavily in equities to provide necessary growth.

While segmenting the portfolio by line of business is useful and became popular some years ago for insurance companies, it can be overdone. Companies that created too many segments created control issues and sub-optimal results. Companies have moved toward limiting the number of segments of the total portfolio. Each segment is then viewed in isolation versus its liabilities, but the total aggregate portfolio is also analyzed to determine the final optimal allocation of assets.

> **For the Exam:** On the exam, the specifics of the individual segments would have to be provided and you would select a suitable allocation for each based on its return and risk objectives and its constraints. Tax laws vary considerably from country to country, so any tax differences will have to be clearly noted for you on the exam. Also be prepared to discuss, if asked, why companies have moved to limit the segmentation. As is common at Level III, the basic core issues are generally well-tested. Occasionally, some of the sub-details will be tested.

Banks. The strategic allocation for banks is determined by their product mix and the goals of the securities portfolio. As we discussed in Study Session 5, the primary goals for a bank's securities portfolio are:

- Provide liquidity.
- Manage credit risk.
- Manage duration (gap management).
- Generate income.

Of the listed goals, managing duration (interest rate risk) is the most important, although managing credit risk and providing a source of liquidity are also very important. The strategic allocation is determined through an ALM process. You saw in Study Session 6 that bank portfolios are allocated primarily to fixed-income securities, and the equity (surplus) duration (asset duration minus liability duration) is managed by altering the duration of the securities portfolio.

TACTICAL ALLOCATION

LOS 17.t: Formulate and justify tactical asset allocation (TAA) adjustments to strategic asset class weights, given a TAA strategy and expectational data.

Tactical asset allocation (TAA) involves short-term deviations from the strategic asset allocation in an attempt to capitalize on capital market disequilibria (mispricing). The goal is to add value relative to an already established SAA or benchmark. A primary challenge is whether the expected benefits will outweigh the upfront costs to implement the TAA deviation away from SAA. The TAA could be undertaken at infrequent intervals or as part of a regular tactical allocation program that monitors market conditions, sectors, or asset classes, and reacts accordingly. TAA can be performed by internal personnel or by outside firms that specialize in TAA.

A disciplined approach to TAA could consist of:

- Periodically review market prices and expected returns for asset classes. For fixed income, the YTM is often taken as an initial proxy for expected return. If the manager believes the market return is attractive (unattractive), fixed income can be overweighted (or underweighted). Estimating market expectations for equity tends to be more difficult but the manager might take observed stock index prices and back-solve for the implied return using a dividend discount model or other valuation model. The managers can then react to the implied return and under- or overweight the asset class.
- These expected returns could be adjusted for the manager's perception of risk. For example, if the manager believes current conditions are more risky than normal, the manager could assess expected returns as needing to be higher than normal just to maintain a neutral weight.
- Many TAA approaches (but not all) are based on an assumption that returns are mean reverting to some long-term level.

Adding value through TAA is challenging and should be used as an increment to SAA, not a replacement for SAA. The decision to pursue TAA must consider both expected value added but also cost.

Example: Adjusting Global Allocation

Foundations Ltd., manages the portfolio of a large endowment fund with a strategic allocation of 70% to equities. The 70% is split with 40% in UK equities and the remaining 30% in international equity. The firm's economics staff has made the following return projections.

Asset Class	Long-term E(R)	Short-term E(R)
UK Equity	8%	4%
International Equity	9%	7%

1. **Calculate** the long- and short-term expected return for equity.

(4 minutes)

2. The manager is not willing to change the SAA to equity of 70%. Is there a TAA opportunity? If so, what is it?

(2 minutes)

---

3. The same portfolio normally holds a laddered portfolio of bonds as a 20% allocation to fixed income. A tactical band is established by policy of 5% around this (a maximum of 25% and a minimum of 15%). The current allocation is 20%. The portfolio manager expects the central bank to loosen monetary policy, resulting in a small reduction in real interest rates and a large increase in inflation expectations. The manager proposes to tactically move 10% of the portfolio from bonds to alternative investments. Is the action appropriate? What other information should be considered? If the action is not appropriate, could it be made appropriate? How?

(6 minutes)

Answer:

1. LT: $(40/70)(8\%) + (30/70)(9\%) = 8.42\%$

   ST: $(40/70)(4\%) + (30/70)(7\%) = 5.29\%$

2. Yes, there is an opportunity. The short-term view of equities is less attractive with the larger shortfall for UK equity. The manager could tactically asset allocate funds from UK to international equity but keep the total equity at 70%.

3. The small fall in real rates and large increase in inflation expectations will raise interest rates and reduce bond prices and returns. Reducing bond exposure may make sense, but a reduction from 20% to 10% is too large and exceeds the tactical band.

   The manager needs to compare the projected bond returns to alternative investment returns and consider the costs of the trade before making a smaller shift. The often high transaction cost and low liquidity of alternative investments makes this an important consideration.

   After this is done, the action may be appropriate. Change in risk should also be evaluated.

 Professor's Note: This is a broad and rather open-ended question that draws on multiple study sessions, some of which have not yet been covered. Such questions have appeared on the exam. When they do, give answers that are solidly based on the CFA® curriculum, answer all parts of the questions, and pay attention to the assigned point values to decide how much detail to include in the answers.

KEY CONCEPTS

LOS 17.a

Strategic asset allocation combines capital market expectations (formally represented by the efficient frontier) and the investor's risk, return, and investment constraints [from the investment policy statement (IPS)]. Strategic asset allocation is long-term in nature, and hence the weights are called *targets* and the portfolio represented by the strategic asset allocation is called the *policy portfolio*.

Each asset class has its own quantifiable systematic risk. Strategic asset allocation is a conscious effort to gain the desired exposure to systematic risk via specific weights to individual asset classes. Each asset class represents relatively similar investments (e.g., long-term corporate bonds) with similar systematic risk factors. Exposure to specific asset classes in specific proportions enables portfolio managers to effectively monitor and control their systematic risk exposure. In other words, strategic asset allocation reflects the investor's desired systematic risk exposure.

LOS 17.b

Tactical asset allocation is the result of active management wherein managers deviate from the strategic asset allocation to take advantage of any perceived *short-term* opportunities in the market. Hence, tactical asset allocation introduces additional risk, which should be justified by additional return (i.e., positive alpha).

LOS 17.c

Strategic allocation responds to the interaction of the investor's long-term strategic needs and long-run capital market expectations. The investor's goals are in terms of investment policy statement (IPS) objectives and constraints.

It should be remembered that the strategic allocation is based on long-run goals and capital market expectations. Tactical allocation may be used if the market experiences short-term disruptions or the manager recognizes mispriced assets, whereby they can change the allocation for short periods.

Because managers are the *experts* at selecting investments, the question is whether strategic allocation is worth the time and effort. The first response is that without a clearly defined strategic allocation, the portfolio may not reflect the investor's desires. Also, the importance of strategic asset allocation has been well-established empirically. One study showed that 94% of long-term performance is explained by strategic asset allocation.

LOS 17.d

ALM strategic asset allocation is determined in conjunction with modeling the liabilities of the investor. For investors with specific liabilities (e.g., defined benefit pension plans or insurance companies), asset allocation is tailored to meet liabilities and to maximize the surplus, given an acceptable level of risk. This usually results in a relatively high allocation to fixed-income assets. Strategic asset allocation involves specifically modeling liabilities and determining the asset allocation appropriate to fund them. Even for those investors who don't have specific (contractual) liabilities, future obligations (e.g., providing for post-retirement living expenses for an individual investor) can be modeled as liabilities, and an ALM approach to strategic asset allocation can be applied.

In asset-only strategic asset allocation, the focus is on earning the highest level of return for a given (acceptable) level of risk without any consideration for liability modeling. The liability (explicit or implied from future expected cash outflows) is indirectly taken into consideration through the required rate of return. Because the asset-only approach does not specifically model liabilities, the risk of not funding liabilities is not accurately controlled.

LOS 17.e

Dynamic asset allocation takes a multi-period view of the investment horizon. In other words, it recognizes that asset performance in one period affects the required rate of return and acceptable level of risk for subsequent periods. Dynamic asset allocation is difficult and costly to implement. However, investors who have significant liabilities, especially those with uncertain timing and/or amount, find the cost acceptable. Usually, investors who undertake the asset-liability approach to strategic asset allocation prefer dynamic asset allocation.

Static asset allocation ignores the link between optimal asset allocation across different time periods. For example, the manager using a static approach might estimate the necessary mean-variance inputs at a point in time and then construct the long-term portfolio accordingly. The manager using dynamic allocation allows for changing parameters over time using such techniques as Monte Carlo simulation. This allows the manager to build in expected changes to inputs as well as model unanticipated changes in macroeconomic factors.

LOS 17.f

Individuals display *loss aversion* rather than risk aversion and approach investing from a segmented perspective. Because of *mental accounting*, they meet goals one at a time. Their overall asset allocation is likely to be different from their optimal strategic allocation and inconsistent with their risk tolerance.

LOS 17.g

The portfolio's return objective is based on portfolio size, liquidity needs, time horizon, and maintenance of the principal. Unless stated otherwise, we always assume the investor will maintain the principal, so the portfolio must not only meet spending needs but expected inflation and management fees as well.

The risk objective should be specified in light of the investor's risk aversion. Investors can be classified using a numerical scheme, such as scoring investors from 1 to 10 based on their risk tolerance, with 1 indicating very high tolerance and 10 indicating very low tolerance.

The utility-adjusted (risk-adjusted) return the investor will realize from the portfolio can be found by using the following equation:

$$U_P = \hat{R}_P - 0.005(A)\left(\sigma_P^2\right)$$

where:

$\hat{R}_P$ = portfolio expected return

A = investor's risk aversion score

σ_P^2 = portfolio variance

In addition to standard deviation as a measure of risk (volatility), the acceptable level of risk can be stated in terms of *downside risk* measures such as shortfall risk, semivariance, and target semivariance.

LOS 17.h
Asset classes have been appropriately specified if:
- Assets in the class are similar from a descriptive as well as a statistical perspective.
- They are not highly correlated, so they provide the desired diversification.
- Individual assets cannot be classified into more than one class.
- They cover the majority of all possible investable assets.
- They contain a sufficiently large percentage of liquid assets.

LOS 17.i, 17.r
The capital allocation line (CAL) is the straight line drawn from the risk-free rate to tangency portfolio on the efficient frontier. The corner portfolio with the highest Sharpe ratio will approximate that tangent portfolio. If a risk-free asset exists and an investor is willing to lend or borrow at the risk-free rate, allocations on the CAL will be superior to allocations on the EF (which only considers risky assets). Investors wishing lower/higher risk than the tangent portfolio will hold a combination of the tangent portfolio and invest/borrow at the risk free rate.

If an ongoing allocation to the risk-free asset is not available, the investor can approximate the optimal efficient frontier asset allocation with a weighted average allocation between the two corner portfolios that most closely bracket the desired return. The asset class weights and the estimated standard deviation of the portfolio will be a weighted average of the asset classes and standard deviation of those two CPs.

LOS 17.j
There are advantages and disadvantages to adding different asset classes to a portfolio:
- Inflation-protected securities provide protection against inflation and automatically increase or decrease portfolio cash flows with inflation and deflation. U.S. Treasury Inflation Protection Securities (TIPS) are highly liquid and virtually risk free.
- The theoretical justification for adding global securities is the potential to increase return at all levels of risk. The practical implications of including global securities relate to other concerns associated with global investing that are not experienced in a domestic-only setting.

- The primary benefit to including alternative investments in an asset allocation is the diversification benefit. However, the practical drawbacks include the typically large amount of capital required and the need to carefully select out-performers.
- In some cases, information on alternative investments can be sparse or even nonexistent.

LOS 17.k

A decision rule based on the new investment's Sharpe ratio, the current portfolio Sharpe ratio, and the correlation of the returns on the two is used. If the Sharpe ratio of the new investment is greater than the current portfolio Sharpe ratio multiplied by the correlation of the new investment's returns with the portfolio's returns, adding the investment to the portfolio will improve the portfolio Sharpe ratio:

If $S_i > S_p \times \rho_{i,p}$ adding the investment will improve the portfolio Sharpe ratio

where:
S_i = Sharpe ratio of proposed investment
S_p = current portfolio Sharpe ratio
$\rho_{i,p}$ = correlation of the returns on the proposed investment with the portfolio returns

Sharpe Ratio is the: (expected return of the asset less the risk free rate) divided by the standard deviation of the asset.

LOS 17.l

Currency risk: Investing in a foreign-denominated security exposes the investor to changes in value of foreign asset and changes in value of the foreign currency. This has implications for the return of the asset and for its volatility.

Empirical evidence suggests that the standard deviation of currency is only about half the standard deviation of stock prices. It is the less important determinant of risk. (In the bond market, the currency volatility is generally higher than bond volatility, reflecting bonds are generally less volatile than stocks, making it a more important consideration for bond investors).

Political risk: Exists when a country has (1) irresponsible fiscal and/or monetary policy, and/or (2) lacks reasonable legal and regulatory rules to support but not stifle financial markets. It could arise if a government confiscates property without compensation, unduly restricts foreign investment or suspends capital and currency movement, manipulates the currency or taxes foreign investors unfairly, is unstable or defaults on its debt, and allows or requires companies to be managed for goals inconsistent with those of the shareholders.

Home country bias: Refers to the observation that investors tend to overweigh investments in their own country, creating a suboptimal portfolio allocation.

Costs in International Assets
- Transaction costs can be higher and liquidity can be lower.
- Withholding taxes on foreign investors may not be fully offset by tax treaties.
- Free-float can be an issue. The stated market capitalization may include shares held by the government or other investors who will not sell.
- Inefficient market infrastructure can result in high costs for security registration, settlement, custody, management, or information.

Opportunities in International Assets
1. Foreign markets could be undervalued and, thus, offer better expected return.

2. While the investor's home market may have had the best returns in the past, that is not a reliable indicator of future returns.

3. Even if correlations rise in the short run during crises, the long-run benefits of diversification can remain.

4. Correlations among bond markets tend to be lower than among equity markets. Adding international bonds to domestic-only portfolios can be particularly beneficial in reducing risk for risk averse investors.

LOS 17.m

A mean-variance based approach that assumes correlations and standard deviations are stable over time. The observation that correlations increase during financial crises is inconsistent with this assumption and indicates **conditional return correlations** (i.e., correlations that depend on market volatility and conditions). Diversification benefits fail when they are most needed.

Alternative methods exist to calculate correlation conditioned on the level of return. A portfolio could be optimized both assuming normal conditions and assuming crisis conditions.

A simpler method to determine what is happening to correlation is to plot rolling correlations between markets over time. The plot reveals:

- Correlations have been rising over time, and potential diversification benefits have decreased as markets integrate.
- Correlations did rise during crises periods and then fell back after the crises, within a generally rising upward trend.

LOS 17.n

As markets integrate and move through emerging market status to developed market status, the general progression is:

- Equity share prices rise as (1) capital can now flow into the formerly uninvestable market, and (2) to reflect declining stand-alone risk.
- Expected returns increase as capital flows into the market but then declines after the initial inflow to be consistent with the now higher stock prices and lower risk going forward.
- Long-run return volatility should decline as prices reflect information that is more freely available and political risk declines.

©2016 Kaplan, Inc.

LOS 17.o

The asset allocation process is essentially the portfolio management process that has been identified throughout the CFA curriculum. The steps are as follows:

- Determine the investor's return requirement and risk tolerance, subject to the investor's current wealth and constraints.
- Formulate long-term capital market expectations and their potential effects on the various asset classes.
- Determine the asset allocation that best meets the objectives defined in the investment policy statement (IPS), subject to any other limitations specified by the investor.
- Monitor the portfolio regularly as specified in the IPS. A feedback loop should be included so changes in long-term market factors can be incorporated into the *model* and to determine whether adjustments to the strategic allocation are justified. If market changes are short-term, tactical allocation measures should be considered.

LOS 17.p

Mean-Variance Approach

The **mean-variance approach** begins with estimated return, standard deviation, and correlations for asset classes. The optimizer then solves for the asset class weight that produces the highest return for each level of risk. A serious problem is the instability of those asset class weights for even small changes in estimated asset class returns.

Resampled Efficient Frontier

Resampling begins with an initial mean variance optimization analysis. Small variations in the inputs around the initial estimates [particularly E(R)] are used to generate a series of efficient frontiers. The resampled EF (REF) is an average of these multiple EFs, and the asset allocation for each point on the REF is an average of the asset allocations for a given return on each of the multiple EFs. Resampling tends to produce portfolios with more asset classes (better diversified) and allocations that do not change as much for a subsequent change in estimated inputs.

Black-Litterman (BL)

BL uses world market asset class weights with analyst estimates of risk and correlations in a MVO to solve for consensus asset class expected returns. The analyst can then adjust the model-generated returns using personal return expectations (and confidence in those expectations). BL tends to produce portfolios with more asset classes (better diversified) and is less dependent on the analyst's initial estimates of expected return by asset class.

Monte Carlo Simulation (MSC)

MCS is a complement to the other approaches. It can take one asset allocation and simulate how that allocation will perform over time. Small random variations around inputs (such as expected returns) generate potential future return paths. Additional factors such as distributions and path dependency issues can be incorporated into the analysis.

Asset-Liability Management

Asset-liability management considers the allocation of assets with respect to a given liability or set of liabilities. The ALM approach searches for the set of allocations, which maximize the *difference* (the *surplus*) between assets and liabilities at each level of risk.

Experience-Based Techniques

Experience-based techniques are practical rules-of-thumb that are generally consistent with more complex methods of asset allocation in many situations. The risk is that it may not be appropriate in some situations.

LOS 17.q

The efficient frontier is the set of portfolios with the highest return for the portfolio risk taken. A constrained frontier allows only positive or zero weight for any asset class and no short sales. This is a normal constraint, as most investors do not short sell, and it allows corner portfolios to be determined and used to interpolate the risk and asset allocation between any two adjacent CPs.

LOS 17.s

Institutional investors. The typical institutional investor is concerned more with meeting liabilities than with generating wealth.

Individuals. Individuals' goals include meeting living expenses, funding children's educational expenses, funding retirement, setting up trusts, etc. In other words, the individual typically looks primarily at wealth accumulation to meet required as well as *desired* expenditures.

Unlike the institutional investor, the typical individual's wealth is accumulated over many years, while the ability to generate income reaches a peak and falls to zero at retirement. The individual's *human capital*, therefore, is greatest at an early age, while his financial capital increases over time and reaches a maximum at retirement.

At younger ages, then, he has a considerable allocation to *bonds* (his human capital) and the allocation of his financial assets should be toward riskier, higher-return assets like equities. As he ages and accumulates financial capital, his human capital becomes a smaller and smaller component of his total portfolio, and the financial assets require more protection (i.e., an allocation to safer assets).

Two other factors that separate individuals from institutions are **longevity risk** and **mortality risk**.

LOS 17.t

Tactical asset allocation (TAA) involves short-term deviations from the strategic asset allocation in an attempt to capitalize on capital market disequilibria (mispricing). If used it should be a compliment to SAA and expected added value should be compared to cost of implementation.

CONCEPT CHECKERS

1. Jack Manning, CFA, and Tess Brown, CFA, have just joined a financial planning firm. They will work as a team assessing and managing the portfolios of individual clients. Manning will specialize in forming long-term capital market expectations. Brown focuses on relative value models to assess shorter-term over- and undervaluation. Based upon this, we would define the focus of:
   A. both Manning and Brown as tactical asset allocation.
   B. both Manning and Brown as strategic asset allocation.
   C. Manning as strategic asset allocation and Brown as tactical asset allocation.

2. North East Fellowship University's endowment fund has $20 million in assets. The fund has a targeted spending rate of 4.50%. The fund has been incurring 0.75% as management costs. The trustees would like to preserve the purchasing power of the fund and curtail the risk in terms of standard deviation to no more than 10%. Inflation expectation is 2% per year over the foreseeable future. The fund's required rate of return is *closest* to:
   A. 7.00%.
   B. 7.40%.
   C. 8.00%.

3. Tom Wright is evaluating the following portfolios for his retirement. The risk-free rate is 3%, and Wright is moderately risk averse with a numerical ranking of 5.

Portfolio	Return	Std. Dev.
A	15.50%	19%
B	10.85%	12%
C	8.50%	14%
D	14.25%	16%

   The utility adjusted return for the portfolio Wright will *most likely* accept is *closest* to:
   A. 6.48%.
   B. 7.25%.
   C. 7.85%.

Use the following information to answer Question 4.

Portfolio	Exp. Return	Std. Dev.	Asset Class Weights			
			1	*2*	*3*	*4*
A	12.00%	10.50%	65%	–20%	35%	20%
B	16.50%	15.00%	15%	20%	50%	15%
C	18.00%	20.00%	30%	20%	25%	25%
D						

4. Given that Portfolio D is composed of 35% Portfolio A and 65% Portfolio B, the asset class weights in Portfolio D (in percent) are *closest* to:

	1	2	3	4
A.	32.50	20.00	30.75	16.75
B.	14.85	6.00	32.50	46.65
C.	32.50	6.00	44.75	16.75

Use the following information to answer Questions 5 through 8.

Alpa Singh, 56, was recently widowed. She was married to Robert Singh, MD, for 29 years and has two daughters, a 26-year-old and a 23-year-old. Upon the death of her husband, Mrs. Singh received $2 million from his life insurance policy. The Singhs had also set aside $1,350,000 towards their retirement. Mrs. Singh has no income of her own and was dependent on her husband. They lived comfortably, and Mrs. Singh estimates that she would need about $100,000 next year, after taxes. Even though her daughters are not dependent on her, she would like to gift them each $15,000 next year out of the after-tax return on the portfolio. She also would like to be able to pay $200,000 for the younger daughter's wedding in one year. As she will set aside the appropriate amount in T-bills earning 2% after tax, it will not be considered part of her investable portfolio. Her house is completely paid for, and she would like to leave it to her daughters upon her death as part of their inheritance. She would also like to leave a sizable inheritance for her grandchildren.

Mrs. Singh would like to keep her investments in the United States and not use any leverage in her portfolio. She considers herself to be moderately risk averse but recognizes that she has a long-term time horizon after taking gifts to her grandchildren into account. Her numerical risk aversion is 6. Her tax bracket is 30%, and inflation is estimated to be 1.50% per year. To be conservative, she and her advisor assume 100% of all return is taxed at 30% each year.

David Wells has been the financial adviser for the Singhs. To plan for changes in her portfolio and to invest the proceeds from the life insurance policy, he has prepared the following long-term capital market expectations:

	Asset Class	Expected Return	Exp. Std. Dev.	Correlations			
				1	2	3	4
1	U.S. Lg Cap	14.23%	14.74%	1.00			
2	U.S. Sm Cap	13.36%	17.32%	0.793406	1.00		
3	U.S. LT corp	9.47%	6.90%	0.317803	0.097134	1.00	
4	U.S. LT Gov	9.55%	8.99%	0.325103	0.075176	0.95754	1.00

Using the long-term capital market expectations, the mean-variance optimization yields four corner portfolios as follows:

Corner Portfolio	Expected Return	Exp. Std. Dev.	Sharpe Ratio	Asset Class Weights			
				1	2	3	4
1	9.90%	6.60%	1.197	0.00%	11.10%	88.90%	0.00%
2	10.06%	6.64%	1.214	0.00%	14.90%	85.10%	0.00%
3	12.10%	9.58%	1.054	55.22%	0.00%	44.78%	0.00%
4	14.23%	14.74%	0.830	100.00%	0.00%	0.00%	0.00%

The efficient frontier from the same data is shown in the following graph:

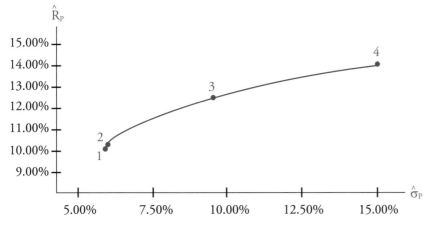

5. Assuming Mrs. Singh wants to protect the real value of her portfolio, the required nominal, before-tax rate of return her portfolio must generate to meet her combined expenses next year is *closest* to:
    A. 6.21%.
    B. 7.45%.
    C. 8.03%.

6. Suppose that Mrs. Singh agrees with her adviser to seek a required rate of return of 11%. Wells then calculates the asset class weights of the efficient portfolio that has an expected return of 11%. His results are *closest* to (with weights given in percentages):
    A. weights = 35.43; 6.32; 58.25; 0.00.
    B. weights = 27.26; 7.25; 65.49; 0.00.
    C. weights = 25.44; 8.03; 66.52; 0.00.

7. Wells then determines the efficient portfolio that provides the highest level of utility for Mrs. Singh and calculates the utility she will derive from it. He decides on:
    A. Portfolio 2 with U_2 = 0.0879.
    B. Portfolio 3 with U_3 = 0.0935.
    C. Portfolio 1 with U_1 = 0.0859.

8. Using Roy's Safety-First Measure, **determine** which of the corner portfolios is the *most appropriate* given that the minimal acceptable return on the portfolio is 6%.

9. **Explain** how Black-Litterman (BL) uses the three inputs required for mean variance optimization (MVO) and **explain** the two primary benefits of using BL rather than MVO.

Use the following information to answer Questions 10 and 11.

Bill Mosley is the Chief Investment Officer for Trinity Endowment Fund. The trustees of the fund have asked Bill to recommend a strategic asset allocation for the fund. The trustees have determined that the required rate of return for the fund should be 12% and that the fund standard deviation should not exceed 15%. Further, the fund should be diversified in broad asset categories including foreign equities and precious metals. The fund charter does not allow negative weights in any asset classes.

Based on his capital market expectations, Bill ran a constrained optimization, and the results are shown below:

Corner Portfolio	Expected Return	Exp. Std. Dev.	Sharpe Ratio	Asset Class Weights					
				1	2	3	4	5	6
1	7.86%	5.05%	1.259	59.59%	0.00%	4.90%	0.00%	6.87%	28.63%
2	8.52%	5.18%	1.355	61.11%	0.00%	6.56%	0.00%	9.74%	22.58%
3	10.88%	7.23%	1.297	66.97%	0.00%	7.47%	4.78%	20.78%	0.00%
4	14.10%	13.96%	0.903	0.00%	0.00%	4.75%	8.22%	87.03%	0.00%
5	14.18%	14.19%	0.894	0.00%	0.00%	0.00%	6.40%	93.60%	0.00%
6	14.29%	14.65%	0.873	0.00%	0.00%	0.00%	0.00%	100.00%	0.00%

The efficient frontier is shown below.

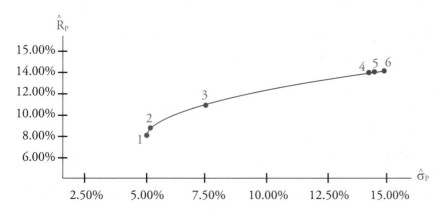

10. What would be the asset class weights of the efficient portfolio that would be recommended for the endowment fund?
    A. Weights = (43.68%; 0%; 6.52%; 5.98%; 43.82%; 0.00%).
    B. Weights = (35.22%; 0%; 6.23%; 5.67%; 21.71%; 0.32%).
    C. Weights = (45.98%; 0%; 6.21%; 5.45%; 33.72%; 0.21%).

11. **Discuss** and **contrast** asset-only versus asset-liability portfolio management.

12. **Describe** expected return estimation bias associated with traditional mean-variance allocation and **describe** how resampling can be used to help solve the problem.

13. Due to the recent decline in gold prices, Thomas Goetz, a banking executive in Spain, is considering adding gold to his portfolio, which currently contains no precious metals. Goetz has gathered the following information:
   - Risk free rate = 3%.
   - Correlation between gold and his current portfolio = 0.42.
   - Expected return of his current portfolio = 11%.
   - Expected return of gold = 8%.
   - Standard deviation of his current portfolio = 15%.
   - Standard deviation of gold = 20%.

   Goetz has two objectives: (1) to make the right decision regarding whether to add gold to the portfolio, and (2) to make the decision in the most efficient manner possible. Considering both objectives, he should:
   A. not add gold to his portfolio because the return of gold is lower, and the risk is higher than his current portfolio.
   B. run a mean-variance optimization creating an efficient frontier comparing the current and proposed portfolios to determine whether to add gold to the portfolio.
   C. add gold to his portfolio because the Sharpe ratio of gold is higher than the product of the Sharpe ratio of his current portfolio and the correlation between gold and his current portfolio.

14. Hannah Tremblay is a Canadian investor who has the following asset allocation in her portfolio:
   - 30% invested in a mixture of Canadian bonds of different maturities and risk levels.
   - 10% invested in a foreign bond index fund.
   - 40% invested in Canadian equities.
   - 15% invested in foreign stocks.
   - 5% invested in alternative investments.

   Which of the following is an issue she should be most concerned with in her portfolio?
   A. Political risk.
   B. Currency risk.
   C. Lack of diversification.

15.   **Explain** conditional return correlation and its implication on asset allocation in the portfolio construction process.

16.   Which of the following is *least accurate* regarding what happens to stocks in an emerging market when it becomes a developed market?
       A. Volatility decreases as information flows more freely and political risk decreases.
       B. Expected return will be higher when the economy reaches developed market status.
       C. Equity prices rise as investors are able to buy the stock that was previously unavailable.

For more questions related to this topic review, log in to your Schweser online account and launch SchweserPro™ QBank; and for video instruction covering each LOS in this topic review, log in to your Schweser online account and launch the OnDemand video lectures, if you have purchased these products.

ANSWERS – CONCEPT CHECKERS

1. **C**   Manning is using longer term capital market expectations to form SAA, while Brown is looking at shorter term indicators, which is TAA.

2. **B**   Required rate of return = $(1.045)(1.02)(1.0075) - 1 = 0.0739 = 7.39\%$

    Generally, either addition or compounding of returns have been shown as acceptable on the exam. The recommended preference is to use compounding for multiperiod ongoing situations (such as foundations and endowments) or if the question references path dependency or specifies compounding.

3. **C** $U_A = \hat{R}_A - 0.5(R_Z)(\sigma_A^2) = 0.1550 - 0.5(5)(0.19)^2 = 0.0648 = 6.48\%$
    $U_B = \hat{R}_B - 0.5(R_Z)(\sigma_B^2) = 0.1085 - 0.5(5)(0.12)^2 = 0.0725 = 7.25\%$
    $U_C = \hat{R}_C - 0.5(R_Z)(\sigma_C^2) = 0.0850 - 0.5(5)(0.14)^2 = 0.0360 = 3.60\%$
    $U_D = \hat{R}_D - 0.5(R_Z)(\sigma_D^2) = 0.1425 - 0.5(5)(0.16)^2 = 0.0785 = 7.85\%$

    Because U_D is the highest of all four, Tom gets the highest utility by investing in Portfolio D with a utility-adjusted return of 7.85%.

    Hint: Remember this function can also be presented as –0.005 instead of –0.5. If –0.005 is used, the inputs must be in whole numbers. For example, $U_A = 15.5\% - 0.005(5)(19)^2 = 6.48\%$. Either approach is acceptable on the exam.

4. **C**   Investing 35% in Portfolio A and 65% in Portfolio B, the resulting asset class weights in Portfolio D are:

    $$\text{asset class weight} = (w_A)(\text{wt in A}) + (w_B)(\text{wt in B})$$
    $$\text{weight of 1} = (0.35)(65) \quad + (0.65)(15) = 32.50\%$$
    $$\text{weight of 2} = (0.35)(-20) \quad + (0.65)(20) = 6.00\%$$
    $$\text{weight of 3} = (0.35)(35) \quad + (0.65)(50) = 44.75\%$$
    $$\text{weight of 4} = (0.35)(20) \quad + (0.65)(15) = 16.75\%$$
    $$\sum_{i=1}^{4} W_i = 100\%$$

5. **C**   The total value of Singh's portfolio is $3,350,000 ($2,000,000 life insurance proceeds + $1,350,000 retirement portfolio). To provide $200,000 in one year, she will set aside the present value of $200,000 at 2% = $196,078 in T-bills. Therefore, she has an investable portfolio of $3,350,000 – $196,078 = $3,153,922.

    Singh's after-tax living expenses and gifts over the coming year total $130,000. This represents an after-tax real spending rate of $130,000 / $3,153,922 = 4.12%. Adding 1.5% inflation to protect the real value of the portfolio, the required after-tax nominal return becomes 5.62%. The before-tax nominal return = 5.62% /(1 – 0.30) = 8.03%.

    Note that the case facts explicitly say the $200,000 will not be considered part of her investable portfolio, so its PV is properly excluded from the investable asset base. The two $15,000 gifts are to be made from the after-tax return of the portfolio, so they are not to be deducted from the investable asset base, and they are part of the required return amount. The case provided these specific directions to follow.

6. **C** The expected return of 11% lies between Corner Portfolios 2 and 3 with expected returns of 10.06% and 12.10%, respectively. We solve for w in the following equation:

$$0.11 = w_2(0.1006) + (1 - w_2)(0.1210)$$
$$w_2 = 0.5392; \ w_3 = 1 - 0.5392 = 0.4608$$

In other words, the efficient portfolio with an expected return of 11% has 53.92% weight in Corner Portfolio 2 and 46.08% weight in Corner Portfolio 3. With respect to asset classes, the weights then are derived as follows:

US Lg Cap	$= (0.5392)(0) + (0.4608)(0.5522)$	$= 0.2544 = 25.45\%$
US Sm Cap	$= (0.5392)(0.149) + (0.4608)(0)$	$= 0.0803 = 8.03\%$
US LT Corp bonds	$= (0.5392)(0.851) + (0.4608)(0.4478)$	$= 0.6652 = 66.52\%$
US LT Gov bonds	$= (0.5392)(0) + (0.4608)(0)$	$= 0\%$

Note: The approximate standard deviation of the efficient portfolio with 11% expected return is the weighted average standard deviations of Corner Portfolios 2 and 3.

Standard deviation = (0.5392)(0.0664) + (0.4608)(0.0958) = 0.08 = 8%

7. **B** Risk aversion is 6.

$$U_1 = \hat{R}_1 - 0.5(R_Z)(\sigma_1^2) = 0.0990 - 0.5(6)(0.0660)^2 = 0.0859$$
$$U_2 = \hat{R}_2 - 0.5(R_Z)(\sigma_2^2) = 0.1006 - 0.5(6)(0.0664)^2 = 0.0874$$
$$U_3 = \hat{R}_3 - 0.5(R_Z)(\sigma_3^2) = 0.1210 - 0.5(6)(0.0958)^2 = 0.0935$$
$$U_4 = \hat{R}_4 - 0.5(R_Z)(\sigma_4^2) = 0.1423 - 0.5(6)(0.1474)^2 = 0.0771$$

Portfolio 3 has the highest utility for Mrs. Singh.

8. Corner Portfolio 3 is the most appropriate. Roy's Safety-First criterion for Portfolio 3 is:

$$RSF_{P3} = \frac{\hat{R}_P - R_{MAR}}{\sigma_P} = \frac{12.1\% - 6\%}{9.58\%} = 0.637$$

Portfolio	Expected Return	Std. Dev.	Roy's Safety First Measure
1	9.90%	6.60%	0.591
2	10.06%	6.64%	0.611
3	12.10%	9.58%	0.637
4	14.23%	14.74%	0.558

9. MVO requires expected return, standard deviation, and correlations among asset classes as inputs. BL differs by using market asset class weights, standard deviation, and correlations among asset classes as inputs. BL then uses MVO to back-solve for asset class expected returns.

The primary benefits of BL are (1) it is less dependent on the analyst's initial estimates of expected returns by asset class and (2) it reduces the instability of the efficient frontier, which refers to large changes in asset weights due to even small changes in expected return inputs for traditional MVO. BL also tends to produce allocations with a larger number of asset classes (i.e., better diversified).

Candidate Discussion: Arguably, the answer gave three benefits and the question asked for the two "primary benefits." Worst case scenario, the grader will only read the first two, but here we provided three, as there really are three. If you wish, only give two. Not every question will be self-evident as to what the single correct answer is.

10. **A**   The required rate of return of 12% lies between Corner Portfolios 3 and 4 with expected returns of 10.88% and 14.10% respectively. We solve for w_3 in the following equation:

$$0.12 = w_3(0.1088) + (1 - w_3)(0.1410)$$

$$w_3 = 0.6522$$

65.22% is in Corner Portfolio 3 and 34.78% is in Corner Portfolio 4, so the asset class weights are:

AC 1: $(0.6522)(0.6697) + (0.3478)(0)$ $= 0.4368 = 43.68\%$
AC 2: $(0.6522)(0) + (0.3478)(0)$ $= 0$
AC 3: $(0.6522)(0.0747) + (0.3478)(0.0475)$ $= 0.0652 = 6.52\%$
AC 4: $(0.6522)(0.0478) + (0.3478)(0.0822)$ $= 0.0598 = 5.98\%$
AC 5: $(0.6522)(0.2078) + (0.3478)(0.8703)$ $= 0.4382 = 43.82\%$
AC 6: $(0.6522)(0) + (0.3478)(0)$ $= 0$

11.   Asset-liability portfolio management allocates assets within the framework of funding liabilities. The optimal allocation is the one that maintains risk within an acceptable range while providing the return necessary to meet the liabilities. The manager can employ an ALM efficient frontier framework. The ALM frontier plots surplus at various levels of risk, and the manager selects the allocation on the frontier that produces an acceptable mix of expected surplus and risk.

In contrast, asset-only allocation looks solely at risk and return with the goal of maximizing return for the acceptable level of risk. Although liabilities can be modeled into the required return, the surplus (assets minus liabilities) is not specifically considered. To avoid the estimation uncertainty associated with projecting expected returns, the Black-Litterman approach can be employed in an asset-only allocation.

12.   Traditional mean variance optimization begins with estimating expected return, standard deviation, and correlation among asset classes. The expected returns are the most difficult to estimate inputs and are subject to bias (i.e., the analysts may over- or understate return estimates). Unfortunately, the resulting MVO asset allocations are highly sensitive to small changes in estimated returns.

Resampling addresses this by starting with a single set of estimated asset class returns and then generating multiple data sets around those estimates. While there can still be bias in the initial estimates, the distribution of data inputs produces an average asset allocation for any given target return that is less sensitive to any further change in expected return.

Candidate Discussion: Resampling does not fully solve the bias issue, but it does mitigate the problem. Stating either that it does nothing or that it fully solves the problem is incorrect and would reduce the score. The correct answer is to accurately reflect what resampling does and does not do.

13. **C**   If Sharpe$_G$ > Sharpe$_P$ × $\rho_{G,P}$ then add gold to the portfolio:
Sharpe ratio = (ER – R$_f$) / Std
Sharpe ratio of gold = (8 – 3) / 20 = 0.25
Sharpe ratio of current portfolio = (11 – 3) / 15 = 0.53
Sharpe$_P$ × $\rho_{G,P}$ = 0.53 × 0.42 = 0.22
0.25 > 0.22, therefore, add gold to the portfolio.

Note that generating a new efficient frontier including gold in the analysis will answer whether or not Goetz should add gold to his portfolio; however, it is a cumbersome process. This decision rule is an efficient way to determine if the new asset is beneficial. Full MVO is still required to determine the percentage asset allocation.

14. **B**   Tremblay should be considering the impact of foreign currency (non-Canadian dollars) on her portfolio risk and return. There is no specific indication of political risk, and she has reasonable diversification.

15.   Conditional return correlation means that correlation is dependent upon the amount of volatility in the global markets at any point in time. Unfortunately, markets tend to be more positively correlated in crisis conditions and decline together, reducing the diversification benefit when it is most needed. Conditional correlation assumes one set of correlations in normal periods and a second, more positive set of correlations in periods of high volatility. This allows for a more complete analysis and could be used for a joint optimization considering both market environments or to examine a range of potential outcomes.

16. **B**   As an emerging market transitions to a developed market, expected return increases at first when capital flows into the market causing stock prices to increase and then expected return falls. The expected return should remain positive in the newly classified developed market but at a lower level due to lower risk than during the transitional phase from developing to developed market.

CURRENCY MANAGEMENT: AN INTRODUCTION

Study Session 9

EXAM FOCUS

Globalization of financial markets is an important topic in portfolio management and for the CFA exam. This section reviews currency math and then discusses an extensive list of currency management tools and techniques.

INTRODUCTION

Professor's Note: Good technique always matters but particularly with currency. This material emphasizes (1) thinking of a currency quote as a base currency in the denominator and a pricing currency in the numerator, and (2) being prepared to interpret a currency quote from the perspective of either the base or pricing currency.

This assignment is new as of the 2014 exam. It consolidates and replaces several other readings and follows some conventions you may not have seen before. Our introduction is longer than usual and is important. It is drawn from material marked optional or included later in the CFA text and you will need it to understand the assignment.

The Price and Base Currencies: The **base currency** is the denominator of the exchange rate and it is **priced** in terms of the numerator. Unless clearly identified otherwise, the terms "buy" and "sell" refer to the base currency. But remember, there are two currencies involved. For example, sell spot 1,000,000 at CAD/USD 0.9800 is assumed to mean sell for "immediate delivery" 1,000,000 U. S. dollars and buy 980,000 Canadian dollars. (The convention is settlement in two business days but this detail is ignored in most cases; the FX swap is an exception where the two business days are considered).

Buy 500,000 USD/CHF six months forward at 1.07 is assumed to mean buy 500,000 Swiss francs, settling in six months versus sell USD 535,000.

Bid/Asked Rules: Currencies are quoted with a **bid/offered** or **bid/asked price**. By convention, the smaller number is written first and the larger number is second. However, both the bid and the asked can be interpreted as the sale of one currency versus the purchase of the other currency. The difference is the dealer's profit margin to buy or sell the currencies. The customer pays the bid/ask spread, paying more and/or receiving less in the transaction. A quote of 0.9790/0.9810 CAD/USD has four interpretations.

Deliver more CAD can be phrased as:

- Buy 1.0000 USD and deliver (sell) 0.9810 CAD.
- Sell 0.9810 CAD and receive (buy) 1.0000 USD.

Receive less CAD can be phrased as:

- Sell 1.0000 USD and receive (buy) 0.9790 CAD.
- Buy 0.9790 CAD and deliver (sell) 1.0000 USD.

Spot Versus Forward: Spot exchange transactions are for immediate settlement and a **forward transaction** is a price agreed to on a transaction date for delayed (longer than spot) settlement. The forward quote can be given directly or in forward points (an adjustment from the spot quote).

Forward points are an adjustment to the spot price to determine the forward price. The points are interpreted based on the number of decimal places in which the spot price is quoted. The rule is to move the decimal in the points to the left by the same number of decimal places shown in the right for the spot price. For example:

Spot Quote	Forward Points	Points with Decimal Adjusted	Forward Price
1.33	1.1	1.1 / 100 = 0.011	1.33 + 0.011 = 1.341
2.554	−9.6	−9.6 / 1,000 = −0.0096	2.554 − 0.0096 = 2.5444
0.7654	13.67	13.67 / 10,000 = 0.001367	0.7654 + 0.001367 = 0.766767

There is a myth that the forward points are always divided by 10,000. That is only true if the spot quote is given to four decimal places. To continue the pattern, if the spot quote shows five decimals on the right, move the forward point decimal five places (/100,000) to the left.

Example 1: Spot and forward bid/asked quotes of the Australian dollar/euro

Maturity/ Settlement	Spot Quote/ Forward Points
Spot AUD/EUR	1.2571/ 1.2574
30 days	−1.0/−0.9
90 days	+11.7/+12.0

1. What is the 30 day forward bid/offered quote?

2. If a manager sells 1,000,000 AUD forward 90 days, **calculate** what the manager will deliver and receive. When will the exchange take place?

Answer:

1. The spot quote is given to four decimal places making the forward points for 30 days: –1.0 / 10,000 = –0.00010 and –0.9 / 10,000 = –0.00009, a four decimal place adjustment to match the spot quote. The 30-day forward bid/asked are: 1.2571 – 0.00010 = 1.25700 and 1.2574 – 0.00009 = 1.25731.

2. The exchange will be 90 days from the trade date, at contract expiration. The manager will deliver AUD 1,000,000.

   The 90-day forward quotes are 1.2571 + 0.00117 by 1.2574 + 0.00120, which is 1.25827/1.25860 for the AUD/EUR. The manager is delivering AUD and receiving EUR. The manager must deliver more AUD or receive fewer EUR. In this case, the bid/asked quotes are both for 1 EUR and the manager will deliver AUD. The manager must deliver at AUD/EUR 1.25860.

   The manager will receive EUR: AUD 1,000,000 / (1.25860 AUD/EUR) = EUR 794,533.61.

Offsetting Transactions and Mark to Market: While forward contracts do not require market to market cash flow exchanges prior to settlement, it is often desirable or required for regulatory purposes to mark the position to market value. The mark-to-market value is the present value of any gain or loss that would be realized if the contract were closed early with an offsetting contract position.

Example 2: Offsetting transactions

Based on the initial quotes given in the previous example, a different manager entered into a trade to sell (deliver) 90 days forward, EUR 10,000,000 at the "all-in" forward quote of AUD/EUR 1.25827. Thirty days have passed and exchange rates are now the following:

Maturity/ Settlement	Spot Quote/ Forward Points	LIBOR Rates AUD
Spot AUD/EUR	1.3189/1.3191	
30 days	+1.1/+1.2	1.10%
60 days	+10.3/+10.5	1.20%
90 days	+15.3/+16.1	1.25%

1. **Identify** the offsetting position the manager would take to close the initial transaction and **calculate** the resulting gain or loss. When will this gain or loss be settled?

2. **Calculate** the mark to market the manager would report on day 30 of the original trade if the trade were not closed out early.

Answers:

1. Thirty days have passed and the initial trade to sell EUR 10,000,000 forward has 60 days until expiration. The offsetting transaction is to buy 10,000,000 EUR 60 days forward. The solution is done in steps.

   Step 1: Identify the forward exchange rate for the offsetting position. The manager must buy EUR 10,000,000 (which requires delivering AUD) 60 days forward at AUD/EUR 1.3191 + 0.00105, which is AUD/EUR 1.32015.

   Step 2: In 60 days, the manager will do the following:
   - On the original trade: sell EUR 10,000,000 and buy AUD at AUD/EUR 1.25827. The manager will receive AUD 12,582,700.
   - On the offsetting trade: buy EUR 10,000,000 and sell AUD at AUD/EUR 1.32015. The manager will pay AUD 13,201,500.

   The difference, a loss of AUD 618,800, will be settled and paid 90 days after the initial transaction and 60 days after the offsetting transaction.

   Alternatively, this can be solved directly. The base currency (euro) is sold at 1.25827 AUD and then bought at 1.32015 AUD for a loss of 1.32015 − 1.25827 = 0.06188 AUD per euro. On the trade of 10,000,000 euros, this is a loss of AUD 618,800.

2. The current mark to market is the present value of the gain or loss that would be locked in with an offsetting transaction. That offsetting loss was calculated in Solution 1 as AUD 618,800. The 60-day LIBOR rate on the AUD is 1.20%

   Mark-to-market loss = AUD 618,800 / (1 + (0.012 (60 / 360))) = AUD 617,564.87

An FX Swap: The FX swap is not a currency swap or even a swap as that term is otherwise used. The FX swap rolls over a maturing forward contract using a spot transaction into a new forward contract. An existing forward is "swapped" for another forward transaction.

Example 3: An FX swap

A manager purchased 10,000,000 South African rand (ZAR) three months forward at ZAR/USD 0.1058.

Two days before contract expiration the manager decides to extend the transaction for another 30 days. **Explain** the FX swap used to implement this decision.

Answer:

The manager sells spot ZAR 10,000,000 to offset the maturing contract. Both the initial forward and offsetting spot transaction will settle in two business days. The manager enters a new 30-day forward contract to buy ZAR 10,000,000 versus the USD to rollover the trade.

Option Basics: A call option is a right to buy the underlying and gains value as the underlying rises above the strike price; its delta approaches 1.00 (a 100-delta). The call loses value as the underlying falls below the strike price and its delta approaches 0.00 (a 0-delta).

A put is the right to sell the underlying and gains value as the underlying falls below the strike price; its delta approaches −1.00 (this can also be referred to as a 100-delta, the negative sign is assumed and not written). The put loses value as the underlying rises above the strike price and the delta approaches 0.00 (a 0-delta).

For a call and a put with identical parameters (time to expiration, strike price, and price of the underlying), the sum of the absolute deltas is 1.00 or 100-delta.

Currency Option Basics: Currency options require two currencies and a call on one currency is a put on the other currency. Unless otherwise specified, the option is from the base currency perspective. For example, a call option to buy 10,000,000 at a strike price of ZAR/GBP 14.56 is the right to buy 10,000,000 British pounds and sell 145,600,000 South African rand. It is also a put option—the right to sell 145,600,000 South African rand and buy 10,000,000 British pounds.

A put option to sell 100,000 at MXN/EUR at 20.1 is the right to sell 100,000 euros and buy 2,010,000 Mexican pesos. It is also a call option to buy 2,010,000 Mexican pesos and sell 100,000 euros.

The important relationships can be summarized as follows:

As the Price of the Base Currency Increases:	The Call Option to Buy the Base Currency:	The Put Option to Sell the Base Currency:
From 0 to the strike price	Is out-of-the-money and rising in value. Delta is shifting from 0.0 toward 0.5 (from a 0-delta to a 50-delta).	Is in-the-money and falling in value. Delta is shifting from −1.0 toward −0.5 (from a 100-delta to a 50-delta).
To the strike price	Is at-the-money. Delta is approximately 0.5 (a 50-delta).	Is at-the-money. Delta is approximately −0.5 (a 50-delta).
From the strike price upward	Is in-the-money and rising in value. Delta is shifting from 0.5 toward 1.0 (from a 50-delta to a 100-delta).	Is out-of-the-money and falling in value. Delta is shifting from −0.5 toward 0.0 (from a 50-delta to a 0-delta).

EFFECTS OF CURRENCY ON PORTFOLIO RISK AND RETURN

Domestic currency or **home currency** is the currency of the investor (or the currency in which portfolio results are reported and analyzed).

Domestic asset is an asset denominated in the investor's domestic currency.

Foreign currency and **foreign asset** are a currency other that the investor's domestic currency and an asset denominated in that foreign currency. These are sometimes called the local currency and local market, respectively.

Foreign-currency return (R_{FC}) is the return of the foreign asset measured in its local (foreign) currency. It can be called the local market return.

The **percentage change in value of the foreign currency** is denoted as R_{FX}. It can be called the local currency return.

Domestic-currency return (R_{DC}) is the return in domestic currency units considering both the **foreign-currency return** (R_{FC}) and the percentage change in value of the foreign currency (R_{FX}).

LOS 18.a: Analyze the effects of currency movements on portfolio risk and return.

An investment in assets priced in a currency other than the investor's domestic currency (a *foreign asset* priced in a *foreign currency*) has two sources of risk and return: (1) the return on the assets in the foreign currency and (2) the return on the foreign currency from any change in its exchange rate with the investor's *domestic currency*. These returns are multiplicative and an investor's returns in domestic currency can be calculated as:

Equation 1: $R_{DC} = (1 + R_{FC})(1 + R_{FX}) - 1 = R_{FC} + R_{FX} + (R_{FC})(R_{FX})$

Example 4: Calculating domestic currency returns

Consider a USD-based investor who invests in a portfolio of stocks that trade in euros. Over a one-year holding period, the value of the portfolio increases by 5% (in euros) and the euro-dollar exchange rate increases from 1.300 USD/EUR to 1.339 USD/EUR.

The EUR has appreciated with respect to the USD, so the investor has positive returns from foreign exchange of:

$R_{FX} = 1.339 / 1.300 - 1 = 0.03 = 3\%$.

The investor's return in domestic currency terms over the one-year holding period is:

$R_{DC} = (1.05 \times 1.03) - 1 = 0.05 + 0.03 + (0.05)(0.03) = 0.0815 = 8.15\%$

This example illustrates two important points. First, simply adding R_{FC} and R_{FX} (5% + 3% = 8%) yields an approximation of the domestic currency return. The approximation is closer to the actual return the smaller the values of the two sources of return.

Second, the exchange rate quotes must use the foreign currency (EUR) as the base currency (the denominator) to calculate the change in value of the currency (R_{FX}). To see why, consider what happens if the domestic currency (USD) had been the base currency.

FX Quotes	Foreign Currency as the Base Currency	1/X for Domestic Currency as the Base Currency
Beginning value	USD/EUR 1.300	EUR/USD 0.76923
Ending value	USD/EUR 1.339	EUR/USD 0.74683

0.74683/0.76923 – 1 = –0.02912 = –2.912%, which is depreciation of the USD relative to the EUR. The appreciation of the EUR is not simply the negative of the depreciation in the USD. R_{FX} is 3.000%, not 2.912%.

> *Professor's Note: The message is to be careful when working with currency. Read the question and determine which is the foreign versus domestic currency. Label the numbers to determine if you are looking at domestic/foreign or foreign/domestic. Always use domestic/foreign (taking reciprocals if needed) and then solve as EV / BV – 1 = R_{FX}.*

CALCULATING PORTFOLIO RETURN FOR MULTIPLE INVESTMENTS IN FOREIGN ASSETS

An investor may invest in multiple markets with different currencies. In that case, the domestic portfolio return is a weighted average of the domestic currency returns for each investment. Formally, we have the following.

Equation 2: $R_{DC} = \sum_{i=1}^{n} w_i(R_{DC,i})$

where:
w_i = the proportion (in domestic currency terms) of the portfolio invested in assets traded in currency *i*
$R_{DC,i}$ = the domestic currency return for asset *i*

The following example illustrates this calculation.

Example 5: Domestic currency returns on an investment in two foreign markets.

A euro-based investor has a 75% position in GBP denominated assets and a 25% position in USD denominated assets. The results for the past year are the following.

R_{FC} for the GBP assets = 12%
R_{FC} for the USD assets = 5%
Beginning EUR/GBP exchange rate: 1.1666
Ending EUR/GBP exchange rate: 1.1437
Beginning USD/EUR exchange rate: 1.332
Ending USD/EUR exchange rate: 1.324

Calculate the investor's return over the period in domestic (EUR) currency terms.

Answer:

First, calculate the R_{DC} (in EUR) for each investment.

For the investment denominated in GBP, we have:

R_{DC} = 1.12 × (1.1437 / 1.1666) − 1 = (1.1200 × 0.9804) − 1 = 9.80%.

The foreign currency (GBP) has depreciated approximately 2% relative to the euro. The negative currency return reduces the 12% return of the foreign market.

For the investment denominated in USD, the exchange rates were given with the foreign currency (USD) in the numerator. These can be inverted to make the investor's currency (the euro) the price currency and the foreign currency (USD) the base currency.

1/1.332 = 0.7508 EUR/USD
1/1.324 = 0.7553 EUR /USD

Allowing the investment denominated in USD R_{DC} (in EUR) to be calculated as:

R_{DC} = [1.05 × (0.7553 / 0.7508)] − 1 = (1.0500 × 1.0060) − 1 = 5.63%

The foreign currency (USD) has appreciated approximately 0.6% relative to the euro. The positive currency return increases the 5% return of the foreign market.

The investor's total portfolio return is the weighted average of the R_{DC} for each market:

(0.75 × 9.80%) + (0.25 × 5.63%) = 7.35 + 1.41 = 8.76%

RISK

An investor investing in a foreign denominated asset has two sources of risk: the fluctuation of the foreign currency and the fluctuation in foreign currency price of the foreign asset. Both will affect the standard deviation of R_{DC}.

The variance of R_{DC} can be calculated using a variation of the basic formula for variance of a two asset portfolio:

$$\sigma^2(R_{DC}) \approx$$
$$w^2(R_{FC})\sigma^2(R_{FC}) + w^2(R_{FX})\sigma^2(R_{FX}) + 2w(R_{FC})w(R_{FX})\sigma(R_{FC})\sigma(R_{FX})\rho(R_{FC},R_{FX})$$

where:
ρ = the correlation between R_{FC} and R_{FX}

However, this basic two asset variance formula can be simplified when a domestic investor holds a single foreign currency denominated asset. The exposures (weights) to R_{FC} and R_{FX} are each 100% with the weights in the formula expressed as 1.0. The formula becomes:

Equation 3: $\sigma^2(R_{DC}) \approx \sigma^2(R_{FC}) + \sigma^2(R_{FX}) + 2\sigma(R_{FC})\sigma(R_{FX})\rho(R_{FC},R_{FX})$

The standard deviation of R_{DC} is the square root of this variance. Examining the equation indicates risk to our domestic investor:

- Depends on the standard deviation of R_{FC} and R_{FX}.
- May be higher for our domestic investor because standard deviation of R_{FX} is an additive term in the equation.
- However, correlation also matters. If the correlation between R_{FC} and R_{FX} is negative, the third component of the calculation becomes negative. The correlation measures the interaction of R_{FC} and R_{FX}.
  - If the correlation is positive, then R_{FC} returns are amplified by R_{FX} returns, increasing the volatility of return to our domestic investor.
  - If the correlation is negative, then R_{FC} returns are dampened by R_{FX} returns, decreasing the volatility of return to our domestic investor. (This is discussed further under this reading's topic of minimum variance hedge ratio).

Professor's Note: The variance formula in Equation 3 is only an approximation but appropriate. It is based on the simple addition of R_{FC} and R_{FX} and ignores the cross product of $(R_{FC})(R_{FX})$. The use of an approximate variance formula relates to the number of correlations that would be required for true variance. Consider a portfolio of two foreign assets that has four variables, two foreign assets, and two foreign currencies resulting in six correlation pairs. With three foreign assets, there are six variables resulting in a total of 15 correlation pairs. A precise variance calculation would require accurately estimating all possible correlation pairs. That is considered unrealistic and the exact formula would create a false impression of precision. The approximation method is used for the CFA text. A special case is discussed below. Think of this special case as risk depends on end of period exposure to the foreign asset.

If R_{FC} is a Risk-Free Return: In this case, its standard deviation and correlation with R_{FX} are zero. When R_{FX} is the only source of risk for the domestic investor in the foreign asset, a direct and precise calculation of the standard deviation of R_{DC} is practical.

Equation 4: $\sigma(R_{DC}) = \sigma(R_{FX})(1 + R_{FC})$

where:
R_{FC} = the return on a foreign currency denominated risk-free asset

STRATEGIC DECISIONS

LOS 18.b: Discuss strategic choices in currency management.

 Professor's Note: This is a lengthy discussion of factors to consider. The next LOS summarizes the conclusions.

Neither academic nor empirical analysis support firm conclusions on currency risk management. Opinions range from doing nothing to active management.

- Arguments made for not hedging currency risk include:
    - It is best to avoid the time and cost of hedging or trading currencies.
    - In the long-run, unhedged currency effects are a "zero-sum game"; if one currency appreciates, another must depreciate.
    - In the long-run, currencies revert to a theoretical fair value.
- The argument for active management of currency risk is that, in the short run, currency movement can be extreme, and inefficient pricing of currencies can be exploited to add to portfolio return. Many foreign exchange (FX) trades are dictated by international trade transactions or central bank policies. These are not motivated by consideration of fair value and may drive currency prices away from their fair value.

Currency management strategies for portfolios with exchange rate risk range from a passive approach of matching benchmark currency exposures to an active strategy that treats currency exposure independently of benchmark exposures and seeks to profit from (rather than hedge the risk of) currency exposures. Different approaches along this spectrum include:

Passive hedging is rule based and typically matches the portfolio's currency exposure to that of the benchmark used to evaluate the portfolio's performance. It will require periodic rebalancing to maintain the match. The goal is to eliminate currency risk relative to the benchmark.

Discretionary hedging allows the manager to deviate modestly from passive hedging by a specified percentage. An example is allowing 5% deviations from the hedge ratio that would match a currency's exposure to the benchmark exposure. The goal is to reduce currency risk while allowing the manager to pursue modest incremental currency returns relative to the benchmark.

Active currency management allows a manager to have greater deviations from benchmark currency exposures. This differs from discretionary hedging in the amount of discretion permitted and the manager is expected to generate positive incremental portfolio return from managing a portfolio's currency exposure. The goal is to create incremental return (alpha), not to reduce risk.

A **currency overlay** is a broad term covering the outsourcing of currency management. At the extreme, the overlay manager will treat currency as an asset class and may take positions independent of other portfolio assets. Seeking incremental return, an overlay manager who is bearish on the Swedish krona (SEK) for a portfolio with no exposure to the SEK would short the SEK. The manager is purely seeking currency alpha (incremental return), not risk reduction.

Overlay managers can also be given a pure risk reduction mandate or restricted to risk reduction with modest return enhancement.

The IPS: The account's policy on whether to hedge or not to hedge currency risk should be recorded in the client's investment policy statement (IPS). Sections of the IPS that will be particularly relevant in reaching this strategic decision include investor objectives (including risk tolerance), time horizon, liquidity needs, and the benchmark to be used for analyzing portfolio results. The IPS should also specify:

- The target percentage of currency exposure that is to be hedged.
- Allowable discretion for the manager to vary around this target.
- Frequency of rebalancing the hedge.
- Benchmarks to use for evaluating the results of currency decisions.
- Allowable (or prohibited) hedging tools.

Example 6: Choosing a hedging approach

A client with a USD based portfolio has little need for liquidity and is focused on short- term performance results. The client evaluates performance relative to a global equity index, which fully hedges currency exposure back to the USD and rebalances the hedge monthly.

1. **Discuss** how this information would affect the manager's views on hedging currency exposure in the portfolio.

2. **Explain** why rebalancing of currency exposure could be needed even if no changes are made to asset holdings.

Answers:

1. The client information leads to two possible strategies. (A) If the manager lacks currency expertise, the manager should also fully hedge currency risk and rebalance monthly, then focus on other areas such as asset selection to add value. (B) If the manager does have views on currency movement, the manager can instead increase exposure to currencies expected to appreciate and decrease exposure to currencies expected to depreciate.

   Given the client's focus on short-term results, the manager must consider the currency exposure of the index and either match it or deliberately deviate. A long-term assumption that "currency does not matter" is not appropriate. The lack of liquidity needs reduces the need for currency hedging as it reduces the likelihood of liquidations of foreign asset positions at depressed values.

2. Suppose both the U.S. client and the index allocate 10% to U.K. equities and sell the GBP forward to fully hedge the currency risk. Then over the course of the month, the U.K. stocks in the benchmark fall in value ($-R_{FC}$) while the U.K. stocks in the portfolio rise in value ($+R_{FC}$). The index will reduce the short GBP position to reflect the decreased GBP asset value. In contrast, the manager needs to increase the GBP short position to reflect increased GBP market value. Rebalancing the hedge must consider not only explicit transactions by the manager but also differentials in R_{FC} between the index and the portfolio.

Strategic Diversification Issues

- In the longer run, currency volatility has been lower than in the shorter run, reducing the need to hedge currency in portfolios with a long-term perspective.
- Positive correlation between returns of the asset measured in the foreign currency (R_{FC}) and returns from the foreign currency (R_{FX}) increase volatility of return to the investor (R_{DC}) and increase the need for currency hedging. Negative correlation dampens return volatility and decreases the need to hedge.
- Correlation tends to vary by time period, providing diversification in some periods and not in others, suggesting a varying hedge ratio is appropriate.
- Empirical evidence indicates higher, positive correlation (between asset and currency returns) in bond than in equity portfolios, suggesting that hedging is more appropriate for bond portfolios. This makes theoretical sense because interest rate movement tends to drive both bond prices and currency values.
- The hedge ratio (the percentage of currency exposure to hedge) varies by manager preference.

Strategic Cost Issues: Hedging is not free and benefits must be weighted versus costs.

- The bid/asked transaction cost on a single currency trade is generally small, but repeated transaction costs add up. Full hedging and frequent rebalancing can be costly.
- Purchasing options to hedge involves an upfront option premium cost. If the option expires out-of-the-money, the premium is lost.

- Forward currency contracts are often shorter term than the hedging period, requiring contracts be rolled over as they mature (an FX swap). The hedge lowers return volatility but the rollover can create cash flow volatility with realized gains and losses on the maturing contracts. Financing cash outflows when interest rates are high can be costly as the interest that would have been earned on the funds is lost.
- Overhead costs can be high. A back office and trading infrastructure are needed for currency hedging. Cash accounts in multiple currencies may have to be maintained to support settlements and margin requirements.
- One hundred percent hedging has an opportunity cost with no possibility of favorable currency movement. Some managers elect to "split the difference" between 0 and 100% hedging and adopt a 50% strategic hedge ratio.
- Hedging every currency movement is costly and managers generally chose partial hedges. They may hedge and rebalance monthly rather than daily or accept some amount of negative currency return rather than zero.

LOS 18.c: Formulate an appropriate currency management program given financial market conditions and portfolio objectives and constraints.

In conclusion, the factors that shift the strategic decision formulation toward a benchmark neutral or fully hedged strategy are:

- A short time horizon for portfolio objectives.
- High risk aversion.
- A client who is unconcerned with the opportunity costs of missing positive currency returns.
- High short-term income and liquidity needs.
- Significant foreign currency bond exposure.
- Low hedging costs.
- Clients who doubt the benefits of discretionary management.

TACTICAL CURRENCY MANAGEMENT

LOS 18.d: Compare active currency trading strategies based on economic fundamentals, technical analysis, carry-trade, and volatility trading.

The strategic decision sets the portfolio's normal currency hedging policy. If discretion is allowed, the manager can make active tactical decisions within defined boundaries, seeking to increase return. In all cases, active management requires that the manager have a view or a prediction of what will happen. Tactical decisions can be based on four broad approaches. Unfortunately, none of the approaches works consistently.

1) Economic Fundamentals

This approach assumes that, in the long term, currency value will converge to fair value. For example, a fundamental approach may assume purchasing power parity will determine long-run exchange rates. If the basket of goods and services produced in Country A costs 100 units of Country A's currency and that basket costs 200 units of Country B's currency in Country B, then the currency exchange rate of A to B is 100/200, a 0.50 A/B exchange rate.

Several factors will impact the eventual path of convergence over the short and intermediate terms. Increases in the value of a currency are associated with currencies:

- That are more undervalued relative to their fundamental value.
- That have the greatest rate of increase in their fundamental value.
- With higher real or nominal interest rates.
- With lower inflation relative to other countries.
- Of countries with decreasing risk premiums.

Opposite conditions are believed to be associated with declining currency values.

2) Technical Analysis

Technical analysis of currency is based on three principals:

1. Past price data can predict future price movement and because those prices reflect fundamental and other relevant information, there is no need to analyze such information.

2. Fallible human beings react to similar events in similar ways and therefore past price patterns tend to repeat.

3. It is unnecessary to know what the currency should be worth (based on fundamental value); it is only necessary to know where it will trade.

Technical analysis looks at past price and volume trading data. FX technical analysis focuses on price trends as volume data is generally less available. Technical analysis works best in markets with identifiable trends. Typical patterns that technicians seek to exploit are the following.

- An **overbought** (or **oversold**) market has gone up (or down) too far and the price is likely to reverse.
- A **support level** exists where there are substantial bids from customers to buy. A price that falls to that level is then likely to reverse and bounce higher as the purchases are executed.
- A **resistance level** exists where there are substantial offers from customers to sell. A price that rises to that level is then likely to reverse and bounce lower as the sales are executed.

At both support and resistance levels, the price becomes "sticky." However, if the market moves through the sticky resistance levels, it can then accelerate and continue in the same direction.

For example, assume technical traders have observed a support level for the GBP at 1.70 USD/GBP. The traders place limit orders to buy GBP at 1.70 USD/GBP. However, to limit their losses, the traders also enter stop loss orders to sell GBP at various prices between 1.70 and 1.69. If the GBP declines to the support level of 1.70, the buy orders are executed, supporting that price and explain the "sticky price behavior." However, if the GBP then declines lower, the stop loss sell orders are executed, driving the GBP lower as the GBP breaks its support level.

Moving averages of price are often used in technical analysis. A common rule is that if a shorter-term moving average crosses a longer-term moving average, it triggers a signal. The 50-day moving average rising above the 200-day moving average is a buy signal, falling below is a sell signal.

3) The Carry Trade

A **carry trade** refers to borrowing in a lower interest rate currency and investing the proceeds in a higher interest rate currency. Three issues are important to understand the carry trade.

1. **Covered interest rate parity** (CIRP) holds by arbitrage and establishes that the difference between spot (S_0) and forward (F_0) exchange rates equals the difference in the periodic interest rates of the two currencies.
    *   The currency with the higher interest rate will trade at a **forward discount**, $F_0 < S_0$

    *   The currency with the lower interest rate will trade at a **forward premium**, $F_0 > S_0$

2. The carry trade is based on a violation of **uncovered interest rate parity** (UCIRP). UCIRP is an international parity relationship asserting that the forward exchange rate calculated by CIRP is an unbiased estimate of the spot exchange rate that will exist in the future. If this were true:
    *   The currency with the higher interest rate will decrease in value by the amount of the initial interest rate differential.
    *   The currency with the lower interest rate will increase in value by the amount of the initial interest rate differential.

    If these expectations were true, a carry trade would earn a zero return.

3. Because the carry trade exploits a violation of interest rate parity, it can be referred to as trading the forward rate bias. Historical evidence indicates that:
    *   Generally, the higher interest rate currency has depreciated less than predicted by interest rate parity or even appreciated and a carry trade has earned a profit.
    *   However, a small percentage of the time, the higher interest rate currency has depreciate substantially more than predicted by interest rate parity and a carry trade has generated large losses.

Generally, the carry trade is implemented by borrowing in the lower interest rate currencies of developed economies (**funding currencies**) and investing in the higher interest rate currencies of emerging economies (**investing currencies**). In periods of financial stress, the currencies of the higher risk emerging economies have depreciated sharply relative to the currencies of developed economies and such carry trades have generated significant losses. Given that periods of financial stress are associated with increasing exchange rate volatility, traders often exit their carry trade positions when exchange rate volatility increases significantly.

Example 7: A carry trade

The spot exchange rate is BRL/USD 2.41. The interest rates in the two countries are 6% and 1%, respectively.

1. **Estimate** the one-year forward exchange rate for the Brazilian Real.

2. **State** the steps to initiate the carry trade and the theory on which it is based.

3. What is the profit on the trade if the spot exchange rate is unchanged and the trade is initiated by borrowing 100 currency units? **Show** your work.

4. What is the primary risk in this trade?

Answers:

1. The forward exchange rate for the Real should be approximately 5% below the current spot exchange rate to reflect the initial interest rate differential. The precise calculation is:

   BRL/USD 2.41 × $(1.06 / 1.01)^1$ = BRL/USD 2.529

2.
   - Borrow USD at 1%.
   - Convert USD to BRL at the spot exchange rate of BRL/USD 2.41.
   - Invest the BRL at 6%.

   The carry trade is based on a violation of uncovered interest rate parity. It is profitable if the spot exchange rate of the higher interest rate currency declines less than predicted by the forward exchange rate.

3. It is 5%, reflecting the initial interest rate difference and unchanged spot exchange rate.
   - Borrow USD 100 creating a loan payable of USD 101.
   - Convert USD 100 to BRL 241 (= 100 × 2.41).
   - Invest the BRL 241 at 6% creating an ending value of BRL 255.46.
   - Convert the BRL 255.46 at the unchanged spot exchange rate back to USD 106.00 (= 255.46 / 2.41).
   - Pay off the USD loan for a profit of USD 5.00 on a USD 100 initial investment.

4. This is an unhedged trade and the profit or loss depends on the ending value of the BRL. If the BRL declines by more than 5%, the trade is unprofitable.

Figure 1: Summary of the Carry Trade

The Carry Trade:		
Is implemented by:	Borrowing and then selling in the spot market the lower yield currency.	To buy and invest in the higher yield currency.
Is trading the forward rate bias:	Selling in the spot market the currency trading at a forward premium.	And buying in the spot market the currency trading at a forward discount.

The carry trade is generally profitable under normal market conditions. But it can generate large losses in periods of financial distress and high volatility as investors flee high risk (yield) currencies.

> *Professor's Note: You should notice this section does not support using the forward exchange rate as a prediction of how currency value will change, sometimes referred as as uncovered interest rate parity (UCIRP). Under IRP, the currency with the higher short-term interest rate will trade at a forward discount. UCIRP asserts that this calculated forward rate is a prediction of what will happen to the spot exchange rate and the higher rate currency will depreciate. This section has (1) noted that empirical evidence indicates the currency with the higher rate tends to appreciate, not depreciate, and (2) the carry trade is based on the higher rate currency appreciating or depreciating less than suggested by UCIRP. You should conclude that the Level III curriculum does not support using the forward exchange rate as a valid prediction of what will happen. The forward exchange rate can be and is used for hedging, but it just is not a good predictor of how the spot exchange rate will move, unless you want a very short career as a currency manager.*

4) Volatility Trading

Volatility or "vol" trading allows a manager to profit from predicting changes in currency volatility. Recall from Level I and Level II that **delta** measures the change in value of an option's price for a change in value of the underlying and that **vega** measures change in value of the option for changes in volatility of the underlying. Vega is positive for both puts and calls because an increase in the expected volatility of the price of the underlying increases the value of both puts and calls.

Delta hedging entails creation of a **delta-neutral position**, which has a delta of zero. The delta-neutral position will not gain or lose value with small changes in the price of the underlying assets, but it will gain or lose value as the implied volatility reflected in the price of options changes. A manager can profit by correctly predicting changes in volatility.

A manager expecting volatility to increase should enter a **long straddle** by purchasing an at-the-money call and put. The manager is buying volatility. The two options will have equal but opposite deltas making the position delta neutral. If volatility increases, the options will rise in net value and the trade will be profitable.

A manager expecting volatility to decrease should enter a **short straddle** by selling both of these options. If volatility declines, the options will fall in net value. The options can be repurchased at lower prices for a profit.

 Professor's Note: Delta hedging will come up several times in the CFA curriculum. An important caveat is that the deltas will change and the positions must be continually rebalanced to maintain a delta-neutral position.

A **strangle** will provide similar but more moderate payoffs to a straddle. Out of-the-money calls and puts with the same absolute delta are purchased. The out-of-the-money options require larger movement in the currency value to create intrinsic value but will cost less. Both the initial cost and the likely profit are lower than for the straddle.

LOS 18.e: Describe how changes in factors underlying active trading strategies affect tactical trading decisions.

Active trading strategies are, by definition, risky. An active manager forms market expectations and implements shorter term tactical strategies seeking to add value. If the manager is wrong or does not cover the transaction costs, return is reduced. Manager expectations that trigger tactical trading decisions include the following.

Expectation:		*Action:*
Relative currency:	Appreciation	Reduce the hedge on or increase the long position in the currency
	Depreciation	Increase the hedge on or decrease the long position in the currency
Volatility:	Rising	Long straddle (or strangle)
	Falling	Short straddle (or strangle)
Market conditions:	Stable	A carry trade
	Crisis	Discontinue the carry trade

Subtle variations on these actions include the following.

- A carry trade may involve a bundle of funding and investment currencies and positions need not be equally weighted. For example, if the manager expects a particular currency to show greater relative increase in value, the trade would be structured with increased long (or decrease short) positions in that currency.
- Delta neutral positions can be "tilted" to net positive or negative based on the manager's view. A manager expecting a currency to appreciate (depreciate) could shift to a net positive (negative) delta.

CURRENCY MANAGEMENT TOOLS

Professor's Note: We now examine a variety of hedging techniques and tools plus special considerations that may arise in some situations. The CFA text includes the warning "rote memorization" is not advised. Instead think of basic "building blocks" that allow an infinite number of combinations; focus on the basic concepts and terminology.

Some useful tips to sort through the material include the following. Some of these may be repeated from other sections.

1. What is the currency exposure that needs to be hedged? A typical situation is a portfolio exposed to fluctuation in value of a foreign currency.

2. It is easier to work with FX quotes when the foreign currency is the base currency. If quotes are given as B/P, take the reciprocal to make it P/B.

3. Assume any statements or directions refer to the base currency unless otherwise indicated in the case. But be explicit in your answers and state the currency you are referring to.

4. Decide whether the case requires buying or selling the base currency.
   - Buying forwards (and futures) or buying call options on the base currency increases exposure to the base currency.
   - Selling forwards (and futures) or buying put options on the base currency decreases exposure to the base currency.
   - Remember that:
     - A call on the base currency is a put on the pricing currency.
     - A put on the base currency is a call on the pricing currency.

5. Hedging is not free.
   - Hedges using forwards have no or minimal initial cost but high opportunity cost because the potential upside of the hedged currency is eliminated.
   - Purchasing options has high initial cost but retains the upside of the hedged currency (the protective put strategy).
   - Lowering the cost of the hedge will require some combination of less downside protection or upside potential. Cost can be lowered through some combination of:
     - Writing options to generate premium inflow.
     - Adjusting the option strike prices.
     - Adjusting the size (notional amount) of the options.
     - Adding exotic features to the options.

6. Discretionary hedging allows the manager to deviate from a policy neutral hedge position. Allowing the manager discretion can lower hedging costs and enhance return but also increases the risk of underperformance.

7. The IPS (or question specifics) should define the strategic, policy neutral hedge position. Generally this is a 100% hedge to match the currency exposure of the portfolio's benchmark.

LOS 18.f: Describe how forward contracts and FX (foreign exchange) swaps are used to adjust hedge ratios.

Typically, **forward contracts** are preferred for currency hedging because:

- They can be customized, while futures contracts are standardized.
- They are available for almost any currency pair, while futures trade in size for only a limited number of currencies.
- Futures contracts require margin which adds operational complexity and can require periodic cash flows.
- Trading volume of FX forwards and swaps dwarfs that of FX futures, providing better liquidity.

A hedge can be a **static hedge**, which is established and held until expiration, or a **dynamic hedge**, which is periodically rebalanced.

Consider a EUR-based manager who must hedge an initial CHF 10,000,000 of asset exposure. One month later, the asset has appreciated to CHF 11,000,000. Assume the manager can initially sell a one- or three-month contract.

1. Initially sell 10,000,000 CHF in the forward market with a one-month forward contract. At contract expiration, roll over the hedge. At rollover, the change in initial contract price will produce a realized gain or loss and cash flow settlement consequences. At the rollover, the size of the new contract can be adjusted to match the new value of the position to be hedged. Over the initial month, the hedge is static but can be dynamic at the rollover.

    If desired, the rollover can be done using an FX swap so that cash flows occur on the expiration date of the initial contract. For an FX swap, the manager would, two days prior to initial contract expiration, buy CHF 10 million in the spot market to cover the short position in the forward and sell forward CHF 11 million to roll over the hedge. This is termed a "mismatched" FX swap because the "near" spot leg and "far" forward leg are not of equal size.

    Both the inital short forward contract and the spot market purchase of CHF are for CHF 10,000,000 and settle in two business days. Any difference between the EUR/CHF rate of the initial forward contract and the current spot price will produce a (positive or negative) cash flow in EUR. For example, if the CHF declined by EUR 0.01, the initial hedge (short forward) will produce a cash gain of EUR 100,000 (= EUR 0.01 × 10,000,000).

2. Initially sell 10,000,000 CHF in the forward market with a three-month forward contract. One month later, the manager is underhedged with a CHF 10,000,000 short position versus an asset now worth CHF 11,000,000.

    A. With a static hedge, the manager would do nothing even though CHF exposure has increased.

B. With a dynamic hedge, the manager would increase the hedge to cover the additional exposure by selling an additional CHF 1 million forward for two months to create a total short position of CHF 11 million. Because no contracts are being closed on the rebalancing date, all realized gain and losses and cash flows are deferred until the end of the three-month period. A dynamic hedging strategy will specify periodicity of rebalancing the hedge.

The choice of hedging approach should consider:

- Shorter term contracts or dynamic hedges with more frequent rebalancing tend to increase transaction costs but improve the hedge results.
- Higher risk aversion suggests more frequent rebalancing.
- Lower risk aversion and strong manager views suggest allowing the manager greater discretion around the strategic hedging policy.

ROLL YIELD

Hedging also exposes the portfolio to **roll yield** or **roll return**. Roll yield is a return from the movement of the forward price over time toward the spot price of an asset. It can be thought of as the profit or loss on a forward or futures contract if the spot price is unchanged at contract expiration. Determining whether the roll yield produces a profit or a loss will depend on two factors: (1) whether the currency is trading at a forward premium or discount and (2) whether is it purchased or sold. Roll yield for a contract held to expiration is determined by initial forward minus spot price divided by initial spot price.

For example, consider an investor who sells CHF 1 million six-month forward for USD 1.05 when the spot rate is 1.04. The forward price is at a premium so the roll yield on a short position will be positive. Think of it as the investor sells at a high price and the price rolls down for a gain. The investor can deliver CHF 1 million for 1.05 USD when its initial cost in the market (at spot) is 1.04 USD, for a gain of USD 10,000. The unannualized roll yield is $0.01/1.04 = 0.96\%$.

Roll yield will affect the cost/benefit analysis of whether to hedge the currency risk. It is a cost of hedging. Positive roll yield will shift the analysis toward hedging and negative roll yield will shift the analysis away from hedging. The relationships of forward premium or discount, initial difference in interest rates, positive or negative roll yield, and impact on hedging cost are summarized in Figure 2.

Figure 2: Forward Premiums or Discounts and Currency Hedging Costs

If the hedge requires:	$F_{P/B} > S_{P/B}$, $i_B < i_P$ The forward price curve is upward-sloping.	$F_{P/B} < S_{P/B}$, $i_B > i_P$ The forward price curve is downward-sloping
A long forward position in Currency B, the hedge earns:	Negative roll yield, which increases hedging cost and discourages hedging.	Positive roll yield, which decreases hedging cost and encourages hedging.
A short forward position in currency B the hedge earns:	Positive roll yield, which decreases hedging cost and encourages hedging.	Negative roll yield, which increases hedging cost and discourages hedging.

Professor's Note: Suppose the initial forward price of the base currency is above its initial spot price. If the base currency is sold forward, F_T and S_T will converge at contract expiration and provide positive roll yield for the short position. The positive roll for the short position does not depend on whether the spot price increases or decreases. This is depicted in the figure below. It shows that the forward and spot price will converege at contract expiration regardless of whether the spot price increases or decreases. Suppose a manager sells the base currency forward when the initial forward price is above the spot price, $F_0 > S_0$. Convergence dictates that at contract expiration, $F_T = S_T$ and the roll return will be positive.

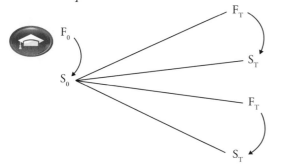

Note that the positive roll for the base currency short position is a negative roll for the long position. This discussion of roll and a contract on the base currency is equally true for contracts on any other assets such as stocks, bonds, and commodities.

Example 8: Roll yield and interest rates

A USD-based investor has exposure to the South African rand (ZAR). The USD interest rate is 2.8% and the ZAR interest rate is 3.6%. **Determine** the roll yield for the investor if he hedges his ZAR exposure with a six-month forward.

Answer:

To hedge the long ZAR exposure, the investor sells the ZAR forward (buy the USD). IRP determines the premium or discount earned (roll yield) on the transaction. From IRP, the periodic risk-free rate of the currency purchased (USD) will be gained and the currency sold (ZAR) will be lost. Over a six-month period, this is approximately + 2.8% / 2 – 3.6% / 2 = –0.4%. The ZAR will trade at approximately a 0.4% forward discount.

A precise calculation of the discount requires first calculating the initial forward price using IRP:

$$F_{P/B} = S_{P/B}\left(\frac{1+i_P}{1+i_B}\right)$$

Then compare that forward price to the initial spot price to calculate the percentage roll yield (i.e., the forward premium or discount):

(F – S) / S

However by "assuming" an initial spot exchange rate between the two currencies of parity, a 1/1 exchange rate, this can be reduced to a single calculation:

% forward premium / discount = % roll yield

$= (1.00)(1.028 / 1.036)^{0.5} - 1 = -0.387\%$

Note that to analyze the ZAR, the ZAR is in the denominator of all terms.

Professor's Note: The CFA text mentions but does not further apply a "similarity" between roll yield and trading the forward rate bias. Both depend on the initial interest rate differential between two currencies. In the previous example, the ZAR traded at a forward discount because it had an initially higher periodic interest rate.

- *The forward rate bias trade (the carry trade) would buy the ZAR in the spot market to invest in and earn the higher interest rate.*
- *An investor who needs exposure to the ZAR would buy the ZAR in the forward market at a discount and earn positive roll yield.*

The "similarity" is buying the higher yielding currency.

Example 9: Hedging and roll yield

A portfolio's reporting currency is the Korean won (KRW) and the portfolio holds investments denominated in EUR, USD, and CHF. Current exchange rate information is provided below along with the manager's expectation for the spot rate in six months.

	Spot EX Rate	Six-Month Forward EX Rate	Manager's forecast
KRW/EUR	1,483.99	1,499.23	1,450.87
KRW/USD	1,108.78	1,112.56	1,146.63
KRW/CHF	1,265.22	1,257.89	1,212.55

1. Which foreign currencies trade at a forward premium or discount?

2. Which foreign currency hedges would earn a positive roll yield?

3. Which foreign currencies would an active currency manager hedge?

4. **Comment** on how the roll yield affects the decision to hedge the EUR or USD.

5. **Calculate** the implied unannualized roll yield of a currency hedged for the portfolio's long exposure to CHF.

Answers:

1. The EUR and USD trade at a forward premium; forward price is above spot price.

2. The hedge will require a forward sale of the currency and sale at a forward premium will earn positive roll yield. Those are the EUR and USD.

3. An active manager will selectively hedge those currencies where the hedge is expected to improve return. The manager will compare expected unhedged with hedged returns. The manager is initially long each foreign currency so increases in the currency's value are a gain.

	Unhedged	*Hedged*
EUR	(1,450.87 / 1,483.99) −1	(1,499.23 / 1,483.99) −1
	= −2.23%	= 1.03%
USD	(1,146.63 / 1,108.78) − 1	(1,112.56 / 1,108.78) − 1
	= 3.41%	= 0.34%
CHF	(1,212.55 / 1,265.22) − 1	(1,257.89 / 1,265.22) − 1
	= −4.16%	= −0.58%

Comparing unhedged expected returns with hedged returns, the manager will hedge the EUR and CHF.

4. Selling forward the USD and EUR will result in positive roll yield which will reduce hedging costs. However, roll yield is only one factor to consider. The positive roll yield for selling the USD forward is not as attractive as the expected appreciation of leaving the USD unhedged.

5. The implied roll yield is the forward premium or discount. It is also the hedged currency return:

$$(F_0 − S_0) / S_0 = (F_0 / S_0) − 1 = (1,257.89 / 1,265.22) − 1 = −0.58\%$$

This example demonstrates two issues involved with forward currency hedging. In essence, they are the same issue viewed from two different perspectives:

1. Positive (negative) roll yield will reduce (increase) hedging cost compared to the initial spot price.
2. Hedging locks in the forward price as an end of period exchange rate.

STRATEGIES TO MODIFY RISK AND LOWER HEDGING COSTS

LOS 18.g: Describe trading strategies used to reduce hedging costs and modify the risk–return characteristics of a foreign-currency portfolio.

The initial forward premium or discount is one cost factor to consider in analyzing the cost/benefit of a currency hedge. To reduce hedging cost, the manager can increase the size of trades that earn positive roll yield and reduce the size of trades that earn negative roll yield.

Forward hedging also incurs **opportunity cost**. Locking in a forward price to hedge currency risk will eliminate downside currency risk but also will eliminate any upside opportunity for gain from changes in exchange rates. Discretionary or option-based hedging strategies are designed to reduce opportunity cost.

Perfect hedging is expensive. If the manager wishes to insure against downside risk and retain upside potential, costs rise further. Reducing those hedging costs involves some form of less downside protection or less upside opportunity, moving the portfolio away from a 100% hedge ratio and/or toward more active decision making. The following discussion of strategies applies to a manager who wishes to hedge long exposure to the CHF (the base currency) and quotations are EUR/CHF.

1. **Over- or under-hedge with forward contracts** based on the manager's view. If the manager expects the CHF to appreciate, she can reduce the hedge ratio, hedging less than the full exposure to CHF risk. If the CHF is expected to depreciate, she can increase the hedge ratio, hedging more than the full exposure to CHF risk. If successful, this strategy creates "positive convexity"; gains will be increased and losses reduced. This is a relatively low cost strategy.

The rest of this discussion proceeds from roughly highest to lowest initial option cost.

2. **Buy at-the-money (ATM) put options** (also called **protective puts** or **portfolio insurance**). This strategy provides asymmetric protection, eliminating all downside risk and retaining all upside potential. But an at-the-money option is relatively expensive and has only time value (no intrinsic value). This strategy has the highest initial cost but no opportunity cost.

3. **Buy out-of-the-money (OTM) put options**. An ATM put would have a delta of approximately –0.50, called a 50-delta put because the sign of the delta is ignored with this terminology. Out-of-the-money puts have deltas that are smaller in magnitude than 0.50, so a 35-delta put is out of the money and a 25-delta put is further out of the money. Puts are less expensive the further they are out of the money, but also offer less downside protection. The manager will have downside CHF exposure down to the strike price of the puts. Compared to buying ATM protective puts, this strategy reduces the initial cost of the hedge but does not eliminate all downside risk.

4. **Collar.** The manager could buy the 35-delta puts on the CHF and sell 35-delta calls on the CHF. The OTM put provides some downside protection while costing less than an ATM put. The sale of the OTM call removes some upside potential (increasing opportunity cost) but generates premium income to further reduce initial cost. This strategy further reduces initial cost but also limits upside potential compared to buying out-of-the money put options only.

A counterparty who buys the OTM call and sells the OTM put has taken on a risk reversal. The risk reversal profits if the underlying rises above the OTM call strike price and loses if the underlying falls below the OTM put strike price. The seller of the call and buyer of the put (used in the collar) can be described as short the risk reversal.

5. **Put spread.** Buy OTM puts on the CHF and sell puts that are further out of the money, (e.g., buy a 35-delta put and sell a 25-delta put). There is downside protection, which begins at the strike price of the purchased puts, but if the CHF falls below the lower strike price of the put sold, that downside protection is lost. This strategy reduces the initial cost and also reduces downside protection compared to buying out-of-the money put options only.

6. **Seagull spread.** This is a put spread combined with selling a call (e.g., buy a 35-delta put, sell a 25-delta put, and sell a 35-delta call). Compared to the put spread, only this hedge has less initial cost and the same down side protection, but limits upside potential.

Further alternatives include varying the degree of upside potential and downside protection. The manager can vary the notional amounts of the options. For example, a 1 × 2 put spread would buy 100 40-delta puts and sell 200 30-delta puts. The sale of additional puts increases premium income, reducing the initial cost of the hedge, but doubles the downside risk if the currency value falls below the strike price on the 30-delta puts.

All of these strategies are considered "plain vanilla" in that they are combinations of standard options. **Exotic options** introduce features not found in standard options.

1. A **knock-in option** is a plain vanilla option that only comes into existence if the underlying first reaches some prespecified level.

2. A **knock-out option** is a standard option that ceases to exist if the underlying reaches some prespecified level.

3. **Binary** or **digital options** pay a fixed amount that does not vary with the difference in price between the strike and underlying price.

Professor's Note: Clearly there are any number of combinations and odd names for hedging strategies that use combinations of options positions. The important thing is to recognize how the above strategies affect the tradeoff between the cost of a hedge, its downside protection, and its upside potential.

The issues involved with selecting a hedge are summarized in the following steps.

1. *Determine the base currency in the P/B quote. In a USD/CHF quote, the CHF is the base and if the quoted price increases (decreases), the CHF appreciates (depreciates).*

2. *Determine whether the base currency will be bought or sold. If bought and the quoted price increases (decreases), there is a gain (loss). If sold and the quoted price increases (decreases), there is a loss (gain).*

3. *If buying the base currency is required to hedge the existing risk, buying forwards or calls can be used. Buying OTM calls or writing options will reduce the hedge cost but also reduce downside protection or upside potential.*

4. *If selling the base currency is required to hedge the existing risk, forwards are sold or puts are purchased. Buying OTM puts or writing options will reduce the hedge cost but also reduce downside protection or upside potential.*

5. *The higher the client's risk tolerance and the stronger the manager's views, the less likely a simple 100% hedge will be used.*

6. *Various combinations of options, strike prices, and position sizes can reduce initial hedging costs, even to zero, but only by reducing downside protection or upside potential.*

HEDGING MULTIPLE CURRENCIES

International portfolios will typically have exposure to more than one foreign currency. Generally, hedging each exposure individually is unnecessary, expensive, and time consuming. Consider a European investor who is underweight the AUD and overweight the NZD. The mechanical solution is a long position in AUD and a short position in NZD to reach neutral weights in both. Because the Australian and New Zealand economies are very similar, their currencies exhibit strong positive correlation. The two currencies are natural hedges for each other. If the initial over- and underweights were equal, there may be no need for any additional hedging.

LOS 18.h: Describe the use of cross-hedges, macro-hedges, and minimum-variance-hedge ratios in portfolios exposed to multiple foreign currencies.

A **cross hedge** (sometimes called a **proxy hedge**) refers to hedging with an instrument that is not perfectly correlated with the exposure being hedged. Hedging the risk of a diversified U.S. equity portfolio with S&P futures contracts is a cross hedge when the portfolio is not identical to the S&P index portfolio. Cross hedges are generally not necessary in currency hedging because forward contracts for virtually all currency pairs are available but cross hedges may improve the efficiency of hedging.

Cross hedges also introduce additional risk to hedging. When the correlation of returns between the hedging instrument and the position being hedged is imperfect, the residual risk increases. The AUD and the NZD have a high positive correlation with each other so hedging an underweighting in the AUD with an overweighting in the NZD has little, but not zero, cross hedge risk.

The historical correlation is not a guarantee of the future. The future correlation may be different from historical correlation. If the correlation between two currencies moves toward zero, the (cross) hedge will not perform as expected. Portfolio performance could benefit or suffer from a change in correlation. The residual risk of the hedge is increased.

A **macro hedge** is a type of cross hedge that addresses portfolio-wide risk factors rather than the risk of individual portfolio assets. A bond portfolio might have interest rate risk, credit risk, and volatility risk exposures that the manager could hedge with bond futures (to hedge interest rate risk by modifying duration), credit derivatives (to hedge credit risk), and with volatility trading (to alter volatility risk).

One type of currency macro hedge uses a derivatives contract based on a fixed basket of currencies to modify currency exposure at a macro (portfolio) level. The currency basket in the contract may not precisely match the currency exposures of the portfolio, but it can be less costly than hedging each currency exposure individually. The manager must make a choice between accepting higher residual currency risk versus lower cost.

The **minimum-variance hedge ratio** (MVHR) is a mathematical approach to determining the hedge ratio. When applied to currency hedging, it is a regression of the past changes in value of the portfolio (R_{DC}) to the past changes in value of the hedging instrument to minimize the value of the tracking error between these two variables. The hedge ratio is the beta (slope coefficient) of that regression. Because this hedge ratio is based on historical returns, if the correlation between the returns on the portfolio and the returns on the hedging instrument change, the hedge will not perform as well as expected.

The practical implications of this are as follows:

1. Our forward hedging examples up to now have been "direct" hedges. For example, a USD portfolio that is long CHF 1,000,000 sells CHF 1,000,000 forward to hedge the risk, a simple one-for-one hedge ratio of the notional exposure. In technical terms, the portfolio is long CHF, the hedging vehicle is a forward contract on the CHF, and the CHF and its forward have a virtually 1.00 correlation; therefore, no MVHR analysis is needed, sell CHF 1,000,000 forward.

2. Cross hedges or macro hedges are considered "indirect" hedges, the correlation between the currency exposure in the portfolio and a currency contract may not be 1.00 and the minimum-variance hedge ratio may not be one-for-one.

3. The MVHR can be used to jointly optimize over changes in value of R_{FX} and R_{FC} to minimize the volatility of R_{DC}.

To illustrate this use of the MVHR, consider the case of a foreign country where the economy is heavily dependent on imported energy. Appreciation of the currency ($+R_{FX}$) would make imports less expensive, which is likely to decrease production costs, increasing profits and asset values ($+R_{FC}$). **Strong positive correlation between R_{FX} and R_{FC} increases the volatility of R_{DC}. A hedge ratio greater than 1.0 would reduce the volatility of R_{DC}.**

Consider the case of a foreign country where the economy is heavily dependent on exports. Appreciation of the currency ($+R_{FX}$) would make its exports more expensive, likely reducing sales, profits, and asset values ($-R_{FC}$). **Strong negative correlation between R_{FX} and R_{FC} naturally decreases the volatility of R_{DC}. A hedge ratio less than 1.0 would reduce the volatility of R_{DC}.**

Example 10: Determining and applying the MVHR

A U.S.-based portfolio is long EUR 2,000,000 of exposure. The portfolio manager decides to jointly hedge the risk of the asset returns measured in EUR and the risk of the currency return to minimize the volatility of the portfolio's returns measured in USD. The manager first adjusts all currency quotes to measure the value of the foreign currency by expressing the currency quotes as USD/EUR. He then calculates weekly percentage changes in value of the EUR (the R_{FX}) and unhedged percentage changes in value of the portfolio position measured in the portfolio's domestic currency (the R_{DC}). He performs a least squares regression analysis and determines based on the historical data that:

$$R_{DC} = 0.12 + 1.25(\%\Delta S_{USD/EUR}) + \varepsilon$$

With a correlation between R_{FX} and R_{FC} of 0.75

1. **Calculate** the size of and **state** the currency hedge to minimize expected volatility of the R_{DC}.

2. **Comment** on how effective the hedge is likely to be.

Answers:

1. EUR 2,000,000 × 1.25 = EUR 2,500,000; the manager will short EUR 2,500,000 to hedge a long EUR 2,000,000 exposure in the portfolio.

2. This is a cross hedge and is based on past correlation. The correlation can change and the hedge may perform better or worse than expected. In addition, a correlation of 0.75 is not perfect and there is random variation even in the past data.

MANAGING EMERGING MARKET CURRENCY

LOS 18.i: Discuss challenges for managing emerging market currency exposures.

The majority of investable asset value and FX transactions are in the six largest developed market currencies. Transactions in other currencies pose additional challenges because of: (1) higher transaction costs, "high markups" and (2) the increased probability of extreme events. Examples of these problems include the following.

- Low trading volume leads dealers to charge larger bid/asked spreads. The problem is compounded as the spreads tend to increase even further during periods of financial crisis.
- Liquidity can be lower and transaction costs higher to exit trades than to enter trades. Consider the carry trade that leads investors to gradually accumulate long positions in higher yield emerging market currencies. During periods of economic crises, the majority of those investors may attempt to exit a carry trade at the same time, driving the value of the emerging market currency down below its fundamental value and disrupting normal trading activity.
- Transactions between two emerging market currencies can be even more costly. Few dealers have the expertise to directly make a market between the currencies of smaller markets. A dealer may quote a transaction between the Malaysian ringgit (MYR) and Hungarian forint (HUF) but would, in fact, execute component transactions in EUR/MYR and EUR/HUF with other dealers who have the expertise to trade only one of the two currencies.
- Emerging market currencies return distributions are non-normal with higher probabilities of extreme events and negative skew of returns. Many trading strategies and risk measures assume a normal distribution and are, therefore, flawed.
- The higher yield of emerging market currencies will lead to large forward discounts. This produces negative roll yield for investors who need to sell such currencies forward.
- Contagion is common. During periods of financial crisis the correlations of emerging markets with each other and with their currencies tend to converge toward +1.0. Both emerging markets and their currencies have declined as a group. At the very time diversification is most needed, it tends to disappear.
- There is *tail risk*; the governments of emerging markets tend to actively intervene in the markets for their currencies, producing long periods of artificial price stability followed by sharp price movements when market forces overwhelm the government's capacity to intervene. The "tail risk" refers to these negative events occurring more frequently than would be assumed in the normal distribution.

Non-deliverable forwards (NDFs): Emerging market governments frequently restrict movement of their currency into or out of the country to settle normal derivative transactions. Such countries have included Brazil (BRL), China (CNY), and Russia (RUB). NDFs are an alternative to deliverable forwards and require a cash settlement of gains or losses in a developed market currency at settlement rather than a currency exchange.

A benefit of NDFs is lower credit risk because delivery of the notional amounts of both currencies is not required. Only the gains to one party are paid at settlement.

An additional point to consider with NDFs is that they exist because the emerging market government is restricting currency markets. Changes in government policy can lead to sharp movements in currency values (i.e., there is tail risk).

Example 11: Calculating cash settlement values for an NDF

A trader buys EUR 1,000,000 six months forward at RUB/EUR 39. Six months later, the spot exchange rate is RUB/EUR 40. **Calculate** the cash flows that will occur at settlement.

Answer:

The trader has agreed to "sell" RUB 39,000,000 for EUR 1,000,000. At settlement, the market value of EUR 1,000,000 is RUB 40,000,000 so the investor has a gain of RUB 1,000,000.

However, NDF settlements are made in the developed market currency at the ending spot exchange rate so we must convert the gain of RUB 1,000,000 to EUR at RUB/EUR 40. The EUR value of RUB 1,000,000 at settlement is 1,000,000 / 40 = 25,000 euros and the trader will receive this payment from the counterparty. There is only a net exchange of gain.

KEY CONCEPTS

LOS 18.a

An investment in assets priced in a currency other than the investor's domestic currency (a *foreign asset* priced in a *foreign currency*) has two sources of risk and return: (1) the return on the assets in the foreign currency and (2) the return on the foreign currency from any change in its exchange rate with the investor's *domestic currency*. These returns are multiplicative and an investor's returns in domestic currency can be calculated as:

Equation 1: $R_{DC} = (1 + R_{FC})(1 + R_{FX}) - 1 = R_{FC} + R_{FX} + (R_{FC})(R_{FX})$

Equation 2: $R_{DC} = \sum_{i=1}^{n} w_i(R_{DC,i})$

Equation 3: $\sigma^2(R_{DC}) \approx \sigma^2(R_{FC}) + \sigma^2(R_{FX}) + 2\sigma(R_{FC})\sigma(R_{FX})\rho(R_{FC},R_{FX})$

Equation 4: $\sigma(R_{DC}) = \sigma(R_{FX})(1 + R_{FC})$

where for Equation 4:
R_{FC} = the return on a foreign currency denominated risk-free asset

LOS 18.b

Passive hedging is rule-based and typically matches the portfolio's currency exposure to the portfolio's benchmark in order to eliminate currency risk relative to the benchmark.

Discretionary hedging allows the manager to deviate modestly from passive hedging. The primary goal is currency risk reduction while seeking some modest value added return.

Active currency management allows wider discretion to selectively hedge or not hedge and to deviate substantially from the benchmark. The goal is value added, not risk reduction. At the extreme, an active manager can treat currency as an asset class and take positions independent of the portfolio assets. For example, a manager who is bearish on the Swedish krona (SEK) can short the SEK even if no SEK assets are owned.

Currency overlay management is a broad term referring to the use of a separate currency manager. The asset manager first takes positions in the markets considered most attractive, without regard to the resulting currency exposures. The overlay manager then adjusts the currency exposures. The overlay manager's mandate can be passive, discretionary, or active.

Arguments made for not hedging currency risk include the following:

- Avoid the time and cost of hedging or trading currencies.
- Currency effects are a "zero-sum game"; if one currency appreciates, another must depreciate.
- In the long run, currencies revert to a theoretical fair value.

Arguments for active currency management include the following:

- In the short run, currency movement can be extreme.
- Inefficient pricing of currencies can be exploited to add to portfolio return. Inefficient pricing of currency can arise as many foreign exchange (FX) trades are dictated by international trade transactions or central bank policies.

LOS 18.c

Factors that favor a benchmark neutral or fully hedged currency strategy are:
- A short time horizon for portfolio objectives.
- High risk aversion.
- High short-term income and liquidity needs.
- Significant foreign currency bond exposure.
- Low hedging costs.
- Clients who doubt the benefits of discretionary management.
- A client who is unconcerned with the opportunity costs of missing positive currency returns.

LOS 18.d

1. Economic fundamentals assumes that purchasing power parity (PPP) determines exchange rates in the very long run. In the shorter run, currency appreciation is associated with:
   - Currencies that are undervalued relative to fundamental value (based on PPP).
   - Currencies with a faster rate of increase in fundamental value.
   - Countries with lower inflation.
   - Countries with higher real or nominal interest rates.
   - Countries with a decreasing country risk premium.

2. Technical analysis:
   - Overbought (or oversold) currencies reverse.
   - A currency that declines to its support level will reverse upward unless it pierces the support level, in which case, it can decline substantially.
   - A currency that increases to its resistance level will reverse downward unless it pierces the resistance level, in which case, it can increase substantially.
   - If a shorter term moving average crosses a longer term moving average, the price will continue moving in the direction of the shorter term moving average.

3. The carry trade exploits the forward rate bias (i.e., forward exchange rates are not a valid predictor of currency market movement).
   - Borrow the lower interest rate currency (often a developed market).
   - Convert it to the higher rate currency (often an emerging market) at the spot exchange rate.
   - Invest and earn the higher interest rate.

   This is a risky, not a hedged, trade. If the higher interest rate currency appreciates or depreciates less than "implied" by the forward rate, the trade will be profitable. In times of severe economic stress, the carry trade can be very unprofitable as the higher interest rate (and riskier) currency collapses.

4. Volatility trading profits from changes in volatility.
   • If volatility is expected to increase, enter a straddle (purchase a call and put with the same strike price, typically using at-the-money options). A strangle (buy an out-of-the-money call and put) can also be used. The strangle will cost less but will have less upside if volatility increases.
   • If volatility is expected to decline, enter a reverse straddle or strangle (i.e., sell the options).

LOS 18.e

Expectation:		Action:
Relative currency:	Appreciation	Reduce the hedge on or increase the long position in the currency
	Depreciation	Increase the hedge on or decrease the long position in the currency
Volatility:	Rising	Long straddle (or strangle)
	Falling	Short straddle (or strangle)
Market conditions:	Stable	A carry trade
	Crisis	Discontinue the carry trade

LOS 18.f

Typically, forward contracts are preferred for currency hedging because:
• They can be customized, while futures contracts are standardized.
• They are available for almost any currency pair, while futures trade in size for only a limited number of currencies.
• Futures contracts require margin which adds operational complexity and can require periodic cash flows.
• Trading volume of FX forwards and swaps dwarfs that of FX futures, providing better liquidity.

A hedge can be a **static hedge**, which is established and held until expiration, or a **dynamic hedge**, which is periodically rebalanced.

The choice of hedging approach should consider:

• Shorter term contracts or dynamic hedges with more frequent rebalancing tend to increase transaction costs but improve the hedge results.
• Higher risk aversion suggests more frequent rebalancing.
• Lower risk aversion and strong manager views suggest allowing the manager greater discretion around the strategic hedging policy.

Hedging also exposes the portfolio to **roll yield** or **roll return**. Roll yield is a return from the movement of the forward price over time toward the spot price of an asset. It can be thought of as the profit or loss on a forward or futures contract if the spot price is unchanged at contract expiration.

Forward Premiums or Discounts and Currency Hedging Costs

If the hedge requires:	$F_{P/B} > S_{P/B}$, $i_B < i_P$ The forward price curve is upward-sloping.	$F_{P/B} < S_{P/B}$, $i_B > i_P$ The forward price curve is downward-sloping
A long forward position in Currency B, the hedge earns:	Negative roll yield, which increases hedging cost and discourages hedging.	Positive roll yield, which decreases hedging cost and encourages hedging.
A short forward position in currency B the hedge earns:	Positive roll yield, which decreases hedging cost and encourages hedging.	Negative roll yield, which increases hedging cost and discourages hedging.

LOS 18.g

The cost of hedging a currency exposure:

- **Positive roll** will reduce and **negative roll** will increase hedging costs.
- Hedging with forward (or futures) has no explicit option premium cost, but it has **implicit cost**; it removes upside as well as downside.
- Active managers can selectively **over- or under-hedge**. Buy more or sell less of the currency expected to appreciate.
- An **at-the-money (ATM) put** (a **protective put** or **portfolio insurance**) is the most expensive (upfront premium cost) form of option hedging (e.g., buy a 50 delta put).

Option hedging costs can be reduced by decreasing upside potential or increasing downside risk. To hedge an existing currency exposure:

- **Buy an out-of-the-money (OTM) put.**
- **Use a collar; buy an OTM put and sell an OTM call.**
- **Use a put spread; buy an OTM put and sell a further OTM put.**
- **Use a seagull spread; buy an OTM put, sell a further OTM put and sell an OTM call.**
- **Use exotic options** that require addition conditions before they can be exercised or which can expire early.

LOS 18.h

A **cross hedge** (sometimes called a proxy hedge) uses a hedging vehicle that is different from, and not perfectly correlated with, the exposure being hedged.

A **macro hedge** is a type of cross hedge that addresses portfolio-wide risk factors rather than the risk of individual portfolio assets. One type of currency macro hedge uses a derivatives contract based on a fixed basket of currencies to modify currency exposure at a macro (portfolio) level.

The **minimum-variance hedge ratio** (MVHR) is a mathematical approach to determining the hedge ratio. Regress past changes in value of the portfolio (R_{DC}) to the past changes in value of the hedging instrument (the foreign currency) to find the hedge ratio that would have minimized standard deviation of R_{DC}. The hedge ratio is the beta (slope coefficient) of that regression.

- Positive correlation between R_{FX} and R_{FC}; MVHR > 1.
- Negative correlation between R_{FX} and R_{FC}; MVHR < 1.

LOS 18.i

Non-deliverable forwards (NDFs) settle the net gain or loss in a single currency (rather than exchanging currencies).

CONCEPT CHECKERS

Use the following information for Questions 1 and 2

A Djiboutian (DJF) investor holds an international portfolio with beginning investments of USD 1,253,000 and EUR 2,347,800. Measured in the foreign currencies, these investments appreciate 5% and depreciate 7%, respectively.

Additional information:

Beginning Spot Exchange Rate	Beginning Forward Exchange Rate	Ending Spot Exchange Rate
DJF/USD 179.54	DJF/USD 185.67	DJF/USD 192.85
EUR/DJF 0.00416	EUR/DJF 0.00413	EUR/DJF 0.00421

1. The ending value of the USD investment is *closest* to:
    A. USD 1,150,000.
    B. DJF 236,200,000.
    C. DJF 253,700,000.

2. The unhedged return to the investor of the U.S. investment is *closest* to:
    A. −3%.
    B. +3%.
    C. +12%.

3. A European investor holds a diversified portfolio. From the euro perspective, the portfolio is weighted 60% and 40% in U.S. and U.K. investments.

Assets	Returns measured in foreign currency	Returns measured from investor's perspective	Standard deviation of asset's returns measured in foreign currency	Standard deviation of the foreign currency's returns
U.S.	5%	6%	4.5%	3.7%
U.K.	7%	8%	3.5%	4.7%

The correlation between the foreign-currency asset's returns and returns on the foreign currency are 0.81 and 0.67, respectively, for the U.S. and English assets. **Compute** the standard deviation for the investor in the U.S. assets. **Show** your work.

4. The strategic decision to hedge currency risk will be *least* affected by the:
    A. manager's market views.
    B. correlation between asset and currency returns.
    C. investor's time horizon, risk aversion, and liquidity needs.

5. Which of the following clients would *most likely* allow a manager to implement discretionary currency hedging?
   A. One with a shorter time horizon and higher liquidity needs.
   B. One with more confidence in the portfolio manager and high income needs.
   C. One very concerned with minimizing regret and higher allocation to equity investments.

6. A currency overlay manager will *most likely* implement a carry trade when the yield of investing currencies is:
   A. lower and volatility is falling.
   B. higher and currency volatility is rising.
   C. higher and currency volatility is stable.

7. Which of the following statements about volatility and interest rates is *most likely* true?
   A. Falling currency volatility leads traders to exit a carry trade.
   B. Rising currency volatility will increase the cost of a collar more than the cost of a protective put.
   C. A delta neutral hedging strategy is more likely to tilt to a net long position in the euro when the euro zone is experiencing rising real interest rates.

8. Jane Simms manages a German portfolio and has a 1,000,000 long position in South Korean won (KRW) through a forward contract that is about to come due. The current spot exchange rate is EUR/KRW 0.00067/0.00068. The forward points for a three-month forward contract are –1.2/–1.1. She expects the KRW to depreciate significantly and has the authority to increase or decrease the hedge size by 10%. **Explain** whether she will increase or decrease the size of the hedge and the forward exchange rate at which she will contract.

9. Peter Perkins has a U.S.-based portfolio and decides to hedge his exposure to the Swiss franc (CHF) with a protective put strategy. However, he also decides he is willing to reduce the downside protection to lower initial cost. Which of the following strategies will accomplish his objective?
   A. Buy 50-delta calls and puts on the CHF.
   B. Buy a 40-delta put and sell a 20-delta put on the CHF.
   C. Buy a 40-delta put and sell a 35-delta call on the CHF.

10. Jane Archer manages a Swiss (CHF)-based hedge fund. A portion of the fund is allocated 60% and 40%, respectively, to EUR and AUD investments. She has collected the following information.

Estimates	Euro zone	Australia
Asset return in foreign currency	2.0%	2.5%
Change in spot exchange rate versus the CHF	–1.0%	3.0%
Asset risk measured in foreign currency (σ)	15.0%	25.0%
Currency risk (σ)	7.0%	9.0%
Correlation of asset and currency return	+0.85	+0.65
Correlation of returns (CHF/EUR, CHF/AUD)		+0.70

The following questions are from the portfolio perspective, measured in CHF.

A. **Calculate** the expected return of the portfolio.

B. **Calculate** the standard deviation of the portfolio.

C. **Calculate** the expected return to the portfolio if Archer takes a leveraged position with a 150% positive weight in Australia and a 150% negative weight in the euro zone.

D. **Calculate** the expected standard deviation of returns to the portfolio if Archer takes a leveraged position with a 150% positive weight in Australia and a 150% negative weight in the euro zone.

11.   Jane Archer manages a Swiss (CHF)-based hedge fund. GBP 1,000,000 is currently invested in a diversified portfolio of U.K. stocks. Archer regresses the monthly returns of a diversified U.K. stock index (returns measured in CHF) versus the monthly change in value of the CHF/GBP. The regression coefficients are intercept = 0.11 and slope coefficient = 1.25. **Determine** the quantity of GBP Archer will short to implement a hedge of direct currency risk and a minimum-variance hedge.

	Direct currency hedge	Minimum-variance hedge
A.	GBP 1,000,000	GBP 1,000,000
B.	GBP 1,000,000	GBP 1,250,000
C.	GBP 1,250,000	GBP 1,250,000

12.   A trader enters a short three-month non-deliverable forward on 2,000,000 CNY at CNY/USD 6.1155. At the end of the period, the spot exchange rate is USD/CNY 0.1612. The trader's gain or loss is *closest* to:
        A.   USD 4,600 loss.
        B.   USD 4,700 loss.
        C.   USD 4,650 gain.

For more questions related to this topic review, log in to your Schweser online account and launch SchweserPro™ QBank; and for video instruction covering each LOS in this topic review, log in to your Schweser online account and launch the OnDemand video lectures, if you have purchased these products.

CONCEPT CHECKERS – ANSWERS

1. **C** The ending value in USD is: USD 1,253,000 × 1.05 = USD 1,315,650.
    The ending value in DJF is: USD 1,315,650 × DJF/USD 192.85 = DJF 253,723,103.

2. **C** $(1 + R_{FC})(1 + R_{FX}) - 1$
    $(1.05)(192.85 / 179.54) - 1 = 12.78\%$

3. It depends on the standard deviation of the asset returns measured in the foreign currency, the standard deviation of the currency, and the correlation between these two sources of return.

    Variance = $(1.0^2)(4.5^2) + (1.0^2)(3.7^2) + 2(1.0)(1.0)(0.81)(4.5)(3.7) = 60.913$
    Standard deviation = 7.8%

4. **A** The manager's market views affect tactical decisions to vary away from the strategic decision. The portfolio and market circumstances determine the strategic decision.

5. **C** Any of the following will shift the portfolio toward active currency management allowing greater manager discretion:
    *   A long time horizon for portfolio objectives.
    *   Low risk aversion.
    *   Concern with regret at missing opportunities to add value through discretionary currency management.
    *   Low short-term income and liquidity needs.
    *   Little foreign currency bond exposure.
    *   High hedging costs.
    *   Clients who believe in the benefits of discretionary management.

6. **C** A carry trade should be more profitable in periods of economic stability (low, stable currency volatility) with lower interest rates in the borrowing currencies and higher interest rates in the investing currencies.

7. **C** Rising real interest rates in the euro zone would attract capital and be associated with a rising currency value, leading a manager to tilt to a long position in the euro. The other two answers are incorrect. Low volatility is favorable to a carry trade. Rising volatility increases the price of both calls and puts. It is likely to have a greater impact on the cost of the protective put, which requires purchase of a put. In contrast, the collar cost is increased to purchase the put but offset by an increased receipt from selling the call.

8. Simms only has authority to increase or decrease the hedge size by 10%. Because she believes the KRW will depreciate, she should reduce the hedge size 10% and will buy only 900,000 KRW rather than the existing 1,000,000 when she rolls over the hedge. The quotes are given in EUR/KRW so she must transact at the higher price of 0.00068 reflecting she is paying more EUR per KRW. The spot quote is given in five decimal places so the forward points decimal must be moved five places to the left for a forward price of 0.00068 – (1.1 / 100,000) = 0.00068 – 0.000011 = 0.000669 EUR/KRW.

9. **B** This question requires you select the strategy that meets the objectives set by Perkins. He has three objectives and only one answer choice meets all three. He wants a protective put on the CHF; all three strategies buy a put on the CHF. He wants to lower the initial cost; one strategy buys a call which will raise the cost, it must be rejected. He is willing to reduce his downside protection in order to lower the initial cost; the only one strategy to do this is the buy a 40-delta put and sell a 20-delta put on the CHF. Note the strategy

that sells an OTM call also lowers the initial cost but does so by limiting upside; this is not what Perkins specified.

10. A. The expected returns measured in the investor's domestic currency (CHF) are:
EUR asset: $(1.02)(0.99) - 1 = +0.98\%$
AUD asset: $(1.025)(1.03) - 1 = +5.58\%$
The weighted average return is: $0.6(0.98\%) + 0.4(5.58\%) = 2.82\%$

B. The standard deviations of asset returns measured in the investor's domestic currency are:
EUR asset: $[(15.0^2) + (7.0^2) + 2(15.0)(7.0)(0.85)]^{1/2} = 21.27\%$
AUD asset: $[(25.0^2) + (9.0^2) + 2(25.0)(9.0)(0.65)]^{1/2} = 31.60\%$

The standard deviation of portfolio returns is:
$[0.6^2(21.27^2) + 0.4^2(31.60^2) + 2(0.6)(0.4)(0.70)(21.27)(31.60)]^{1/2} = 23.42\%$

C. The expected returns measured in the investor's domestic currency (CHF) are:
EUR asset: $(1.02)(0.99) - 1 = +0.98\%$
AUD asset: $(1.025)(1.03) - 1 = +5.58\%$
The weighted average return is: $-1.5(0.98\%) + 1.5(5.58\%) = 6.90\%$

D. The standard deviations of asset returns measured in the investor's domestic currency are:
EUR asset: $[(15.0^2) + (7.0^2) + 2(15.0)(7.0)(0.85)]^{1/2} = 21.27\%$
AUD asset: $[(25.0^2) + (9.0^2) + 2(25.0)(9.0)(0.65)]^{1/2} = 31.60\%$

The standard deviation of portfolio returns is:
$[(-1.5)^2(21.27^2) + (1.5)^2(31.60^2) + 2(-1.5)(1.5)(0.70)(21.27)(31.60)]^{1/2} = 33.87\%$

11. **B** A direct currency hedge is a simple 1.0 hedge ratio; Archer will sell 1,000,000 GBP forward. A MVHR considers the correlation between returns of the foreign asset measured in the portfolio's domestic currency and change in value of the foreign currency. The hedge ratio is the beta (slope coefficient) of the regression. Archer will sell 1,250,000 GBP forward.

12. **C** An NDF settles in the developed market currency; however, the information is presented in a mixture of CNY/USD and USD/CNY which requires additional steps:

Determine the size of the trade in USD at the forward exchange rate:
CNY 2,000,000 / (CNY/USD 6.1155) = USD 327,037.85

Determine the G/L on the USD position in CNY. The two exchange rates need to be in CNY/USD.

Ending spot exchange rate USD/CNY 0.1612 is CNY/USD 6.20347.
G/L = (CNY/USD 6.20347 − 6.1155) × 327,037.85 = CNY 28,769.52

Determine the G/L in USD based on ending spot exchange rate is:
G/L = CNY 28,769.52 × USD/CNY 0.1612 = USD 4,637.65

The CNY was shorted at CNY/USD 6.1155 and declined in value to CNY/USD 6.20347 producing a gain on the trade of USD 4,637.65.

MARKET INDEXES AND BENCHMARKS

Study Session 9

EXAM FOCUS

Benchmarks are the base for performance evaluation. The reading is heavy on vocabulary and concepts, many of which you see discussed in greater depth in other parts of the curriculum.

BENCHMARKS VS. INDEXES

LOS 19.a: Distinguish between benchmarks and market indexes.

Benchmark: A reference point for evaluating portfolio performance.

Index: An index represents the performance of a specified group of securities.

The distinction between the two is that an index may or may not be a valid benchmark to evaluate the performance of a specific portfolio. A valid benchmark will be:

1. *Specified in advance.* The benchmark is known to both the investment manager and the fund sponsor. It is specified at the start of an evaluation period.

2. *Appropriate.* The benchmark is consistent with the manager's investment approach and style as well as the portfolio's objectives and constraints.

3. *Measurable.* Its value and return can be determined on a reasonably frequent basis.

4. *Unambiguous.* Identities and weights of securities constituting the benchmark are clearly defined.

5. *Reflective of the manager's current investment opinions.* The manager has current knowledge and expertise of the securities within the benchmark.

6. *Accountable.* The manager(s) should accept the applicability of the benchmark and agree to accept differences in performance between the portfolio and benchmark as reflecting active management.

7. *Investable.* It is possible to invest in the benchmark as an alternative to active management.

A benchmark that meets these criteria becomes a valid alternative to (paying for) active management. Comparing the performance of the portfolio to the benchmark then determines the amount of value added or lost by the manager.

INVESTMENT USES OF BENCHMARKS

LOS 19.b: Describe investment uses of benchmarks.

- A reference point for portions of a sponsor's portfolio. The sponsor of a defined benefit plan may determine that a 60% allocation to large cap U.S. equities is part of the optimal strategic asset allocation. If so, the S&P 500 Index becomes a suitable reference point to evaluate whether active management adds value to that portion of the portfolio.
- Communication between the plan sponsor, manager, and consultants. The benchmark selection tells the manager what return and risk they will be compared to.
- Communicating to others how a manager wishes to be viewed. A management firm comparing its performance to small-cap U.S. value stocks allows investors to determine if they have any interest in the manager.
- Clearly specifying risk exposures. A style described as small-cap U.S. value is less definitive than identifying a specific benchmark whose characteristics can be analyzed.
- Performance attribution. Attribution models can be used to determine the amount and sources of value added by comparing portfolio to benchmark performance.
- Manager selection. The benchmark a manager selects indicates where he believes his skills lie, allowing a potential investor to qualitatively assess whether the manager has the resources and skills to likely repeat past performances.
- Marketing. GIPS® requires that where a suitable benchmark exists, it be named and results provided, allowing investors to compare the manager's performance to the benchmark. The benchmark a manager selects communicates to prospective clients how that manager views himself.
- Compliance, laws, and regulation (like GIPS) often mandate that comparison benchmark data be provided.

TYPES OF BENCHMARKS

LOS 19.c: Compare types of benchmarks.

Asset–based benchmarks:

Absolute return: Specify a minimum return such as 6% or a minimum spread such as LIBOR + 60bp.

Manager universe or peer group: Outperform the median manager in a specified peer group.

Broad market index: Outperform the U.S. Wilshire 5000 Equity Index.

Investment style: Outperform the U.S. Wilshire 5000 Large-Cap Value Index.

Factor-based models: Portfolio return is related to a set of factors and factor weights.

$$R_P = a_p + b_1F_1 + b_2F_2 + \ldots + b_KF_K + \varepsilon$$

where:
R_p = periodic return on an account
a_p = "zero factor" term, representing the expected value of R_p if all factor values were zero
F_i = factors that have a systematic effect on the portfolio's performance, i = 1 to K
b_i = sensitivity of the returns on the account to the returns generated from factor i
ε = error term; portfolio return not explained by the factor model

For example, an index's return has a 0.4 sensitivity (*b*) to earnings growth (*F*). If earnings increase 6%, then the return will be 2.4% due to that factor.

Return-based: A factor-based model in which the factors are various subgroups of asset return and the sensitivities (*b*) are found by regressing these subgroup returns versus a portfolio's returns.

Custom: Build a benchmark from securities weighted to reflect the manager's style. Reflecting the manager's style, it could be called the manager's **strategy benchmark**.

LOS 19.d: Contrast liability-based benchmarks with asset-based benchmarks.

Asset-based benchmarks focus on return of the assets and the ability of managers to meet or exceed the benchmark return (i.e., adding value). **Liability-based** benchmarks are more appropriate when the objective is to fund a stream of liability payments at relatively low risk. Matching the duration of the assets to the duration of the liabilities leads the two to fluctuate in sync and stabilize the surplus. A defined benefit pension fund benchmark may consist of nominal bonds, real rate bonds, and equities to best mimic the characteristics of the plan liabilities.

USE OF MARKET INDEXES

LOS 19.e: Describe investment uses of market indexes.

In rough order the sequence in which a plan sponsor may uses indexes includes:

Asset allocation proxies: Historical index return data can provide return, risk, and correlation by asset class for asset allocation models.

Investment management mandates: Specifying a benchmark communicates (ex ante) expected return and risk characteristics to a manager. Generally, the assets selected by the manager will be similar to those in the benchmark with an active manager seeking to outperform and a passive manager seeking to match the benchmark.

Performance benchmarks: Ex post the manager's return can be compared to the benchmark return to calculate value added.

Portfolio analysis: More detailed ex post analysis can determine sources of value added (e.g., from security selection versus from over/under-weighting sectors).

Other use of indexes includes:

Gauging market sentiment: Index returns are used to summarize overall market direction, movement, and volatility.

As an investment: Modern portfolio theory postulates and empirical evidence supports that it is difficult for active managers to outperform the market. Index funds, ETFs and derivatives based on market indexes provide a low-cost alternative to active management for a wide variety of asset types and styles.

INDEX CONSTRUCTION

LOS 19.f: Discuss tradeoffs in constructing market indexes.

An index is constructed from a set of rules. The rules define the criteria for selecting the securities to include in the index, how to weight the securities, and how to maintain the index. The construction will require tradeoffs.

Completeness vs. investability: A complete index will include all securities that meet the benchmark criteria and provide complete coverage and greater diversification. The trade off is the inclusion of smaller cap and less liquid securities that are difficult or costly to purchase. Global portfolios may face additional investabilty issues with liquid assets but restrictions on ownership by foreign investors. This tradeoff is more significant for managers who experience larger and more frequent withdrawals and admissions of funds.

Reconstitution and rebalancing (R&R) frequency vs. turnover: Reconstitution is the process of adding and deleting securities while rebalancing is adjusting the weighting of existing securities in an index. Frequent R&R theoretically means the index better reflects the intended characteristics. The tradeoff is increased turnover and transaction costs. Style-based indexes such as S&P Growth typically face a greater tradeoff than broad market indexes such as the S&P 500 as a security remains part of the S&P 500 but can shift from Growth to Value style. An index like the Wilshire 5000 with a fixed number of securities generally has less turnover than one whose number varies based on securities meeting some defined criteria such as market cap above $50 million. International indexes with float adjustment that try to frequently match the changing float (the number of securities actually available for purchase) would also face higher turnover and costs.

Objective and transparent (O&T) rules vs. judgment: Changes to the composition of the index may be based on objective rules that are publically disclosed or on subjective judgments of some defined group. O&T rules allow those who replicate or base holdings around the index holdings to anticipate and plan for changes in the index, thus lowering costs. The fact that when an index adds/removes a security often leads that security's price to increase/decrease makes anticipating changes more important. While O&T is desirable, most index construction includes some judgment in application of the rules to deal with changing or unanticipated situations.

THE PROS AND CONS OF APPROACHES TO INDEX WEIGHTING

LOS 19.g: Discuss advantages and disadvantages of index weighting schemes.

Capitalization weighted (market value weighted, value weighted, market cap weighting, or cap weighted) is the most common form of index construction. The weight of each security is based on its price multiplied by shares outstanding. In some cases, free float is used and shares that are not available to trade are excluded from the calculation. The performance of such indexes is most heavily influenced by the securities with the largest market cap.

Advantages

- Based on an objective measure (the market price) of what every security is worth.
- *Macro consistent* because all securities are owned and therefore the aggregate portfolio of all investors must be market capitalization weighted. A float adjusted, cap weighted index reflects what is available for investors to own.
- Under the assumptions of the capital asset pricing model, it is the only efficient portfolio of risky assets.
- Does not require rebalancing for stock splits and stock dividends.

Disadvantages

- Exposed to market bubbles because it most heavily weights the largest market cap securities, which may also be the most overvalued securities.
- Weighting by market cap can lead to overconcentration in a few securities and less diversification.
- May be unsuited as a benchmark for active managers who take substantially different risk exposures than the market.

Price-weighted indexes reflect initially owning one share of each stock. Their performance is most heavily influenced by the securities with the highest price.

Advantages

- Easy to construct.
- Long price histories are available.

Disadvantages

- Market cap better reflects a company's economic importance.

- Stocks that appreciate are more likely to split and the reduced post split price diminishes the impact of that security on the index. The method effectively tends to reduce the weighting of the more successful companies.
- Does not reflect typical portfolio construction. Most portfolios are not built with an equal number of shares in each security.

Equal-weighted indexes reflect the same initial investment in each security.

Advantages

- Compared to market cap weighting, it places more emphasis on smaller cap securities that (1) may offer a return advantage and (2) provide greater diversification (instead of concentrating in higher market cap assets).
- Some argue it better reflects how the market did because it reflects the average return of each security in the index.

Disadvantages

- Biased to the performance of smaller issuers (when compared to market cap weighted).
- Requires constant rebalancing to maintain equal weight and will result in selling stronger performers and buying weaker performers.
- The emphasis on smaller cap securities can lead to increased liquidity problems and higher transaction costs.

Conclusions

Cap-weighted, float-adjusted construction dominates. Because this method reflects what can be done in aggregate, it generally provides superior benchmarks. As benchmarks, it is:

- Widely used, understood, and readily available.
- Easy to measure, unambiguous, specified in advance, and generally investable.
- Appropriate if it reflects the securities used by and style of the manager.

It also has drawbacks if:

- It does not reflect the manager's investment approach.
- The index construction rules and the rebalancing process are not transparent. The costs of rebalancing increase and the ability to track the index declines.

LOS 19.h: Evaluate the selection of a benchmark for a particular investment strategy.

Non-cap weighting may be used to seek improved risk adjusted return, reflect a particular manager's style, or to better reflect client characteristics.

Example:

A tax-exempt U.S. pension plan is 95% funded and closed to new plan entrants. The plan sponsor is a financially troubled and highly leveraged basic industrial corporation. The average duration of liabilities is five years. Benefits are indexed to inflation and increase with wages for the plan participants. Plan participants may elect a lump sum payout at retirement. The sponsor and plan manager agree to use an inflation-linked bond index of government and high-grade corporate bonds. The bond allocation is expected to provide the primary source of liquidity and reduce overall portfolio risk. Equity is intended to provide diversification, return enhancement, and protection from increasing benefit payouts. A world market stock index is used as the equity benchmark. They agree the portfolio should maintain a strategic underweight in the sponsor's business.

Discuss whether an available market or custom index will be most appropriate to evaluate the plan's long term performance. How often should the benchmark be reviewed?

Answer:

A custom security benchmark should be used. It would include a blend of bonds that reflect the duration of the liabilities and equities with an underweight in basic industrials. A general tilt to lower risk is appropriate given the higher financial risk of the sponsor. The total plan benchmark should be weighted to mimic the plan liabilities distribution between nominal, real rate, and wage inflation exposures. A cash allocation to meet distributions is also needed.

The benchmark should be reevaluated as the nature of the plan liabilities and the sponsor status change.

KEY CONCEPTS

LOS 19.a
- Index: Represents the performance of a specified group of securities.
- Benchmark: A reference point for evaluating portfolio performance.
- Indexes are often used as benchmarks.

LOS 19.b
- Reference point to specify strategic asset allocation and ex post to determine value added.
- Communicate expected risk and return between the plan sponsor, manager, and consultants.
- Clearly specify risk exposures (e.g., large-cap U.S. is less definitive than a specific benchmark).
- Performance attribution for sources of value added.

By the manager to:
- Communicate their perceived skill set.
- Help clients determine if the manager is suitable to client needs.
- Meet GIPS, legal, and regulatory requirements.

LOS 19.c
Asset-based benchmarks include:
- Absolute return: Specify a minimum return.
- Manager universe or peer group.
- Broad market index.
- Investment style index.
- Factor-based models: Portfolio return is related to a set of factors and factor weights:
  - Return-based regression is one type.
  - Custom benchmarks are designed to reflect a specific manager's style.

LOS 19.d
- Asset-based are for managers who focus on matching or exceeding the return of the assets in the benchmark.
- Liability-based are for those who mimic liability characteristics in order to minimize the volatility of surplus.

LOS 19.e
By a plan sponsor:
- Historical market data for asset allocation models.
- To communicate expectations for asset type weights, risk, and return.
- For ex post performance benchmarks and attribution analysis.

Other uses:
- An indicator of how the market is doing.
- Designing securities to match the index (e.g., ETFs, futures contracts).

LOS 19.f

Completeness would include all possible securities but investability would exclude less liquid and higher transaction cost securities.

More frequent reconstitution and rebalancing better controls the characteristics of the index but increases turnover and transaction costs.

Objective and transparent rules for index construction make it easier for users to match the index but allowing judgment in index construction is needed to deal with changing or unanticipated situations.

LOS 19.g

Market-cap weighted: Uses the market's objective opinion of value and is macro consistent with what is owned.

> Cons: Greater exposure to potentially overvalued securities, less diversification, and may not reflect a manager's style.

Price-weighted: Easy to construct and long price histories exist.

> Cons: Price does not reflect economic importance, successful stocks tend to split (lowering their weighting), and is not how most portfolios are constructed.

Equal-weighted: Reflects performance of the average stock and relative to cap-weighted emphasizes smaller cap for better diversification and potentially better return.

> Cons: Overemphasis on small-cap and requires continual rebalancing.

LOS 19.h

Select the benchmark that best matches the portfolio's objectives and constraints, and the manager's investment process.

CONCEPT CHECKERS

1. A global index is offered with returns computed both before dividend withholding taxes and after withholding taxes. Returns computed after withholding taxes are, of course, lower. Assume a client lives in a country with tax treaties that eliminate double taxation of dividend income. **Explain** which version of the index is more suitable for performance evaluation.

2. **Discuss** two benefits to an investment manager of telling a client what benchmark the manager believes the client should use to evaluate the manager's performance.

3. **Discuss** two benefits to a client of the client telling the manager the benchmark the client will use to evaluate the manager's performance.

4. Which of the following benchmark types is *most likely* to meet the characteristics of a valid benchmark?
   A. Investment style.
   B. Manager peer group.
   C. Proprietary return based factor model.

5. For a liability-based benchmark the single most important criteria is to match asset and liability:
   A. duration.
   B. cash flows.
   C. credit quality.

6.   **Explain** the role of market indices in performance evaluation of a total portfolio and by asset class and why investability is a critical characteristic of a valid benchmark.

7.   **List** and **explain** three uses of market indices.

8.   **Explain** the tradeoff between completeness versus investability in index construction.

9.   **Explain** the tradeoff between reconstitution and rebalancing frequency versus turnover. How would float adjustment affect this trade off?

10.   **Discuss** the appropriate type of benchmark for each of the following:
      A. A long and short bond manager with an objective to earn 90-day LIBOR plus 200 basis points.
      B. The sub-portfolio of an insurance company used to fund liabilities that have a duration of 2.7.

      The company is heavily regulated, restricted to investment-grade securities, and has a below average surplus.

For more questions related to this topic review, log in to your Schweser online account and launch SchweserPro™ QBank; and for video instruction covering each LOS in this topic review, log in to your Schweser online account and launch the OnDemand video lectures, if you have purchased these products.

CONCEPT CHECKERS – ANSWERS

1. The higher returns before dividend withholding are appropriate because the investor can claim a credit or otherwise recover the dividend amount withheld.

2. • Tells the client where the manager believes her expertise lies and reduces the chances the client will later be disappointed.
   • Meets requirements of GIPS.
   • Can meet legal and regulatory requirements.

3. • Clearly communicates to the manager the return and risk characteristics the client expects in the portfolio.
   • The client can then fairly use the benchmark in subsequent performance evaluation of portfolio results.

4. **A** Style-based benchmarks are commonly used and if suited to the client needs and manager's approach they meet the characteristics of a valid benchmark. A manager peer group is not normally investable because the median manager cannot be known (specified) in advance. A proprietary model would have the same issue if the specifics of the model are not known.

5. **A** Interest rate risk is normally the most important issue so matching duration is the primary consideration. Matching cash flows would also mean matching duration but matching cash flows is a more restrictive criteria and not necessary.

6. Ex post the return of a portfolio can be compare to its overall benchmark to determine value added or lost by management of the portfolio. Various sectors of the portfolio such as bond and equity can each be compared to their individual benchmark to determine value added or lost by sector. The implicit assumption is the benchmark was an alternative to hiring a manager so if the benchmark is not investable, the analysis has no real value, and the benchmark is no longer a viable alternative.

7. • Asset allocation proxies: Historical data can provide return, risk, and correlation by asset class.
   • Investment management mandates: Specifying a benchmark communicates expected return and risk characteristics to a manager.
   • Performance benchmarks: Ex post the manager's return can be compared to the benchmark return to calculate value added.
   • Portfolio analysis: More detailed ex post analysis can determine sources of value added (e.g., from security selection versus from over/under-weighting sectors).
   • Gauging market sentiment: Index returns summarize overall market direction, movement, and volatility.
   • As an investment: Index funds, ETFs, and derivatives are available based on market indices.

8. A complete index will include more securities for greater diversification. But this means including smaller-cap and less liquid securities that will increase transaction costs for those who replicate the index.

9. Frequent reconstitution and rebalancing will keep the index closely aligned with its intended characteristics. The tradeoff is increased turnover and transaction costs. Frequent float adjustment to match a changing number of investable shares would increase those costs but better reflect what is in aggregate investable.

10. Part A: The 90-day LIBOR plus 200 basis points is appropriate—an absolute return benchmark.

Part B: The appropriate benchmark is driven by the liabilities and constraints on the company. Investment-grade bonds with a duration of 2.7 would best mimic the liabilities.

You have now finished the Asset Allocation topic area. To get immediate feedback on how effective your study has been for this material, log in to your Schweser online account and take the self-test for this topic area. Questions are more exam-like than typical Concept Checkers or QBank questions; a score of less than 70% indicates that your study likely needs improvement. These tests are timed and allow three minutes per question.

The following is a review of the Fixed-Income Portfolio Management (1) principles designed to address the learning outcome statements set forth by CFA Institute. Cross-Reference to CFA Institute Assigned Reading #20.

FIXED-INCOME PORTFOLIO MANAGEMENT—PART I[1]

EXAM FOCUS

The concepts of duration and spread will carry over from earlier levels of the exam with extensions from what has been previously covered. Immunization and its variations is ALM with math. Fixed income will address the details of hedging to modify portfolio risk and touch on some aspects of currency risk management. Don't overlook the seemingly simple discussions of benchmarks and active versus passive management because these are prominent themes at Level III. Expect both math and conceptual questions.

BOND PORTFOLIO BENCHMARKS

LOS 20.a: Compare, with respect to investment objectives, the use of liabilities as a benchmark and the use of a bond index as a benchmark.

Using a Bond Index as a Benchmark

Bond fund managers (e.g., bond mutual funds) are commonly compared to a benchmark that is selected or constructed to closely resemble the managed portfolio. Assume, for example, a bond fund manager specializes in one sector of the bond market. Instead of simply accepting the return generated by the manager, investors want to be able to determine whether the manager consistently earns sufficient returns to justify management expenses. In this case, a custom benchmark is constructed so that any difference in return is due to strategies employed by the manager, not structural differences between the portfolio and the benchmark.

Another manager might be compared to a well-diversified bond index. If the manager mostly agrees with market forecasts and values, she will follow a *passive* management approach. She constructs a portfolio that mimics the index along several dimensions of risk, and the return on the portfolio should track the return on the index fairly closely.

---

1. Much of the terminology utilized throughout this topic review is industry convention as presented in Reading 20 of the 2017 Level III CFA curriculum.

If the manager believes she has a superior ability to forecast interest rates and/or identify under-valued individual bonds or entire sectors, she follows an *active* management approach. She will construct the portfolio to resemble the index in many ways but, through various active management strategies, she hopes to consistently *outperform* the index. Active bond portfolio management strategies are discussed throughout this topic review.

Using Liabilities as a Benchmark

The investment objective when managing a bond portfolio against a single liability or set of liabilities (ALM) is rather straightforward; the manager must manage the portfolio to maintain sufficient portfolio value to meet the liabilities.

BOND INDEXING STRATEGIES

LOS 20.b: Compare pure bond indexing, enhanced indexing, and active investing with respect to the objectives, advantages, disadvantages, and management of each.

As you may surmise from this LOS, there are many different strategies that can be followed when managing a bond portfolio. For example, the manager can assume a completely passive approach and not have to forecast anything. In other words, the manager who feels he has no reason to disagree with market forecasts has no reason to assume he can outperform an indexing strategy through active management. On the other hand, a manager who is confident in his forecasting abilities and has reason to believe market forecasts are incorrect can generate significant return through active management.

The differences between the various active management approaches are mostly matters of degree. That is, bond portfolio management strategies form more or less a continuum from an almost do-nothing approach (i.e., pure bond indexing) to a do-almost-anything approach (i.e., full-blown active management) as demonstrated graphically in Figure 1.

Figure 1: Increasing Degrees of Active Bond Portfolio Management

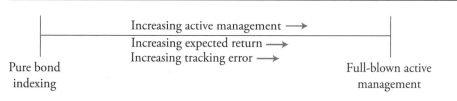

In Figure 1, you will notice the increase of three characteristics as you move from pure bond indexing to full-blown active management. The first, *increasing active management*, can be defined as the gradual relaxation of restrictions on the manager's actions to allow him to exploit his superior forecasting/valuation abilities. With pure bond indexing, the manager is restricted to constructing a portfolio with all the securities in the index and in the same weights as the index. This means the portfolio will have exactly the same risk exposures as the index. As you move from left to right, the restrictions on the manager's actions are relaxed and the portfolio risk factor exposures differ more and more from those of the index.

The next characteristic, *increasing expected return*, refers to the increase in portfolio expected return from actions taken by the manager. Unless the manager has some superior ability that enables him to identify profitable situations, he should stick with pure bond indexing or at least match primary risk factors.

The third characteristic, *increasing tracking error*, refers to the degree to which the portfolio return tracks that of the index. With pure bond indexing, even though management fees and transactions are incurred, the reduced return on the portfolio will closely track the return on the index. As you move to the right, the composition and factor exposures of the portfolio differ more and more from the index. Each enhancement is intended to increase the portfolio return, but is not guaranteed to do so. Thus, the amount by which the portfolio return exceeds the index return can be quite variable from period to period and even negative. The difference between the portfolio and index returns (i.e., the portfolio excess return) is referred to as **active return**. The standard deviation of active return across several periods is referred to as **tracking risk**, thus it is the *variability* of the portfolio excess return that increases as you move towards full-blown active management. This increased variability translates into increased uncertainty.

The five classifications of bond portfolio management can be described as: (1) *pure bond indexing*, (2) *enhanced indexing by matching primary risk factors*, (3) *enhanced indexing by small risk factor mismatches*, (4) *active management by larger risk factor mismatches*, and (5) *full-blown active management*.

> **For the Exam:** Generally, do not expect firm distinctions among these five categories. Instead, view No. 1 as purely passive and No. 5 as having no restrictions on the manager. In between is a continuum and exact distinctions are subjective. Moving from No. 1 to No. 5, the potential for adding value increases compared to the index, but so does risk. Generally:
>
> - No. 1 allows no deviations from the index.
> - Nos. 2 and 3 allow some deviations but will match at least the overall duration of the benchmark.
> - Nos. 4 and 5 involve deviating from the average duration of the benchmark as well as other deviations.

Pure Bond Indexing

This is the easiest strategy to describe as well as understand. In a pure bond indexing strategy, the manager replicates every dimension of the index. Every bond in the index is purchased and its weight in the portfolio is determined by its weight in the index. Due to varying bond liquidities and availabilities, this strategy, though easy to describe, is difficult and costly to implement.

Enhanced Indexing by Matching Primary Risk Factors

Due to the number of different bond issues in the typical bond index as well as the inefficiencies and costs associated with pure bond indexing, that strategy is rarely implemented. Instead, managers will enhance the portfolio return by utilizing a sampling approach to replicate the index's primary risk factors while holding only a percentage of the bonds in the index. Sampling reduces the costs associated with constructing the portfolio, and matching the risk factors means the portfolio is exposed to the same risk factors as the index. This means the portfolio will track the index closely, and since lower transactions costs are incurred, this strategy will outperform a pure bond indexing strategy.

Enhanced Indexing by Small Risk Factor Mismatches

This is the first level of indexing that is designed to earn about the same return as the index. While maintaining the exposure to large risk factors, such as duration, the manager slightly tilts the portfolio towards other, smaller risk factors by pursuing relative value strategies (e.g., identifying undervalued sectors) or identifying other return-enhancing opportunities. The small tilts are only intended to compensate for administrative costs.

Active Management by Larger Risk Factor Mismatches

The only difference between this strategy and enhanced indexing by small risk factor mismatches (the preceding strategy) is the degree of the mismatches. In other words, the manager pursues more significant quality and value strategies (e.g., overweight quality sectors expected to outperform, identify undervalued securities). In addition, the manager might alter the duration of the portfolio somewhat. The intent is earning sufficient return to cover administrative as well as increased transactions costs without increasing the portfolio's risk exposure beyond an acceptable level.

Full-Blown Active Management

There are no restrictions on how the portfolio can deviate from the index. Figure 2 is a summary of the advantages and disadvantages of the bond portfolio strategies discussed. Note that in each case, relative phrases (e.g., lower, increased) refer to the cell immediately above the one in which the phrase is written. For example, *less costly to implement*, under advantages for enhanced indexing by matching primary risk factors, refers to lower costs than those associated with pure bond indexing.

Figure 2: Advantages and Disadvantages of Bond Portfolio Management Strategies

Strategy	Advantages	Disadvantages
Pure bond indexing (PBI)	• Returns before expenses track the index (zero or very low tracking error) • Same risk factor exposures as the index • Low advisory and administrative fees	• Costly and difficult to implement • Lower expected return than the index
Enhanced indexing by matching primary risk factors (sampling)	• Less costly to implement • Increased expected return • Maintains exposure to the index's primary risk factors	• Increased management fees • Reduced ability to track the index (i.e., increased tracking error) • Lower expected return than the index
Enhanced indexing by small risk factor mismatches	• Same duration as index • Increased expected return • Reduced manager restrictions	• Increased risk • Increased tracking error • Increased management fees
Active management by larger risk factor mismatches	• Increased expected return • Reduced manager restrictions • Ability to tune the portfolio duration	• Increased risk • Increased tracking error • Increased management fees
Full-blown active management	• Increased expected return • Few if any manager restrictions • No limits on duration	• Increased risk • Increased tracking error • Increased management fees

SELECTING A BENCHMARK BOND INDEX

LOS 20.c: Discuss the criteria for selecting a benchmark bond index and justify the selection of a specific index when given a description of an investor's risk aversion, income needs, and liabilities.

Out-performing a bond index on a consistent basis is difficult at best, especially when risk and *net* return are considered. The primary benefits to using an indexing approach include diversification and low costs. The typical broad bond market index contains thousands of issues with widely varying maturities, coupon rates, and bond sector coverage. Therefore, a bond portfolio manager should move from a pure indexing position to more active management only when the client's objectives and constraints permit and the manager's abilities justify it.

Regardless of the strategy employed, the manager should be judged against a benchmark, and the benchmark should match the characteristics of the portfolio. Among others, there are four primary considerations when selecting a benchmark: (1) *market value risk,* (2) *income risk,* (3) *credit risk,* and (4) *liability framework risk.*

Market value risk. The market values of long duration portfolios are more sensitive to changes in yield than the market values of shorter duration portfolios. From a market value perspective, therefore, the greater the investor's risk aversion, the shorter the appropriate duration of the portfolio and the selected benchmark.

Income risk. If the client is dependent upon cash flows from the portfolio, those cash flows should be consistent and low-risk. Longer term fixed-rate bonds will lock in an income stream. The longer the maturity of the portfolio and benchmark, therefore, the lower the income risk. Investors desiring a stable, long-term cash flow should invest in longer-term bonds and utilize long-term benchmarks.

Credit risk. The benchmark's credit risk exposure should be consistent with the client's objectives and constraints. If the client seeks higher return and will accept higher credit risk, select a benchmark with greater credit risk exposure.

Liability framework risk. If there are definable liabilities, then ALM is the preferred approach. The benchmark that most closely matches the liabilities should be selected.

LOS 20.d: Critique the use of bond market indexes as benchmarks.

A valid benchmark should be investable in order to provide a valid alternative to hiring a manager. If the index is not investable, it is not a valid benchmark. The bond market provides several challenges to this requirement.

First, bond market securities are more heterogeneous and illiquid. Issues are unique with differences in maturity, seniority, and other features compared to stocks, which are generally issued as one type of stock. Compounding the problem, many issues do not trade regularly and pricing data is frequently based on appraisals and trades are often not publicly reported. These characteristics lead index providers to make choices regarding what to include in an index and full index replication is less common than for equities.

Second, the resulting indexes from various vendors can appear similar but be quite different in characteristics. With different characteristics there can be unapparent risks (e.g., what is the weight of callable and non-callable bonds? Of sinking fund bonds? What countries are included in a global index?).

Third, the risk characteristics can change quickly over time as new issues of bonds are added and those approaching maturity are deleted from the index.

Fourth is the "bums" problem as capitalized-weighted indexes may carry increased exposure to credit downgrades. Large issuance by an issuer leads to greater index weight but large issuance is also related to excessive leverage and subsequent credit problems. To mitigate the bums problem, some index providers impose weight limits, make subjective decisions, or use equal weights.

Lastly, it can be difficult for investors to find an index that matches their risk profile. For example, if long-term interest rates are historically low, bond issuers will finance debt longer term resulting in a higher duration in the index whereas an investor may have a shorter duration time horizon.

The result is many active investors create custom benchmarks from a composite of indexes and sub-indexes to match the characteristics of a particular manager. Passive investors use sampling to replicate an index and ALM portfolios use the liabilities as the benchmark.

ALIGNING RISK EXPOSURES

LOS 20.e: Describe and evaluate techniques, such as duration matching and the use of key rate durations, by which an enhanced indexer may seek to align the risk exposures of the portfolio with those of the benchmark bond index.

An enhanced index portfolio closely mimics its benchmark to minimize tracking error. Enhanced indexing generally allows no deviation from the benchmark's duration but allows smaller deviations in other risk factors in an effort to add value (active return).

The simplest but least precise way to control risk is to **match aggregate portfolio exposure to benchmark exposure**. For example, if the benchmark has a duration of 1.8 and average credit quality of AA, then match the portfolio's duration and credit quality to these two risk factors.

Cell matching (i.e., **stratified sampling**) adds precision by matching individual cell exposure within the risk factor. For example, the benchmark average duration and quality are composed as follows:

Figure 3: Cell Matching

Benchmark Duration	x % Exposure	= Contribution to Duration	Benchmark Quality	x % Exposure	= Contribution to Quality
0 to 1*	40%	0.20	AAA = 1	10%	0.10
+1 to 3	40%	0.80	AA = 2	60%	1.20
+3 to 5	20%	0.80	A = 3	30%	0.90
Average duration =		1.80	Average quality =		2.20 = AA

* midpoint of range used to calculate contribution to duration

The portfolio will match the weights of the benchmark by cell and therefore also match the average risk exposures.

Multifactor modeling of risk exposures produces similar results but with more advance mathematical modeling (The CFA text does not provide details, but think about multifactor regression of past data to find a portfolio allocation by risk factors that would have most closely tracked past benchmark returns.).

The primary risk factors considered in any of the approaches previously mentioned typically include:

1. **Duration** (i.e., **effective duration**) measures exposure to interest rate risk as measured by small parallel changes in the yield curve. A parallel shift means all interest rates change by the same Δr. For larger changes in rates, matching convexity will improve results but convexity also assumes parallel shifts. Matching duration (and convexity) of the benchmark minimizes interest rate risk.

   Think of **interest rate risk** as movement in the general level of interest rates and **yield curve risk** as any non-parallel change in rates and the yield curve. In a non-parallel shift, Δr for different maturities will differ. Non-parallel shifts are normal and this is yield curve risk. The curve can twist (interest rates at shorter and longer maturities move in opposite directions) or the curve can change in other ways. Cell matching duration of the benchmark minimizes both interest rate and yield curve risks. (Note that in spite of parallel shifts being rare, simple duration generally explains *most of* what happens to portfolios when the curve changes.)

2. **Key rate duration** or present value distribution of cash flow matching achieves the same result as cell matching of duration. All three minimize both interest rate and yield curve risk. Key rate duration breaks the yield curve into a finite number of maturity points and analyzes change in price of a security if only one of those points on the yield curve changes. For example, a bond has a 5-year key rate duration of 1.27. If the 5-year interest rate increases 1% and no other rates change, the bond will decline 1.27%. Summing all of a bond's key rate durations will equal the bond's duration.

   Because duration measures price change and price is the PV of a bond's future cash flows, if the **present value distribution of cash flows** are matched, duration and distributions of duration are also matched. Figure 4 and its discussion explain this process:

Figure 4: Present Value Distribution of Cash Flows

	Cash Flow				
Amount	Due in Year	PV at periodic r of: 0.02	PV/Total PV	Duration Contribution	Duration Contributions as % of Total Duration
1.500	0.500	1.471	0.015	0.007	0.005
1.500	1.000	1.442	0.015	0.015	0.010
101.500	1.500	95.646	0.970	1.455	0.985
bond price =		98.559	1.000	1.477	1.000

In the first and second columns, the future cash flows and their timing are projected. Because each cash flow is a onetime event, each is equivalent to a zero-coupon bond, making the timing of each cash flow its duration.

The third column calculates the PV of each cash flow based on the bond's yield. The sum of the PVs is the bond's price.

The forth column shows each PV as a percentage of total PV. The product of column 2 (duration) and column 4 (weighting) is the contribution to total duration of that cash flow and is shown in column 5. Summing each of these products in column 5 is the bond's duration.

The final column finds the % weight of each duration contribution to total duration.

If a manager matches the weights in the final column for a portfolio to those of the portfolio's benchmark, durations will be matched as well as exposure along the yield curve.

> *Professor's Note: The analysis was for one bond; aggregate portfolio cash flows could be used for the total portfolio. Making the calculations is not the point of the reading. The point is that matching duration cells, key rate durations, or PV distributions cash flows is ultimately the same thing; it minimizes both interest rate and yield curve risk. As always, start working practice questions after you have completed each reading to see the application expected.*

3. **Sector and quality percent.** The manager matches the weights of sectors and qualities in the index.

4. **Quality spread duration contribution.** The manager matches the proportion of the index duration that is contributed by each *quality* in the index, where quality refers to bonds with credit risk (i.e., not credit risk-free Treasury bonds). Spread duration measures how the price of one bond will change relative to the price of another bond if the difference in yield between the two bonds (the spread) changes. For example, a portfolio's benchmark has 30% invested in A rated bonds with a spread duration of 5.00. The product of weight and duration is 1.50 and is the spread duration contribution of A rated bonds to the benchmark. If the spread of A rated bonds to Treasury bonds increases 1.0%, then the value of the benchmark would fall 1.5% in relation to Treasury bond prices. (Note: there is no way to know from this data if Treasury prices or the benchmark increases or decreases in price, only that there is a price decline relative to Treasury prices.) If a portfolio matches this 1.50 spread duration contribution for A rated bonds, then change in corporate spreads should not affect the portfolio's performance relative to the benchmark.

5. **Sector duration contributions.** The same analysis applied to quality can be applied to sectors. For example, a portfolio's benchmark has a 2.61 spread duration contribution to industrial bonds. If the portfolio matches this 2.61, then a change in industrial bond spreads should have no effect on the portfolio's performance relative to the benchmark.

6. **Sector/coupon/maturity cell weights.** Convexity is difficult to measure for callable bonds. One way to match the convexity is to match the sector, coupon, and maturity weights in the portfolio to that of the benchmark. For example, hold callable bonds in the portfolio in similar weight and with similar characteristics to those in the benchmark.

7. **Issuer exposure.** After matching all of the risk factors previously mentioned, there is still event risk, and an individual security could underperform for reasons unrelated to market circumstances (e.g., the issuer declares bankruptcy). Holding a smaller number of securities than the benchmark increases this risk because each security will have a relatively larger weight in the portfolio than in the benchmark.

Figure 5 contains a summary of the risk exposures for *non-MBS* bonds.[2] Note that MBS primary risk exposures include sector, prepayment, and convexity risk.

Figure 5: Bond Risk Exposures: Non-MBS

| Risk | *Primary Risk Factors* | | | | |
	Interest Rate	*Yield Curve*		*Spread*	*Credit*	*Optionality*
What is Measured	Exposure to yield curve *shifts*	Exposure to yield curve *twists*		Exposure to spread changes	Exposure to credit changes	Exposure to call or put
Measure Used	Duration	PVD	Key rate durations	Spread duration	Duration contribution by credit rating	Delta

SCENARIO ANALYSIS

LOS 20.f: Contrast and demonstrate the use of total return analysis and scenario analysis to assess the risk and return characteristics of a proposed trade.

Rather than focus exclusively on the portfolio's expected total return under one single set of assumptions, **scenario analysis** allows a portfolio manager to assess portfolio total return under varying sets of assumptions (different scenarios). Possible scenarios would include simultaneous assumptions regarding interest rates and spreads at the end of the investment horizon as well as reinvestment rates over the investment horizon.

Potential Performance of a Trade

Estimating expected total return under a single set of assumptions only provides a point estimate of the investment's expected return (i.e., a single number). Combining total return analysis with scenario analysis allows the analyst to assess not only the return but also its volatility (distribution) under different scenarios.

---

2. Figure 5 is based on Exhibit 3 in the 2017 Level III CFA curriculum, Vol. 4, p. 19.

Example: Scenario analysis

Consider a 7-year, 10% semiannual, $100 par corporate bond. The bond is priced to yield 9% ($105.11), and it is assumed that coupons can be reinvested at 7% over the 1-year investment horizon.

The yield curve is expected to remain flat at its current level. However, the issue's credit spread is expected to change, but by an unknown amount. Thus, the manager has opted to use total return analysis in a scenario analysis framework to assess the range of potential outcomes and has generated the information in the following figure.

Total Return Sensitivity to Horizon Yield: One-Year Horizon

Horizon Yield*(%)	Horizon Price ($)	Bond-Equivalent Yield (%)	Effective Annual Return (%)
11	95.69	0.717	0.718
10	100.00	4.77	4.82
9	**104.56**	**8.96**	**9.16**
8	109.39	13.31	13.76
7	114.50	17.82	18.62
6	119.91	22.50	23.77
5	125.64	27.35	29.22

*Required return on the bond in one year.

Sample calculation, assuming 9% horizon yield (bold in the table):

1. **Horizon price (in one year, the bond will have a 6-year maturity):**
   N = 6 × 2 = 12; FV = 100; I/Y = 9/2 = 4.5%; PMT = 5; CPT → PV = 104.56

2. **Semiannual return:**
   horizon value of reinvested coupons = $5 + $5\left(1 + \dfrac{0.07}{2}\right) = \$10.175$

   total horizon value = 104.56 + 10.175 = $114.735
   PV = −105.11; FV = 114.735; N = 2; CPT → I/Y = 4.478%

3. **BEY** = 4.478% × 2 = 8.96%

4. **EAR** = $(1.04478)^2 - 1 = 9.16\%$

Calculation assuming an 11% horizon yield:

1. Horizon value = horizon price + reinvested coupons = 95.69 + 10.175 = 105.865

2. Semiannual return = PV = –105.11; FV = 105.865; N = 2; CPT $\rightarrow$ I/Y = 0.3585%

3. BEY = 0.3585% × 2 = 0.717%

4. EAR = $(1.003585)^2 - 1 = 0.718\%$

Each row in the table represents a different scenario (possible horizon yield). The last two columns in the table display the bond-equivalent yield and effective annual return, which result under each of the possible scenarios. As shown, as the horizon yield decreases from 11% to 5%, the bond-equivalent yield increases from 0.72% to 27.35%, and the effective annual return increases from 0.72% to 29.22%.

Scenario analysis provides the tools for the manager to do a better job in quantifying the impact of a change in the horizon yield assumption on the expected total return of the bond. A more complete scenario/total return analysis could include the simultaneous impacts of nonparallel shifts in the yield curve, different reinvestment rates, et cetera.

Scenario analysis can be broken down into the return due to price change, coupons received, and interest on the coupons. Examining the return components provides the manager with a check on the reasonableness assumptions. For example, if the price change is large and positive for a decline in rates, but the securities are mortgage-backed with negative convexity, the manager could further examine a somewhat surprising result.

Assessing the performance of a benchmark index over the planning horizon is done in the same way as for the managed portfolio. When you *compare* their performances, the primary reasons for different performance, other than the manager's active bets, are duration and convexity. For example, the convexities (rate of change in duration) for the benchmark and portfolio may be different due to security selection, and the manager may deliberately change the portfolio convexity and/or duration (relative to the benchmark) in anticipation of twists or shifts in the yield curve.

IMMUNIZATION

LOS 20.g: Formulate a bond immunization strategy to ensure funding of a predetermined liability and evaluate the strategy under various interest rate scenarios.

Classical Immunization

Immunization is a strategy used to minimize interest rate risk, and it can be employed to fund either single or multiple liabilities. Interest rate risk has two components: price risk and reinvestment rate risk. *Price risk,* also referred to as market value risk, refers to the decrease (increase) in bond prices as interest rates rise (fall). *Reinvestment rate risk* refers to the increase (decrease) in reinvestment income as interest rates rise (fall).

It is important to note that price risk and reinvestment rate risk cause opposite effects. That is, as interest rates increase, prices fall but reinvestment rates rise. As interest rates decrease, prices rise but reinvestment rates fall.

Suppose you have a liability that must be paid at the end of five years, and you would like to form a bond portfolio that will fully fund it. However, you are concerned about the effect that interest rate risk will have on the ending value of your portfolio. Which bonds should you buy? You should buy bonds that result in the effects of price risk and reinvestment risk exactly offsetting each other. This is known as classical immunization.

Reinvestment rate risk makes matching the maturity of a coupon bond to the maturity of a future liability an inadequate means of assuring that the liability is paid. Because future reinvestment rates are unknown, the total future value of a bond portfolio's coupon payments plus reinvested income is uncertain.

Classical Single-Period Immunization

Classical immunization is the process of structuring a bond portfolio that balances any change in the value of the portfolio with the return from the reinvestment of the coupon and principal payments received throughout the investment period. The goal of classical immunization is to form a portfolio so that:

- If interest rates increase, the gain in reinvestment income ≥ loss in portfolio value.
- If interest rates decrease, the gain in portfolio value ≥ loss in reinvestment income.

To accomplish this goal, we use effective duration. If you construct a portfolio with an effective duration equal to your liability horizon, the interest rate risk of the portfolio will be eliminated. In other words, price risk will exactly offset reinvestment rate risk.

 Professor's Note: Recall duration works best for small, immediate, parallel shifts in the yield curve. Therefore, additional rules will be added shortly.

Immunization of a Single Obligation

To effectively immunize a single liability:

1. *Select* a bond (or bond portfolio) with an effective duration equal to the duration of the liability. For any liability payable on a single date, the duration is taken to be the time horizon until payment. For example, payable in 3 years is a duration of 3.0.

2. *Set* the present value of the bond (or bond portfolio) equal to the present value of the liability.

For example, suppose you have a $100 million liability with a duration of 8.0 and a present value of $56,070,223. Your strategy should be to select a bond (or bond portfolio) with a duration of 8.0 and a present value of $56,070,223.

Theoretically, this should ensure that the value of your bond portfolio will equal $100 million in eight years, even if there is a small one-time instantaneous parallel shift in yields. Any gain or loss in reinvestment income will be offset by an equal gain or loss in the value of the portfolio.

What does it mean if the duration of the portfolio is not equal to the duration of the liability?

- If portfolio duration is less than liability duration, the portfolio is exposed to reinvestment risk. If interest rates are decreasing, the *losses* from reinvested coupon and principal payments would more than offset any gains from appreciation in the value of outstanding bonds. Under this scenario, the cash flows generated from assets would be insufficient to meet the targeted obligation.
- If portfolio duration is greater than liability duration, the portfolio is exposed to price risk. If interest rates are increasing, this would indicate that the *losses* from the market value of outstanding bonds would more than offset any gains from the additional revenue being generated on reinvested principal and coupon payments. Under this scenario, the cash flows generated from assets would be insufficient to meet the targeted obligation.

Adjustments to the Immunized Portfolio

Without rebalancing, classical immunization only works for a one-time instantaneous change in interest rates. In reality, interest rates fluctuate frequently, changing the duration of the portfolio and necessitating a change in the immunization strategy. Furthermore, the mere passage of time causes the duration of both the portfolio and its target liabilities to change, although not usually at the same rate.

Remember, portfolios cease to be immunized for a single liability when:

- Interest rates fluctuate more than once.
- Time passes.

Thus, immunization is not a buy-and-hold strategy. To keep a portfolio immunized, it must be rebalanced periodically. Rebalancing is necessary to maintain equality between the duration of the immunized portfolio and the decreasing duration of the liability. Rebalancing frequency is a cost-benefit trade-off. Transaction costs associated with rebalancing must be weighed against the possible extent to which the terminal value of the portfolio may fall short of its target liability.

Bond Characteristics to Consider

In practice, it is important to consider several characteristics of the individual bonds that are used to construct an immunized portfolio. Bond characteristics that must be considered with immunization include the following:

- *Credit rating.* In immunizing a portfolio, it is implicitly assumed that none of the bonds will default.

- *Embedded options.* For bonds with embedded options, it may be difficult to estimate duration because cash flows are difficult to forecast.
- *Liquidity.* If a portfolio is to be rebalanced, it will be necessary to sell some of the bonds. Thus, liquidity is an important concern.

Optimization procedures are often used to build immunized portfolios. These procedures consider the many variations that typically exist within the universe of available bonds.

Immunization Against Nonparallel Shifts

An important assumption of classical immunization theory is that any changes in the yield curve are parallel. This means that if interest rates change, they change by the same amount and in the same direction for all bond maturities. The problem is that in reality, parallel shifts rarely occur. Thus, equating the duration of the portfolio with the duration of the liability does not guarantee immunization.

Immunization risk can be thought of as a measure of the relative extent to which the terminal value of an immunized portfolio falls short of its target value as a result of arbitrary (nonparallel) changes in interest rates.

Because there are many bond portfolios that can be constructed to immunize a given liability, you should select the one that minimizes immunization risk.

How do you do this? As it turns out, immunized portfolios with cash flows that are concentrated around the investment horizon have the lowest immunization risk. As the dispersion of the cash flows increases, so does the immunization risk. Sound familiar?

In general, the portfolio that has the *lowest reinvestment risk* is the portfolio that will do the best job of immunization:

- An immunized portfolio consisting entirely of zero-coupon bonds that mature at the investment horizon will have zero immunization risk because there is zero reinvestment risk.
- If cash flows are concentrated around the horizon (e.g., bullets with maturities near the liability date), reinvestment risk and immunization risk will be low.
- If there is a high dispersion of cash flows about the horizon date (as in a barbell strategy), reinvestment risk and immunization risk will be high.

The Target Immunization Return

The target rate of return for an immunized portfolio is determined by the yield curve at the start of the immunization period. That immunization rate is the initial discount rate used to determine the initial PV of future liabilities. There is no one universally agreed upon method to determine the immunization rate.

The most conservative rate is to use the YTM of zero-coupon Treasury bonds with the same time horizon as the liabilities (i.e., the Treasury spot rate curve). This will produce the lowest target rate, the highest initial PV of liabilities, and require the largest initial funding of the portfolio.

An alternative is to use the implied zero-coupon yield of bonds with comparable duration and quality to the portfolio assets. Another variation is to make assumptions regarding changes in the yield curve and reinvestment rates to determine expected total return on the portfolio assets.

More generally, the target return is based on the initial yield curve and, assuming no changes in its shape, the resulting projected total return. This is consistent with using spot rates because the spot rate will be the target return under that assumption. In this case, the target return will be related to initial YTM of the bonds in the portfolio:

- In a flat yield curve, target return will be the initial YTM of the assets.
- In an upward sloping yield curve, target return will be lower than YTM as the cash flows coming in will be reinvested for progressively shorter periods and at lower rates to meet the approaching ending time horizon.
- In a downward sloping yield curve, target return will be higher than YTM as the cash flows coming in will be reinvested for progressively shorter periods and at higher rates to meet the approaching ending time horizon.

WARM-UP: DURATION AS A MEASURE OF BOND PORTFOLIO RISK

> **For the Exam:** This material on duration, dollar duration, and duration contribution is provided solely as a review of the basics required for a complete understanding of the material in LOS 20.h.

The major factor that drives bond price movements (and returns) is changing interest rates, and duration is used to measure individual bond and portfolio exposure to changes in interest rates. Duration is often considered a more useful measure of bond risk than standard deviation derived from historical returns, because the number of estimates needed to calculate standard deviation increases dramatically as the number of bonds in the portfolio increases, and historical data may not be readily available or reliable. Estimating duration, on the other hand, is quite straightforward and uses easily obtainable price, required return, and expected cash flow information.

Effective Duration

Effective duration of a portfolio or index is the *weighted average* of the individual effective durations of the bonds in the portfolio.

Example: Calculating portfolio effective duration

Brandon Mason's portfolio consists of the bonds shown in the following figure.

Bond Portfolio of Brandon Mason

Bond	Market Value ($ million)	Effective Duration
A	$37	4.5
B	$42	6.0
C	$21	7.8
Portfolio	$100	?

Calculate the effective duration of Mason's portfolio and **interpret** the significance of this measure.

Answer:

The duration of Mason's portfolio is:

$$D_p = w_A D_A + w_B D_B + w_C D_C$$

$$D_p = \frac{37}{100} 4.5 + \frac{42}{100} 6.0 + \frac{21}{100} 7.8 = 5.8$$

A duration of 5.8 indicates that the market value of the portfolio will change by approximately 5.8% for every 1.0 percentage point (100 bps) parallel change in interest rates.

The effective duration for a bond index is computed in the same way as that for a bond portfolio. In this case, however, we can use the average effective duration of the sectors rather than the durations of the individual bonds in the sectors, which would be far more tedious:

$$D_{Index} = \sum_{i=1}^{n} w_i D_i = w_1 D_1 + w_2 D_2 + w_3 D_3 + ... + w_n D_n$$

where:
D_{Index} = the effective duration of the index
w_i = the weight of sector i in the index
D_i = the effective duration of sector i

DURATION CONTRIBUTION

Effective Duration

Managers sometimes rely on a bond or sector's market-value weight in their portfolio as a measure of the exposure to that bond or sector. An alternative way to measure exposure is to measure the contribution of a sector or bond to the overall portfolio duration. Specifically, the contribution of an individual bond or sector to the duration of the portfolio is the weight of the bond or sector in the portfolio. Duration contribution is the product of the duration of an asset (or group of assets) and their weight in the portfolio. It captures both their volatility (duration) and also relative size (weight) in the portfolio.

contribution of bond or sector i to the portfolio duration $= w_i D_i$

where:

w_i = the weight of bond or sector i in the portfolio

$$= \frac{\text{market value of bond or sector i in the portfolio}}{\text{total portfolio value}}$$

D_i = the effective duration of bond or sector i

Example: Duration contribution

Assume you have a 10-year corporate bond in an actively managed portfolio. The bond has a market value of $5 million and a duration of 4.7, and the portfolio has a total value of $20 million and a duration of 6. **Calculate** the contribution of the corporate bond to the overall *duration* of the portfolio.

Answer:

The contribution of the corporate bond to the duration of the actively managed portfolio is:

contribution to portfolio duration = ($5 million / $20 million) × 4.7 = 1.175

It contributes 19.6% of the portfolio's duration, 1.175 / 6.0.

Dollar Duration

Duration measures percent change in value. Dollar duration is related and measures dollar change in value. By convention, it is calculated for a 100 basis points (bp), a 1% change in rates, and shown as a positive number. (It can be calculated for changes other than 100 bp. For example, price value of a basis point is dollar duration for a 1 bp change.) If rates increase, the bond or portfolio declines in percent and dollar amount. DD can be calculated for an individual bond or for a portfolio as:

DD = (duration)(0.01)(price)

Example: Dollar duration

A portfolio with a market value of GBP 47,500,000 and a par value of GBP 50M has a duration of 7.0. The manager uses cash in the portfolio (duration = 0) to purchase GBP 1,000,000 market value and par of a bond with a duration of 4.0. **Calculate** the initial and after purchase "dollar duration" of the portfolio.

Answer:

Initial DD = GBP 47,500,000(7.0)(0.01) = GBP 3,325,000

DD after purchase:

DD is a simple addition of the DD of the assets in the portfolio. It is not a weighted average. The cash used had no duration and contributed no DD to the initial portfolio. The purchased bond has a DD of GBP 1,000,000(4.0)(0.01) = GBP 40,000.

DD after purchase = GBP 3,325,000 + 40,000 = GBP 3,365,000

Example: Contribution to portfolio dollar duration

Assume you have a 10-year corporate bond in an actively managed portfolio. The bond has a market value of $5 million and a duration of 4.7. The portfolio has a total value of $20 million and a duration of 6.8. **Calculate** the contribution of the corporate bond to the *dollar duration* of the portfolio.

Answer:

The dollar duration of the portfolio and bond (assuming a 100 bp change) is:

$$DD = (P)(D)(\Delta y)$$

$$DD_P = (\$20 \text{ million})(6.8)(0.01) = \$1,360,000$$

$$DD_B = (\$5 \text{ million})(4.7)(0.01) = \$235,000$$

The bond contributes $235,000 to the portfolio dollar duration of $1.36 million or about 17.3% of the portfolio dollar duration.

ADJUSTING DOLLAR DURATION

LOS 20.h: Demonstrate the process of rebalancing a portfolio to reestablish a desired dollar duration.

Dollar duration, just like any other duration measure, changes as interest rates change or simply as time passes. Therefore, the portfolio manager must occasionally adjust the portfolio's dollar duration. There are two primary steps:

Step 1: Calculate the new dollar duration of the portfolio.
Step 2: Calculate the *rebalancing ratio* which is the ratio of the desired (target or original) DD to the new DD of the portfolio. Subtracting 1 from this ratio gives the percent change to make in the holding of each asset in the portfolio to restore the desired DD.

Example: Reestablishing the portfolio dollar duration

A portfolio with a dollar duration of $162,658 consists of four bonds with the indicated weights, durations, and dollar durations:

	Market Value	×	Duration	× 0.01 =	Dollar Duration
Bond 1	$1,000,000		5.0		$50,000
Bond 2	1,350,000		4.5		60,750
Bond 3	965,000		3.0		28,950
Bond 4	883,000		2.6		22,958
Portfolio	$4,198,000				$162,658

One year later, the yield curve has shifted upward with the following results:

	Market Value	×	Duration	× 0.01 =	Dollar Duration
Bond 1	$958,500		4.1		$39,299
Bond 2	1,100,000		3.6		39,600
Bond 3	725,000		2.2		15,950
Bond 4	683,000		1.8		12,294
Portfolio	$3,466,500				$107,143

$$\text{rebalancing ratio} = \frac{\text{target DD}}{\text{new DD}} = \frac{162{,}658}{107{,}143} = 1.52$$

To readjust back to the original dollar duration as well as maintain *the current proportions* of each bond in the portfolio, we subtract 1.0 from the rebalancing ratio to arrive at the necessary increase in the value of each bond in the portfolio and, thus, the total increase in the portfolio value (i.e., required additional cash):

$$1.52 - 1 = 0.52; \ 0.52 \times \$3,466,500 = \$1,802,580$$

The increases (in dollars) required for the individual bonds in the portfolio are:

Bond 1:	$958,500	× 0.52 =	$498,420
Bond 2:	$1,100,000	× 0.52 =	$572,000
Bond 3:	$725,000	× 0.52 =	$377,000
Bond 4:	$683,000	× 0.52 =	<u>$355,160</u>
			$1,802,580

Professor's Note: The next example extends the concept of adjusting proportionately all bonds in the portfolio to the often more practical approach of making the adjustment in only one bond.

To return the portfolio back to its original dollar duration, the manager could add cash and purchase the bonds in the amounts indicated. Alternatively, the manager could select one of the bonds to use as a *controlling position*. Because the dollar duration has fallen dramatically and Bond 1 has the longest duration, the manager could use less additional cash by increasing only the holding in Bond 1 (i.e., using Bond 1 as the controlling position):

$$\text{desired increase in DD} = \$162,658 - \$107,143 = \$55,515$$

$$\text{increase in Bond 1: new DD of Bond 1} = \$39,299 + \$55,515 = \$94,814$$

$$\text{required new value of Bond 1} = \frac{\$94,814}{\$39,299} \times \$958,500 = \$2,312,507$$

Thus, instead of investing $1,802,580 in all the bonds, the manager could purchase another $1,354,007 (= $2,312,507 – $958,500) of Bond 1 and return the portfolio dollar duration back to its original level.

	Market Value	×	Duration	×0.01 =	Dollar Duration
Bond 1	$2,312,507		4.1		$94,813
Bond 2	1,100,000		3.6		39,600
Bond 3	725,000		2.2		15,950
Bond 4	<u>683,000</u>		1.8		<u>12,294</u>
Portfolio	$4,820,507				$162,657

(Note: The slight difference in total dollar duration is due to rounding.)

SPREAD DURATION

LOS 20.i: Explain the importance of spread duration.

Duration measures the sensitivity of a bond to a one-time parallel shift in the yield curve. *Spread duration* measures the sensitivity of non-Treasury issues to a change in their spread above Treasuries of the same maturity.

Although yield spread and spread duration can be defined and measured for individual bonds, they are typically used for entire classifications of bonds, where classification is by rating and/or sector. Calculating the spread duration for a sector allows the manager to both forecast the future performance of the sector and select superior bonds to represent each sector in the portfolio.

For example, the manager might forecast a widening of the spread for one sector of bonds and a narrowing of the spread for a second. The manager would want to reduce the weight of the first sector to minimize the impact of the increase in interest rates (falling prices). He would want to increase the weight of the second sector to maximize the impact of falling rates (rising prices). The manager may then focus on selecting superior bonds within each sector.

There are three spread duration measures used for fixed-rate bonds:

1. **Nominal spread** is the spread between the nominal yield on a non-Treasury bond and a Treasury of the same maturity. When spread duration is based on the nominal spread, it represents the approximate percentage price change for a 100 basis point change in the nominal spread.

2. **Zero-volatility spread** (or **static spread**) is the spread that must be added to the Treasury spot rate curve to force equality between the present value of a bond's cash flows (discounted at the Treasury spot rates plus the static spread) and the market price of the bond plus accrued interest. Computing spread duration using the zero-volatility spread measures the percentage change in price given a one-time, 100 basis point change in the zero-volatility spread.

3. **Option-adjusted spread** (OAS) is determined using a binomial interest rate tree. Suffice it to say that when spread duration is based on OAS, it is the approximate percentage change in price for a 100 basis point change in the OAS.

Spread duration may be computed using any of these methods. As a result, observed discrepancies among reported values for spread duration may be a result of the different methods used.

A portfolio's spread duration is the market value-weighted average of the individual sector spread durations.

Example: Spread duration

Compute the spread duration for the following portfolio.

Spread Duration

Sector	Weight	Spread* Duration
Treasury	30	0.00
Mortgage	40	3.41
Corporate	30	5.89

* Spread defined in terms of OAS.

Answer:

$$\text{spread duration} = 0.30(0) + 0.40(3.41) + 0.30(5.89) = 3.13$$

Interpretation: If the OAS of each sector increases by 100 basis points with no change in Treasury yields, the value of the portfolio will decrease by approximately 3.13%.

A portfolio's duration, which is a weighted average of the individual bond durations, measures the percentage change in the total value of the portfolio for a 100 bps change in the required return on the portfolio. Duration assumes a one-time parallel shift in the yield curve, which causes the yields on all bonds to increase or decrease the same amount. Spread duration measures the percentage change in the total value of the portfolio given a parallel 100 bps change in the spread over Treasuries.

In the former (duration), the parallel shift in the yield curve could be caused by a change in inflation expectations, which causes the yields on all bonds, including Treasuries, to increase/decrease the same amount. In the latter (spread duration), the shift is in the spread only, indicating an overall increase in risk aversion (risk premium) for all bonds *in a given class*.

By weighting classes (sectors) differently in the bond portfolio, the manager exposes the portfolio to spread risk (i.e., the risk that the spread for a given class will change). Of course, the active manager typically weights the sectors in a portfolio differently from the benchmark in an effort to capture favorable changes in spreads.

EXTENSIONS TO CLASSICAL IMMUNIZATION

LOS 20.j: Discuss the extensions that have been made to classical immunization theory, including the introduction of contingent immunization.

Thus far, we have looked at classical immunization as if there were few uncertainties. For instance, we assumed any changes in the yield curve were parallel and instantaneous so that we could immunize our portfolio using duration strategies.

When the goal is to immunize against a liability, however, we must also consider changes in the value of the liability, which in turn could change the amount of assets needed for the immunization. We must also consider the ability to combine indexing (immunization) strategies with active portfolio management strategies. Note that since active management exposes the portfolio to additional risks, immunization strategies are also *risk-minimizing strategies*.

The bottom line is that classical immunization strategies may not be sufficient in managing a portfolio to immunize against a liability. To address the deficiencies in classical immunization, four extensions have been offered: (1) *multifunctional duration*, (2) *multiple-liability immunization*, (3) *relaxation of the minimum risk requirement, and* (4) *contingent immunization*.

The first modification or extension to classical immunization theory is the use of **multifunctional duration** (a.k.a. **key rate duration**). To incorporate multifunctional duration into our immunization strategy, the manager focuses on certain key interest rate maturities. For example, the manager's portfolio might contain mortgage-backed securities, which are exposed to prepayment risk. Unlike other fixed-income securities that increase in value when interest rates fall, MBS act like callable corporate bonds that are retired when rates fall. Thus, MBS and callable corporates do not increase in value as much as non-callables when rates fall below their coupon rates, so the portfolio's sensitivity to changes in different interest rate maturities can be unique, making the analysis of its exposures to key rates very important.

The second extension is **multiple-liability immunization**. The goal of multiple-liability immunization is ensuring that the portfolio contains sufficient liquid assets to meet all the liabilities as they come due. That is, rather than monitor the value of the portfolio as if the liability is its minimum target value at a single horizon date, there can be numerous certain or even uncertain liabilities with accompanying numerous horizon dates.

The third extension is allowing for **increased risk,** or otherwise relaxing the minimum risk requirement of classical immunization. As will be demonstrated when we discuss contingent immunization, as long as the manager does not jeopardize meeting the liability structure, he can pursue increased risk strategies that could lead to excess portfolio value (i.e., a terminal portfolio value greater than the liability).

The fourth extension is **contingent immunization**, which mixes active and passive (i.e., immunization) strategies.

Contingent Immunization

Contingent immunization is the combination of active management with passive immunization techniques. Like immunization, there must be a defined liability or liabilities for known amounts on known dates allowing a present value of liabilities to be computed. Unlike immunization, the beginning value of the portfolio must exceed the PV of the liabilities. The difference is called an economic surplus or surplus. The initial surplus is related to and can only exist if the investor will accept a floor return less than the available immunization rate. The immunization rate available in the market minus the investor's minimum floor return is called the cushion spread.

The basic steps in contingent immunization consist of determining the PV of the liability and comparing this to the PV of the assets (their market value) to determine the value of the surplus. As time and/or market conditions change, the PV of assets and liabilities will change as well. The surplus must be continually recomputed. As long as the surplus is positive the portfolio can be actively managed.

©2016 Kaplan, Inc.

Example: Contingent immunization

An investor decides to pursue a contingent immunization strategy over a 3-year time horizon. The investor has $20,000,000 to invest, the available 3 year immunization rate is 4%, and the investor will accept a minimum safety net return of 3.2%.

Determine the: (a) cushion spread, (b) required terminal value [future value of liability (FVL)], (c) present value of liabilities (PVL), and (d) initial surplus amount.

- (a) The cushion spread is 4% – 3.2% = 0.8%, which means there must be an initial positive surplus.
- (b) The required terminal value (FVL) is usually given. In this case it is not and must be computed from the initial invested amount [the PV of assets (PVA)] and minimum acceptable return: $20,000,000 [1 + (.032/2)]^{3×2} = $21,998,458$
- (c) The PVL is the FVL discounted at the available immunization rate:

$21,998,458 / [1 + (.04/2)]^{3×2} = $19,534,001$

- (d) The surplus is PVA – PVL, initially this is:

$20,000,000 – 19,534,001 = $465,999$

Assume the investor had initially expected a fall in interest rates and had purchased $20,000,000 par of 4.5%, 10-year bonds. Now assume one year has passed and the bond now trades at a 3.9% YTM and the 2-year immunization rate is 3.4%. **Determine** the: (e) required terminal value, (f) present value of liabilities (PVL), and (g) PV of assets (PVA).

- (e) Required terminal value only changes if a new target value is set by the client and manager; it is still $21,998,458 and is now due in 2 years.
- (f) The new PVL is based on the terminal value, remaining 2-year time horizon, and new available immunization rate. The PVL is now:

$21,998,458 / [1 + (0.034 / 2)]^{2×2} = $20,564,039$

- (g) The original purchase of $20,000,000 par of 4.5%, 10-year bonds had a 4.5% YTM and is now a 9-year bond yielding 3.9%. Its new market value is:
  PMT = $20,000,000 × (0.045 / 2) = $450,000, N = 9 × 2 = 18
  I/Y = 3.9/2 = 1.95%, FV = $20,000,000:
  CPT → PV = $20,903,489

Assuming the manager also collected $900,000 of coupons and reinvestment earnings of $2,500, (h) **compute** the new surplus amount, (i) **determine** if the manager can continue to actively manage the portfolio, and (j) **state** and **explain** what will happen to the surplus if rates immediately rise (no calculations).

- (h) The surplus is the new PVA – PVL. The PVA is the ending market value plus coupons collected and reinvestment earnings:

  $20,903,489 + 900,000 + 2,500 − 20,564,039 = $1,241,950

- (i) With a positive surplus the manager can continue to actively manage.
- (j) The results of the previous year demonstrate that the asset duration exceeds the liability duration. The higher asset duration would be the reason the assets rose in value more than the liabilities when rates fell and created a larger surplus. If rates immediately rise then the asset value will drop by more than the liability value and surplus will decline.

For the Exam: A contingent immunization strategy is a complex time value of money strategy. The data can be presented in a variety of ways so examine the information carefully to determine how to solve the question. Determining the surplus or what has happened to surplus is generally important. Surplus is a concept that pervades any form of asset liability management and contingent immunization is a form of ALM. To compute surplus be prepared to calculate the PVA and PVL if not given directly. A couple of hints:

- Assume semiannual compounding as in the example unless directed otherwise.
- If asset duration and convexity match those of the liability the surplus will be relatively stable (essentially this means the portfolio is immunized). If duration and convexity of assets and liability do not match, the surplus will change as market conditions change and time passes.
- If the initial surplus and cushion spread are large, a larger adverse movement in market conditions can occur before the surplus is exhausted.
- Before the surplus becomes negative, the portfolio must be immunized and active management is no longer allowed. If the surplus becomes negative, it is no longer possible to immunize and reach the target value because the current value of assets is not large enough to reach the terminal value at the prevailing market immunization rates.

IMMUNIZATION RISKS

LOS 20.k: Explain the risks associated with managing a portfolio against a liability structure including interest rate risk, contingent claim risk, and cap risk.

Three risks that the portfolio manager must be aware of relate to market interest rates and the structure of the bonds in the portfolio. They are (1) interest rate risk, (2) contingent claim risk (i.e., call or prepayment risk), and (3) cap risk.

Interest rate risk is the primary concern when managing a fixed-income portfolio, whether against a liability structure or a benchmark. Because the values of most fixed-income securities move opposite to changes in interest rates, changing interest rates are a continual source of risk. As already mentioned, to help avoid interest rate risk, the manager will match the duration and convexity of the liability and the portfolio. Convexity can be difficult to measure for some fixed-income securities, especially those with *negative* convexity. This is the concern when fixed-income securities are subject to early retirement (e.g., mortgage-backed securities, callable corporate bonds).

Contingent claim risk (a.k.a. call risk or prepayment risk). Callable bonds are typically called only after interest rates have fallen. This means that the manager not only loses the higher stream of coupons that were originally incorporated into the immunization strategy, she is faced with reinvesting the principal at a reduced rate of return. Thus, contingent claim risk has significant potential to affect the immunization strategy through its effect on the value of the portfolio. To adjust for this potential, rather than simply comparing the portfolio duration to that of the liability, the manager must consider the convexity of the bonds.

Cap risk. If any of the bonds in the portfolio have floating rates, they may be subject to *cap risk*. If the coupon on the floating rate bond does not fully adjust upward for rising interest rates, the market value of the bond will adjust downward. The assets and liabilities will not adjust in sync and the surplus will deteriorate.

IMMUNIZING SINGLE LIABILITIES, MULTIPLE LIABILITIES, AND GENERAL CASH FLOWS

LOS 20.l: Compare immunization strategies for a single liability, multiple liabilities, and general cash flows.

If a manager could invest in a zero-coupon Treasury with a maturity equal to the liability horizon, he has constructed an immunization strategy with no risk. Because this is rarely the case, however, the manager must take steps to *minimize risk*.

One strategy is *minimizing reinvestment risk* (i.e., the risk associated with reinvesting portfolio cash flows). To reduce the risk associated with uncertain reinvestment rates, the manager should minimize the *distribution* of the maturities of the bonds in the portfolio around the (single) liability date. If the manager can hold bullet securities with maturities very close to the liability date, reinvestment risk is low.

Concentrating the maturities of the bonds around the liability date is known as a **bullet strategy**. Think of a strategy employing two bonds. One bond matures one year before the liability date and the other matures one year after the liability date. When the first matures, the proceeds must be reinvested for only one year. At the date of the liability, the maturity of the other is off only one year. Thus, the reinvestment rate on the first will have a minimal impact on the terminal value of the portfolio and the value of the second is only minimally sensitive to interest rates.

Now consider a **barbell strategy** where the first bond matures several years before the liability date and the other several years after the liability date. The face value of the first must be reinvested when it matures, so the manager must be concerned with both the reinvestment rate and, since the new bond will have several years until maturity, all the other risk factors associated with such a bond. The second bond, since it matures several years after the liability date, is subject to significant interest rate risk.

Obviously, as the maturities of the bullet strategy move away from the liability date and the maturities of the barbell move toward the liability date, the distinction between the two will begin to blur. Rather than base the strategy on subjective judgment, the manager can minimize M-Square (M^2) (a.k.a. *maturity variance*).

Maturity variance is the variance of the differences in the maturities of the bonds used in the immunization strategy and the maturity date of the liability. For example, if all the bonds have the same maturity date as the liability, M^2 is zero. As the dispersion of the maturity dates increases, M^2 increases.

Multiple Liabilities

The key to immunizing multiple liabilities is to decompose the portfolio payment streams in such a way that the component streams separately immunize each of the multiple liabilities. Multiple-liability immunization is possible if the following three conditions are satisfied (*assuming parallel rate shifts*):

1. Assets and liabilities have the same present values.

2. Assets and liabilities have the same aggregate durations.

3. The range of the distribution of durations of individual assets in the portfolio exceeds the distribution of liabilities. This is a necessary condition in order to be able to use cash flows generated from our assets (which will include principal payments from maturing bonds) to sufficiently meet each of our cash outflow needs.

It is not unusual to find some liabilities with duration in excess of 30 years (e.g., in defined benefit pension plans). However, coupon-bearing bonds rarely have such long durations. Immunization is still possible as it only requires that the average asset duration match the average liability duration. In such cases, no single asset duration will exceed the longer liability durations, and the third condition will not be met. This increases the amount of immunization risk.

It is important to note that satisfying these three conditions will assure immunization only against parallel rate shifts. In the case of *nonparallel rate changes*, linear programming models can be used to construct minimum-risk immunized portfolios for multiple liabilities. The procedure is to minimize a measure of immunization risk for multiple liabilities and nonparallel rate changes. The minimization procedure is subject to the constraints imposed by the conditions required for immunization under the assumption of a parallel shift along with any other relevant investment constraints.

General Cash Flows

General cash flows in this case refers to using cash as part of an immunization strategy even though the cash has not yet been received. For example, expecting a cash flow in six months, the portfolio manager does not put the entire amount required for immunization into the portfolio today. Instead he looks at the expected cash flow as a zero and incorporates its payoff and duration into the immunization strategy.

Let's assume the manager expects to receive a cash flow in six months. Treating this like a zero, the duration is 0.5. To construct the portfolio to immunize a liability due in 1.5 years with a duration of 1.0, the manager could *combine* the cash to be received with an appropriate amount of bonds with durations greater than 1.0, so that the conditions for immunization are met, including a weighted average portfolio duration of 1.0.

RISK MINIMIZATION VS. RETURN MAXIMIZATION

LOS 20.m: Compare risk minimization with return maximization in immunized portfolios.

One standard condition for classical immunization is **risk minimization**. As we have discussed in several sections of this topic review, the portfolio manager has many tools to minimize exposure to risks faced when immunizing a portfolio to meet a liability. We have neglected to mention the relationship of risk minimization to the level of portfolio expected return.

Return maximization is the concept behind *contingent immunization*. Consider the manager who has the ability to lock in an immunized rate of return equal to or greater than the required safety net return. As long as that manager feels he can generate even greater returns, he should pursue active management in hopes of generating excess value.

CASH FLOW MATCHING

LOS 20.n: Demonstrate the use of cash flow matching to fund a fixed set of future liabilities and compare the advantages and disadvantages of cash flow matching to those of immunization strategies.

Cash flow matching is used to construct a portfolio that will fund a stream of liabilities with portfolio coupons and maturity values. Cash flow matching will also cause the durations to be matched, but it is more stringent than immunization by matching duration. The timing and amounts of asset cash flows must also correspond to the liabilities. Because of this, the durations will stay matched as time passes and rebalancing should not be needed. To construct the portfolio, the manager:

- Selects a bond with a maturity date equal to that of the last liability payment date.

- Buys enough in par value of this bond such that its principal and final coupon fully fund the last liability.
- Using a recursive procedure (i.e., working backwards), chooses another bond so that its maturity value and last coupon plus the coupon on the longer bond fully fund the second-to-last liability payment and continues until all liability payments have been addressed.

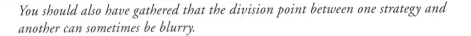

Professor's Note: An easy way to construct a cash flow match is to purchase only zero-coupon bonds. Simply buy face amounts equal to each liability on the needed payout dates. However, this is more restrictive in the bonds that can be used and, hence, could be more expensive than using coupon bonds. Know that zeros is the easy way and be prepared for the tougher coupon bond calculations if asked on the exam.

While a pure cash flow match is the safest way to fund the liabilities, some clients and their managers allow a slight deviation in matching the dates. A bond might be used that provides a cash flow slightly before it is needed and a modest reinvestment rate might be factored in. Alternatively, a bond with a cash flow just after what is needed could be selected on the assumption it could be used as collateral and the funds borrowed for a brief period to make the distribution.

The following are the differences between cash flow matching and multiple-liability immunization:

- Cash flow matching depends upon all the cash flows of the portfolio, so expectations regarding short-term reinvestment rates or borrowing rates are critical. For this reason, managers must use conservative assumptions. Deviations from a true cash flow match should be modest and be associated with a significant expected cost saving. This tends to increase the overall cost to purchase the cash flow matched portfolio. Immunization by matching duration is less restrictive and may cost less.
- Owing to the exact matching problem, only asset flows from a cash-flow-matched portfolio that occur prior to the liability may be used to meet the obligation. An immunized portfolio is only required to have sufficient *value* on the date of each liability because funding is achieved through portfolio rebalancing. (Hint: the statement about cash flows occurring just prior to the payout date and the earlier discussion about allowing cash flows to occur after the payout date are both in the CFA text. Yes, they contradict each other. The focus here is that the control of cash flows is much more restrictive for cash flow matching than for immunization.)

Professor's Note: You should conclude cash flow matching is more restrictive, simpler to understand, and safer (though both are very safe when done correctly) but generally makes the purchase price of the required portfolio higher.

You should also have gathered that the division point between one strategy and another can sometimes be blurry.

These approaches can also be combined and blended together.

Combination matching, also known as *horizon matching*, is a combination of multiple-liability immunization and cash flow matching that can be used to address the asset cash flow/liability matching problem. This strategy creates a portfolio that is *duration* matched. During the first few years, the portfolio would also be cash flow matched in order to make sure that assets were properly dispersed to meet the near-term obligations.

Combination matching offers the following *advantages* over multiple-liability immunization:

- Provides liquidity in the initial period.
- Reduces the risk associated with nonparallel shifts in the yield curve. The initial cash needs are met with asset cash flows. There is no rebalancing needed to meet the initial cash requirements.

The primary *disadvantage* of combination matching is that it tends to be more expensive than multiple-liability immunization.

KEY CONCEPTS

LOS 20.a

Portfolios that are being used to fund measurable liabilities typically use the liabilities as the portfolio benchmark. The low risk strategy is to match the asset characteristics to those of the liabilities. The most important match is duration.

Portfolios without definable liabilities often use a bond index as a benchmark and their performance is evaluated versus that benchmark. The low risk strategy is to match the characteristics of the benchmark.

LOS 20.b

Strategy	Advantages	Disadvantages
Pure bond indexing (PBI): manager replicates the index	• Tracks the index (zero or very low tracking error) • Same risk factor exposures as the index • Low advisory and administrative fees	• Costly and difficult to implement • Lower expected return than the index
Enhanced indexing by matching primary risk factors (sampling)	• Less costly to implement • Increased expected return • Maintains exposure to the index's primary risk factors	• Increased management fees • Lowered ability to track the index (i.e., increased tracking error) • Lower expected return than the index
Enhanced indexing by small risk factor mismatches: earns the same return as the index; tilt the portfolio towards smaller risk factors by pursuing return-enhancing opportunities	• Same duration as index • Increased expected return • Reduced manager restrictions	• Increased risk • Increased tracking error • Increased management fees
Active management by larger risk factor mismatches: pursue more significant quality and value strategies	• Increased expected return • Reduced manager restrictions • Ability to tune the portfolio duration	• Increased risk • Increased tracking error • Increased management fees
Full-blown active management: actively pursues tilting, relative value, and duration strategies	• Increased expected return • Few if any manager restrictions • No limits on duration	• Increased risk • Increased tracking error • Increased management fees

LOS 20.c

A bond portfolio manager should move from a pure indexing position to more active management only when the client's objectives and constraints permit and the manager's

abilities justify it.
- *Market value risk* varies directly with maturity. The greater the risk aversion, the lower the acceptable market risk, and the shorter the benchmark maturity.
- *Income risk* varies indirectly with maturity. The more dependent the client is upon a reliable income stream, the longer the maturity of the benchmark.
- *Credit risk*. The credit risk of the benchmark should closely match the credit risk of the portfolio.
- *Liability framework risk* is applicable only to portfolios managed according to a liability structure and should always be minimized.

LOS 20.d
If the index is not investable, it is not a valid benchmark.

1. Bond securities are heterogeneous and illiquid. Issues have unique differences in maturity, seniority, and other features; plus many issues do not trade regularly and pricing data is frequently based on appraisals and trades are often not publically reported.

2. Indexes can appear similar but be quite different in risks.

3. Risk characteristics can change quickly over time as new issues of bonds and those approaching maturity lead to significant annual additions and deletions for the bonds in an index.

4. The "bums" problem as large issuance by an issuer leads to greater index weight but large issuance is also related to excessive leverage and subsequent credit problems.

5. Difficulty for investors in finding an index that matches their risk profile.

LOS 20.e
Duration. Effective duration (a.k.a. option-adjusted or adjusted duration), which is used to estimate the change in the value of a portfolio given a small parallel shift in the yield curve, is probably the most obvious risk factor to be measured. Due to the linear nature of duration, which causes it to underestimate the increase and overestimate the decrease in the value of the portfolio, the convexity effect is also considered.

Key rate duration measures the portfolio's sensitivity to twists in the yield curve by indicating the portfolio's sensitivity to certain interest rates. Due to the nearly endless combinations of assets that will have the same duration as the index, the manager must take the time to ensure that the portfolio also matches the index's exposure to important key rates. Mismatches can occur when the portfolio and benchmark contain different combinations of bonds with varying maturities and key rate durations but the same overall effective duration.

LOS 20.f
Scenario analysis allows a portfolio manager to assess portfolio total return under a varying set of assumptions (different scenarios). Possible scenarios would include simultaneous assumptions regarding interest rates and spreads at the end of the investment horizon as well as reinvestment rates over the investment horizon.

Estimating expected **total return** under a single set of assumptions (predictions) only provides a point estimate of the investment's expected return (i.e., a single number). Combining total return analysis with scenario analysis allows the analyst to assess not only the return but also its volatility (distribution) under different scenarios.

LOS 20.g
To effectively immunize a single liability:
1. *Select* a bond (or bond portfolio) with an effective duration equal to the duration of the liability.
2. *Set* the present value of the bond (or bond portfolio) equal to the present value of the liability.

Without rebalancing, classical immunization only works for a one-time instantaneous change in interest rates. *Immunization risk* can be thought of as a measure of the relative extent to which the terminal value of an immunized portfolio falls short of its target value as a result of arbitrary (nonparallel) changes in interest rates. In general, the portfolio that has the *lowest reinvestment risk* is the portfolio that will do the best job of immunization:

- An immunized portfolio consisting entirely of zero-coupon bonds that mature at the investment horizon will have zero immunization risk because there is zero reinvestment risk.
- If cash flows are concentrated around the horizon (as in a bullet), reinvestment risk and immunization risk will be low.
- If there is a high dispersion of cash flows about the horizon date (as in a barbell strategy), reinvestment risk and immunization risk will be high.

LOS 20.h
Δvalue = (effective duration)(decimal change in interest rates)(price)

dollar duration = (effective duration)(0.01)(price)

Portfolio dollar duration is the sum of the dollar durations of the individual bonds in the portfolio.

A manager must occasionally adjust the portfolio's dollar duration due to interest rate changes or the passing of time. The two steps in adjusting dollar duration are (1) calculate the new dollar duration and (2) calculate the rebalancing ratio and use it to determine the required percentage change in the value of the portfolio.

rebalancing ratio = target DD / new DD

LOS 20.i
Spread duration measures the sensitivity of non-Treasury issues to a change in their spread above Treasuries of the same maturity. Calculating the spread duration for a sector allows the manager to both forecast the future performance of the sector and select superior bonds to represent each sector in the portfolio. There are three spread duration measures used for fixed-rate bonds:
1. **Nominal spread** is the spread between the nominal yield on a non-Treasury bond and a Treasury of the same maturity.

2. **Zero-volatility spread** (or **static spread**) is the spread that must be added to the Treasury spot rate curve to force equality between the present value of a bond's cash flows and the market price of the bond plus accrued interest.

3. **Option-adjusted spread** (OAS) is determined using a binomial interest rate tree.

LOS 20.j

To address the deficiencies in classical immunization, four extensions have been offered:

- **Multifunctional duration** (a.k.a. **key rate duration**). Where the manager focuses on certain key interest rate maturities.
- **Multiple-liability immunization.** Where the portfolio contains sufficient liquid assets to meet all the liabilities as they come due.
- **Increasing risk**, or otherwise relaxing the minimum risk requirement, the manager can pursue increased risk strategies that could lead to excess portfolio value (i.e., a terminal portfolio value greater than the liability).
- **Contingent immunization** is the combination of active management strategies and passive management techniques (immunization). As long as the rate of return on the portfolio exceeds a prespecified *safety net return*, the portfolio is managed actively. If the portfolio return declines to the safety net return, the immunization mode is triggered to *lock in* the safety net return. The safety net return is the minimum acceptable return as designated by the client.

LOS 20.k

Interest rate risk: Because the values of most fixed-income securities move opposite to changes in interest rates, changing interest rates are a continual source of risk. To help avoid interest rate risk, the manager will match the duration and convexity of the liability and the portfolio.

Contingent claim risk (a.k.a. **call risk** or **prepayment risk**): Callable bonds are typically called only after interest rates have fallen. This means that the manager not only loses the higher stream of coupons that were originally incorporated into the immunization strategy, but they are faced with reinvesting the principal at a reduced rate of return.

Cap risk refers to a cap on the adjustment to the coupon on a floating rate security. If the bonds are subject to caps when interest rates rise, they might not fully adjust and thus would affect the immunization capability of the portfolio.

LOS 20.l

Single liability: One strategy is *minimizing reinvestment risk* (i.e., the risk associated with reinvesting portfolio cash flows). To reduce the risk associated with uncertain reinvestment rates, the manager should minimize the *distribution* of the maturities of the bonds in the portfolio around the (single) liability date. If the manager can hold bullet securities with maturities very close to the liability date, reinvestment risk is low.

Multiple liabilities: The key to immunizing multiple liabilities is to decompose the portfolio payment streams in such a way that the component streams separately immunize each of the multiple liabilities. Multiple liability immunization assumes parallel rate shifts.

General cash flows in this case refers to using cash as part of an immunization strategy even though the cash has not yet been received. For example, a portfolio manager expecting a cash flow in six months does not put the entire amount required for immunization into the portfolio today. Instead he looks at the expected cash flow as a zero coupon bond and incorporates its payoff and duration into the immunization strategy.

LOS 20.m

A cash flow match will minimize risk in an ALM portfolio. However, it is the most restrictive in security selection and will likely minimize return as well. Return maximization looks at the trade off between E(R) and variability of surplus. Some portfolios may choose higher return and risk. Generally, the lower-to-higher risk tradeoff is: cash flow matching, immunize, contingent immunization, active management.

LOS 20.n

Cash flow matching with zero coupon bonds is easy; buy default free bonds in amount and maturity to meet the liability payouts. Cash flow matching using coupon bearing bonds is possible for some sequential multiperiod liabilities but more complicated:

- Start with the longest liability and buy a coupon bearing bond with par and final coupon amount that matches the liability.
- Repeat this process for the next longest liability, first considering the coupon payment on the bond purchased for the longest liability will fund part of this next longest liability.
- Keep repeating the process for remaining liabilities working from longest to shortest.

CONCEPT CHECKERS

Use the following information to answer Questions 1 through 3.

Brian Reid is the portfolio manager of AA Corporate Bond Investors, Inc. His current $10 million bond position is as follows:

Bond	Market Value Weight (%)	Effective Duration
1	50	2.00
2	40	3.00
3	10	4.00

The Investment Policy Statement (IPS) allows the portfolio manager to leverage the portfolio by 20%, or $2 million.

1. What is the duration of the bond portfolio?
    A. 1.5.
    B. 2.0.
    C. 2.6.

2. What is the contribution of Bond 2 to the duration of the bond portfolio?
    A. 1.0.
    B. 1.2.
    C. 1.4.

3. Reid's bond portfolio is potentially exposed to:
    A. spread risk.
    B. default risk.
    C. both spread risk and default risk.

4. Which of the following spreads is determined using binomial interest rate trees?
    A. Nominal spread.
    B. Zero-volatility spread.
    C. Option-adjusted spread.

5. Drew Promadi and Louie Cheung are both employed by FI Associates, a bond trading firm. Promadi is a trader and Cheung is a performance analyst. After a performance tracking meeting, Promadi and Cheung discuss alpha and tracking error. Promadi states that he doesn't think it is fair that his portfolio tracking error is being criticized, since his performance is evaluated against a custom benchmark containing Treasury bonds, which he does not hold. Promadi also argues that he should have some tracking error because he pursues an active strategy. In response, Cheung makes the following statements:

    Statement 1: I agree that over the period, your portfolio didn't contain exactly the same allocations as the benchmark, and you deliberately constructed your portfolio that way with the goal of generating positive alpha.

    Statement 2: However, the fact that you have a non-zero tracking error implies that you occasionally generate a negative alpha.

    Regarding these statements, is Cheung correct?
    A. Both statements are correct.
    B. Both statements are incorrect.
    C. One statement is correct.

6. Kirsten Radomski analyzes spread duration (based on OAS) for SAM Advisors, a fixed-income firm. One of her smaller portfolios consists of $5 million in U.S. Treasuries and $10 million in corporate bonds. If the portfolio's spread duration is 5.6, the spread duration of the corporate bonds is *closest* to:
    A. 3.75.
    B. 5.70.
    C. 8.40.

7. Given a market value of $100,000 for a bond and an effective duration of 6, **calculate** the bond's contribution to portfolio effective duration and dollar duration, if the portfolio is valued at $15 million and has a duration of 9.
    Contribution to:

	Effective duration	Dollar duration
A.	0.00450	$4,500
B.	0.04000	$6,000
C.	0.66009	$6,600

8.   A bond portfolio manager is contemplating the purchase of a corporate bond
       with the following characteristics:
       - A coupon rate of 11%, paid semiannually.
       - Four years remain until maturity.
       - The current price of the bond is 98.4321 with a yield to maturity of
         11.50%.
       - The Treasury yield curve is flat at 8.0%.
       - The credit spread for the issuer is 350 basis points at all maturities.

       Calculate the total effective return on this investment, assuming a 1-year
       investment horizon, a coupon reinvestment rate of 6%, no change in the
       Treasury yield curve at the horizon date, and a 250 basis point decline in the
       credit spread for all maturities at the horizon date.
       A. 8.71%.
       B. 17.42%.
       C. 18.18%.

9.   Two components of interest rate risk are:
       A. duration and convexity.
       B. reinvestment risk and price risk.
       C. duration sensitivity and price risk.

10.   To immunize a portfolio consisting of a single coupon bond against a future
       liability, an investor should select a bond that:
       A. has a duration that equals the liability horizon.
       B. has a duration that exceeds the liability horizon.
       C. has a maturity date that extends beyond the liability horizon.

11.   An extension of immunization that uses cash matching during the early years of
       a liability schedule and duration matching in the later years is referred to as:
       A. combination matching.
       B. dual horizon matching.
       C. immunization matching.

12.   An investor wishes to immunize a single liability payment that will occur six
       years from today. Which of the following portfolios *most likely* has the *least*
       immunization risk?
       A. A 12-year annually compounded coupon bond with duration of six years.
       B. 50% invested in a 2-year zero-coupon bond and 50% invested in a 10-year
           zero-coupon bond.
       C. 50% investment in a 5-year zero-coupon bond and 50% investment in a
           7-year zero-coupon bond.

Use the following information to answer Questions 13 through 17.

An investor has $100 million and would like to institute a contingent immunization strategy over the next six years. Current rates of return for immunization strategies are 10%, but the investor is willing to accept an 8.5% rate of return. His active strategy is to purchase $100 million in 8% coupon, semiannually compounded, 25-year bonds priced to yield 10%.

13. The cushion spread is *closest* to:
    A. 50 basis points.
    B. 150 basis points.
    C. 200 basis points.

14. The required terminal value is *closest* to:
    A. $163,146,750.
    B. $164,783,136.
    C. $169,588,143.

15. The amount of assets necessary to achieve the required terminal value is *closest* to:
    A. $91,757,416.
    B. $92,092,087.
    C. $93,015,784.

16. The current dollar safety margin is *closest* to:
    A. $5,566,976.
    B. $8,242,584.
    C. $71,389,334.

17. If interest rates fall to 8% immediately after the purchase of these bonds, is immunization necessary?
    A. No, because the dollar safety margin is positive.
    B. No, because the dollar safety margin is negative.
    C. Yes, because the dollar safety margin is negative.

18. **Explain** how using key rate duration in addition to effective duration is more beneficial to measuring a portfolio's sensitivity to yield curve changes than effective duration alone.

19. Portfolio LTG has a dollar duration of 80,000 and a market value of $3 million. Suppose that one year later the yield curve shifted upward, which consequently decreased the dollar duration to 65,000 and decreased the market value to $2.5 million. What is the portfolio's rebalancing ratio and total increase in portfolio value required to readjust the portfolio back to its original dollar duration?

	Rebalancing ratio	Dollar adjustment
A.	0.81	$475,000
B.	1.23	$575,000
C.	0.81	$575,000

20. Tim Owens is currently managing his portfolio against a liability structure. However, interest rates have recently declined and some of the bonds in his portfolio have been called. Owens is faced with having to reinvest the principal of those bonds at a lower rate of return. **Identify** the risk(s) that Owens is facing while managing his portfolio.

21. Which of the following is the *most* important issue with using a bond market index as a benchmark?
     A. Investability because the index is illiquid.
     B. The index may be inappropriate due to frequent changes.
     C. Accountability because the manager may not be familiar with some of the securities in the index.

For more questions related to this topic review, log in to your Schweser online account and launch SchweserPro™ QBank; and for video instruction covering each LOS in this topic review, log in to your Schweser online account and launch the OnDemand video lectures, if you have purchased these products.

ANSWERS – CONCEPT CHECKERS

1. **C** Portfolio duration is computed as a weighted average of the individual bond durations.

   duration = (0.50 × 2) + (0.40 × 3) + (0.10 × 4) = 2.60

2. **B** Contribution of Bond 2 to the portfolio duration = 0.4 × 3 = 1.2.

3. **C** The bond portfolio is potentially exposed to spread risk, default risk, and interest rate risk.

4. **C** The option-adjusted spread (OAS) is determined using a binomial interest-rate tree. The nominal spread is based on the nominal spread between non-Treasury and Treasury securities. The zero-volatility spread uses present value methodology to determine what spread must be added to the Treasury spot rate curve to equate the present value of a bond's cash flows with the market price of the bond plus accrued interest.

5. **C** Tracking error is the standard deviation of alpha, the return to active management. Whenever the manager deviates the composition of the portfolio from that of the index, the portfolio has the potential for generating alpha and, hence, tracking error. However, the non-zero tracking error does not automatically indicate that the manager generated negative alphas over the period. Any time alpha is not exactly the same for each period, even if it is always positive, it will have a standard deviation.

6. **C** The spread duration for the U.S. Treasuries is zero, and the spread duration of the portfolio is a weighted average of the individual (sector) durations. We can solve for the spread duration (SD) of the corporates as follows:

   $$SD_p = w_C SD_C + w_T SD_T = 5.6$$

   since:

   $$SD_T = 0; \ w_T = \frac{5,000,000}{15,000,000} = 0.333; \ w_C = \frac{10,000,000}{15,000,000} = 0.667$$

   $$0.667(SD_C) + 0.333(0) = 5.6 \Rightarrow SD_C = \frac{5.6}{0.667} = 8.395$$

7. **B** The contribution of a bond or sector to the portfolio duration = $w_i D_i$. In this case, the bond is valued at $100,000 and the portfolio is valued at $15 million. The bond's duration is 6, so its contribution to the portfolio duration is (100,000 / 15,000,000) × 6 = 0.04.

   The contribution of a bond or sector to the portfolio dollar duration is the dollar duration of the individual bond or sector. The bond is worth $100,000 and its duration is 6, so its dollar duration (contribution to the portfolio dollar duration) is (6)(100,000)(0.01) = $6,000.

   Note: Unless you are asked to specify percentage contributions, the effective duration of the portfolio is irrelevant (i.e., extraneous information).

8. **C** *Step 1:* Compute the horizon price of the bond using a yield of 9%:

   The horizon yield of 9% is determined by adding the credit spread of 100 bps to the treasury yield of 8%. The new credit spread of 100 bps is computed as

©2016 Kaplan, Inc.

the difference between the original credit spread of 350 bps and the 250 bps reduction in the spread at the horizon date.

Recognizing that the bond has three years to maturity after one year, the price of this bond when discounted at a flat rate of 9% is:

N = 6; PMT = 5.5; I/Y = 4.5; FV = 100; CPT → PV = $105.16

Step 2: Calculate the end-of-period value of accumulated coupon income, assuming an annual reinvestment rate of 6% (semiannual rate of 3%):

N = 2; I/Y = 3; PMT = 5.5; PV = 0; CPT → FV = $11.165

Step 3: Compute the semiannual total return. The end of period value to use in this step is the total value of all cash flows at the end of the investment horizon. This is the sum of the horizon price and the value of the accumulated coupon income that was calculated in Step 1 and Step 2, respectively. This value is: $105.16 + $11.17 = $116.33.

N = 2; PV = –98.4321; FV = 116.33; PMT = 0; CPT → I/Y = 8.71%

Step 4: Compute the effective annual return: rate = $(1.0871)^2 - 1 = 18.18\%$.

Note: The BEY for the investment is 8.71% × 2 = 17.42%.

9. **B** Interest rate risk is made up of two components: *reinvestment risk* and *price risk*. If interest rates rise, bond prices will fall. At the same time, the amount received from reinvested coupons will rise. The net result is that the two components of interest rate risk move in *opposite* directions.

10. **A** The conditions for immunizing a portfolio against a future liability are (1) the portfolio's duration must equal the duration of the liability and (2) the present value of the assets must equal the present value of the liabilities.

11. **A** Combination matching, also known as horizon matching, involves creating a portfolio that is duration matched with the added constraint that it be cash matched in the early years.

12. **C** The higher the dispersion of cash flows around the horizon date, the greater the reinvestment risk and, hence, the immunization risk. The portfolio in answer choice C contains less dispersion of cash flows than answer choice B. The bond in answer choice A is subject to significant reinvestment risk.

13. **B** The *cushion spread* or *excess achievable return* is the difference between the current immunization rate and minimum acceptable return. In this case, cushion spread = 10% − 8.5% = 1.5% = 150 basis points.

14. **B** The required terminal value = $I(1 + s/2)^{2H}$ (using semiannual compounding), where I = initial portfolio value, s = safety net return, and H = number of years in investment horizon.

In this case, the required terminal value = $100,000,000(1.0425)^{12}$ = $164,783,136.

Using your financial calculator, PV = $100,000,000; I/Y = 4.25; PMT = 0; N = 12; CPT → FV = $164,783,136.

15. **A** Required assets at any time t = required terminal value / $(1 + i_t)^{2(H-t)}$ (assuming semiannual compounding), where i_t = the immunization rate at time t.

In this case, the required assets = $164,783,136 / (1.05)^{12}$ = $91,757,416.

Using your financial calculator, FV = $164,783,136; PMT = 0; I/Y = 5; N = 12; CPT → PV = $91,757,416.

16. **B** The dollar value of the safety margin at any time t equals the difference between the required assets at time t and the actual value of the assets in the portfolio.

The assets required to meet the minimum required terminal value are $164,783,136 / (1.05)^{12}$ = $91,757,416, and the actual value of the assets in the portfolio is $100,000,000. Therefore, the dollar safety margin is $100,000,000 – $91,757,416 = $8,242,584.

17. **A** You initially purchased 122,333 bonds at an individual price of $817.44 (N = 50; I/Y = 5; PMT = 40; FV = 1,000). The number of bonds is calculated as the funds expended divided by the price paid per bond ($100,000,000 / $817.44 per bond). At the new immunization rate of 8%, your bonds are priced at par ($1,000 per bond), and your portfolio is worth $122,333,000.

At 8%, the assets required to meet the required terminal value at 8% are: $164,783,136 / (1.04)^{12}$ = $102,923,061.

Using your financial calculator, FV = $164,783,136; PMT = 0; I/Y = 4; N = 12; CPT → PV = $102.92 million.

Because your portfolio is currently worth more than the required assets, the dollar safety margin is positive, and you should not immunize.

18. The use of effective duration will capture a portfolio's sensitivity to parallel shifts in the yield curve. However, in order to capture twists in the yield curve a portfolio manager should also incorporate key rate durations.

19. **B** The rebalancing ratio is the target DD / new DD. 80,000 / 65,000 = 1.23. The adjustment to dollar duration is an increase of the new market value of the portfolio times the rebalancing ratio minus 1. 2,500,000 × (1.23 – 1) = $575,000.

20. Because Owens is managing his portfolio against a liability structure, he should be concerned about interest rate risk, contingent claim risk (a.k.a. call risk), and cap risk. Note that the risk of having to reinvest the principal of bonds at a lower rate is call risk, but since he is managing a portfolio against a liability structure he should be concerned with all three of the aforementioned risks.

21. **A** An index is selected to use in evaluating the subsequent success of a manager in adding value. If the index is not investable, it is not a valid alternative to hiring a manager and not a valid benchmark. Investability is the most important factor in benchmark selection. In selecting the best benchmark, choosing an index with less turnover and securities the manager is familiar with are desirable characteristics, but they are not the most important issue.

RELATIVE-VALUE METHODOLOGIES FOR GLOBAL CREDIT BOND PORTFOLIO MANAGEMENT[1]

EXAM FOCUS

This topic review focuses on terminology. Have a working knowledge of the vocabulary as presented here. Much of it should be familiar from earlier levels.

RELATIVE VALUE ANALYSIS

LOS 21.a: Explain classic relative-value analysis, based on top-down and bottom-up approaches to credit bond portfolio management.

In relative value analysis, assets are compared along readily identifiable characteristics and value measures. With bonds, some of the characteristics used include sector, issuer, duration, and structure, which are used to rank the bonds across and within categories by expected performance. You are familiar with two of these methodologies:

1. In the **top-down approach**, the manager uses economy-wide projections to first allocate funds to different countries or currencies. The analyst then determines what industries or sectors are expected to outperform and selects individual securities within those industries.

2. The **bottom-up approach** starts at the *bottom*. The analyst selects undervalued issues.

Classic relative-value analysis combines the best bond investment opportunities using both the top-down and bottom-up approaches. This methodology combines many sources of information from portfolio managers, quantitative analysts, credit analysts, economists, strategists, and chief investment officers.

Any bond analysis should focus on total return. The analyst performs a detailed study of how past total returns for markets or individual securities were affected by macroeconomic events, such as interest rate changes and general economic performance.

---

1. The terminology presented in this topic review follows industry convention as presented in Reading 21 of the 2017 Level III CFA exam curriculum.

Any trends detected are used to estimate future total returns, based upon predictions for those same macro-trends.

CYCLICAL AND SECULAR CHANGES

LOS 21.b: Discuss the implications of cyclical supply and demand changes in the primary corporate bond market and the impact of secular changes in the market's dominant product structures.

Cyclical changes. Supply and demand analysis can be used to understand bond price and resulting spread changes, with sometimes surprising results. Increases in the number of new corporate bond issues are sometimes associated with narrower spreads and relatively strong returns. Even though this seems counter-intuitive, corporate bonds often perform best during periods of heavy supply. A possible explanation is that the valuation of new issues validates the prices of outstanding issues, which relieves pricing uncertainty and reduces all spreads. Another way to think of this is that the increase in supply attracts attention and could be associated with an even larger increase in demand. That demand raises the corporate bond prices relative to Treasury bonds, resulting in lower relative corporate bond yields and spreads associated with the increase in supply.

In similar fashion, corporate bond returns on both a relative and an absolute basis sometimes decline when supply falls unexpectedly. An explanation for this occurrence is the loss of the validation provided by the primary markets, which causes uncertainty and declines in value with accompanying higher spreads.

 Professor's Note: This is just classic supply and demand analysis from economics where supply change may also elicit demand change.

Secular changes. In all but the high-yield market, intermediate-term and bullet maturity bonds have come to dominate the corporate bond market. Bullet maturities are not callable, putable, or sinkable. Callable issues still dominate the high-yield segment, but this situation is expected to change as credit quality improves with lower interest financing and refinancing.

There are at least three implications associated with these product structures:

1. Securities with embedded options may trade at premium prices due to their scarcity value.

2. Credit managers seeking longer durations will pay a premium price for longer duration securities because of the tendency toward intermediate maturities.

3. Credit-based derivatives will be increasingly used to take advantage of return and/or diversification benefits across sectors, structures, and so forth.

Study Session 10

Cross-Reference to CFA Institute Assigned Reading #21 – Relative-Value Methodologies for Global Credit Bond Portfolio Management

LIQUIDITY

LOS 21.c: Explain the influence of investors' short- and long-term liquidity needs on portfolio management decisions.

As you would expect, there is generally a positive relationship between liquidity and bond prices. That is, as liquidity decreases, investors are willing to pay less (increasing yields), and as liquidity increases, investors are willing to pay more (decreasing yields).

The corporate debt market has shown variable liquidity over time, influenced to a great extent by macro shocks (i.e., a variety of economic conditions). And while some investors are willing to give up additional return by investing in issues that possess greater liquidity (e.g., larger-sized issues and government issues), other investors are willing to sacrifice liquidity for issues that offer a greater yield (e.g., smaller-sized issues and private placements). The move in debt markets has been toward increased liquidity (i.e., faster and cheaper trading) mainly due to trading innovations and competition among portfolio managers.

RATIONALES FOR SECONDARY BOND TRADES

LOS 21.d: Discuss common rationales for secondary market trading.

The following are some of the reasons why managers actively trade in the secondary bond markets, rather than simply hold their portfolios. In all cases, the manager must determine whether trading will produce returns greater than the associated costs or not.

Yield/spread pickup trades. The most common rationale for trading is the pickup of additional yield, which is possible within specified duration and credit-quality bounds. For example, suppose that a 10-year, A-rated bond is trading at a spread of 93 basis points, and a 10-year, BBB-rated bond is trading at a spread of 98 basis points. A bond portfolio manager holding the A-rated issue could consider the quality difference virtually meaningless and swap for the BBB issue and pick up a yield of five basis points.

The potential flaw in this rationale is that it does not recognize the limitations of yield measures as an indicator of potential performance (i.e., it is not based within a total return framework). For instance, if the spread on the A bond narrowed during the investment period and the BBB spread remained constant, the A bond would increase in price and outperform the BBB bond on a total return basis.

Credit-upside trades. In credit-upside trades, the bond portfolio manager attempts to identify issues that are likely to be upgraded in credit rating before the upgrade is incorporated into their prices. When the upgrade is officially announced, the prices of the affected bonds will increase as their spreads narrow.

Credit upside trades occur most often at the juncture of the highest speculative rating and the lowest investment rating. If the issues that warrant the highest speculative rating (e.g., BB) are considered creditworthy enough to be upgraded to investment grade (e.g., BBB or better), the bonds will benefit from decreased credit spread and increased liquidity.

Credit-defense trades. In credit-defense trades, the opposite of credit-upside trades, managers reduce exposure to (sell) sectors where they expect a credit downgrade.

New issue swaps. Managers often prefer to move into new issues, because new issues, particularly on-the-run Treasuries, are often perceived to have superior liquidity.

 Professor's Note: On-the-run implies the most recent issue of bonds.

Sector-rotation trades. Similar to strategies in the equity market, the idea behind preferred sector trades in the corporate bond market is to shift out of a sector or industry that is expected to underperform and into one that is expected to outperform on a total return basis.

Yield curve-adjustment trades. Yield curve-adjustment trades attempt to align the portfolio's duration with anticipated changes/shifts in the yield curve. That is, if long-term (only) interest rates are expected to fall, the manager may want to shift into longer durations to maximize the positive effect of the change in interest rates.

Structure trades. The rationale behind bond structure trades is to swap into structures that will have strong performance given an expected movement in volatility and yield curve shape. For example, higher volatility tends to result in decreased prices for callable securities because of the increased value to the issuer of the embedded option. Put structures tend to fare better in environments where interest rates are not expected to decrease. Holders of putable bonds sacrifice a small amount of yield for the ability to put the bond to the issuer and seek out higher yielding investments. If interest rates decline, putable bonds tend to underperform nonputable issues as the put feature becomes less valuable.

Cash flow reinvestment trades. The need to reinvest cash flows is a common reason for portfolio managers to trade in the secondary market. This is particularly true when portfolio cash flows do not coincide with new issues in the primary market for corporate bonds.

DURATION MANAGEMENT

Bond portfolio trades can be based on changes in the general level of interest rates. This can be referred to as a parallel shift in the yield curve because it means all interest rates will move by the same amount. With all Δr the same, duration will determine superior performance:

- If interest rates are expected to rise, buy shorter-duration bonds and sell longer-duration bonds.
- If interest rates are expected to fall, buy longer-duration bonds and sell shorter-duration bonds.

Study Session 10

Cross-Reference to CFA Institute Assigned Reading #21 – Relative-Value Methodologies for Global Credit Bond Portfolio Management

RELATIVE VALUE ANALYSIS

LOS 21.e: Discuss corporate bond portfolio strategies that are based on relative value.

Another strategy (relative value) assumes the Δr of two bonds or bond sectors will not change by the same amount. Making the implicit assumption that portfolio duration is kept the same, the difference in the two Δr [i.e., the spread change (Δs)] will determine which bond will have superior relative performance. This means that regardless of whether the general level of rates is increasing or decreasing and whether the level of return is negative or positive, it is possible to determine which bond will have the best relative performance:

- If the yield spread is expected to narrow, choose the higher yield bond.
- If the yield spread is expected to widen, choose the lower yield bond.

Another approach to relative value trading is to focus on the portfolio's overall spread duration:

- If the yield spread is expected to narrow, increase spread duration.
- If the yield spread is expected to widen, decrease spread duration.

MEASURING SPREAD

Option-adjusted spread (OAS) has been the preferred way to measure spread for investment grade securities. If the securities have embedded options, it is the most appropriate measure; however, these securities have become less common and OAS usage less prevalent. It is less suited to evaluating high yield securities because it does not consider credit spread volatility and default.

Nominal spread is the difference in yield to maturity of a higher credit risk to a lower credit risk security. Typically U.S. Treasuries are used as the lower risk and default-free bond to compute nominal spread. Nominal spread is the most commonly used measure of spread. Some practitioners have modified this and use agency yields rather than Treasury yields.

Static or zero-volatility spread is similar to OAS but ignores the effect of embedded options. For bonds without embedded options, static and OAS will be the same and will be similar to the nominal spread.

Swap spread is another approach to measuring spread and is particularly useful in comparing floating and fixed rate debt. Swap spread developed in Europe, where most non-government debt was fairly uniform with 10-year maturity and AA credit quality.

> **Example: Computing swap spread**
>
> A hypothetical 10-year bond of Giant Foods is priced to yield 73 basis points above the 10-year Treasury, a nominal spread of 73 basis points. Fixed rates on 10-year swaps are 41 basis points above the Treasury rate. The Treasury rate is 3.00%. Compute the swap spread.
>
> **Answer:**
>
> | | |
> |---|---|
> | Purchase Giant and receive (3.00 + 0.73) | 3.73% |
> | Pay on swap (3.00 + 0.41) | – 3.41% |
> | Receive on swap | LIBOR |
> | Net swap spread | LIBOR + 32 bp |
>
> The Giant bond's swap spread is 32 bp. Note that this is simply the difference in the two spreads (73 – 41 bp). It is treating fixed rate in the swap market as the base line to compute the bond's spread.

SPREAD ANALYSIS

Mean-reversion analysis is simple and widely used. It assumes spreads revert to the mean.

- If the spread is significantly greater than the historic mean, buy the sector or issue. (If yield is high on a relative basis, price is low.)
- If the spread is significantly less than the historic mean, sell the sector or issue. (If yield is low on a relative basis, price is high.)

Quality-spread analysis. Quality-spread analysis is based on the spread differential between low- and high-quality credits. Based on this analysis, a manager may buy an issue with a spread wider than that which is justified by its intrinsic quality. However, there is risk that the spread will not narrow or will become even greater.

Percentage yield spread analysis. Percentage yield spread analysis *divides* the yields on corporate bonds by the yields on Treasuries with the same duration. If the ratio is higher than justified by the historical ratio, the spread is expected to fall, making corporate bond prices rise. Methodological deficiencies render this form of analysis of little use. For example, the denominator in the ratio (government yields) is just one of many factors that contribute to corporate yields. Supply, demand, profitability, default, liquidity, and other factors can enhance or diminish any insights derived from the ratio of corporate yields to government yields.

BOND STRUCTURES

Structural analysis is the analysis of the performance of structures (e.g., bullet, callable, putable, and sinking fund) on a relative-value basis. This type of analysis is becoming less useful, however, as the U.S. and global corporate bond markets move toward the homogeneous bullet structure of the European corporate bond market. However, it

Study Session 10

Cross-Reference to CFA Institute Assigned Reading #21 – Relative-Value Methodologies for Global Credit Bond Portfolio Management

is still a valuable tool that can be used to enhance risk-adjusted returns of corporate portfolios.

Bullet Structures

Short-term bullets have maturities of one to five years and are used on the short end of a barbell strategy. A **barbell** is a portfolio that contains short- and long-term bonds. As opposed to using short-term Treasuries, corporate securities are used at the front end of the yield curve with long-term Treasuries at the long end of the yield curve.

Medium-term bullets (maturities of five to 12 years) are the most popular sector in the United States and Europe. When the yield curve is positively sloped, 20-year structures are often attractive, because they offer higher yields than 10- or 15-year structures but lower duration than 30-year securities.

Long-term bullets (30-year maturities) are the most commonly used long-term security in the global corporate bond market. They offer managers and investors additional positive convexity at the cost of increased effective duration.

Early Retirement Provisions

Callable bonds. An important consideration in valuing bonds is that the difference between the prices of otherwise identical non-callable and callable bonds is the value of the embedded option. Thus, their price and return differentials are driven by the value of the embedded option.

Due to the *negative convexity* caused by the embedded option, *callable* bonds:

- **Underperform** non-callables when interest rates fall. They do not realize the gains from a bond market rally (falling rates), because, due to the embedded option, their prices do not rise as much as those of similar non-callables.
- **Outperform** non-callables in bear bond markets with rising rates as the probability of being called falls. (When the current rate is lower than the coupon rate, their negative convexity makes callables respond less to increasing rates.)
- When yields are very high, relative to coupon rates, the callable bond will behave much the same as the non-callable (i.e., the call option has little or no value).

Professor's Note: Unless rates are very high (relative to the coupon rate), the embedded option in a callable bond has value. Anytime the option has value, a callable bond will have less interest rate sensitivity than a comparable non-callable.

Sinking funds. Sinking funds provide for the early retirement of a portion of an issue of bonds. Sinking fund structures priced at a discount to par have historically retained upside price potential during interest rate declines as long as the bonds remain priced at a discount to par (the firm can call the bonds back at par). Furthermore, given that the issuer is usually required to repurchase part of the issue each year, the price of sinking fund structures does not fall as much relative to callable and bullet structures when interest rates rise.

Putable bonds. Due to the relative scarcity of bonds with put options, it is difficult to reach a conclusion regarding their performance and valuation. Thus, managers and investors should only consider putable bonds as an alternative, when there is a strong belief that interest rates will rise (i.e., increases in interest rates increase the value of the embedded put option).

It is worth noting that valuation models for bonds with embedded put options often fail to incorporate the probability that the issuer will be unable to fulfill its obligation to repurchase its bonds. This is particularly relevant to the valuation of putable bonds issued by high-yield issuers. It may be that the creditworthiness of the high-yield issuer is a more relevant indicator of the value of the bond than that calculated using a valuation model.

CREDIT ANALYSIS

Credit analysis involves examining financial statements, bond documents, and trends in credit ratings. It provides an analytic framework in assessing key information in sector selection. It could include:

- Capacity to pay in corporate credit analysis.
- The quality of the collateral and the servicer are important in the analysis of asset-backed securities.
- The ability to assess and collect taxes for municipal bonds.
- An assessment of the country's ability to pay (economic risk) and willingness to pay (political risk) for sovereign bond issuers.

The main disadvantage to credit analysis is the need to continually search out and interpret information, which is becoming more arduous with the expansion in the universe of global bonds. In order to be effective, managers must establish and support an effective credit analysis system within their managerial domains to assure that appropriate information is available to make the best possible choices.

Figure 1 is a compilation of the primary relative valuation methodologies along with their descriptions.

Study Session 10

Cross-Reference to CFA Institute Assigned Reading #21 – Relative-Value Methodologies for Global Credit Bond Portfolio Management

Figure 1: Relative Valuation Methodologies

Methodology	Description	Strategy
Total return analysis	Consider coupons (yield) as well as potential price increases or decreases.	Study past bond reactions to macroeconomic changes to project future returns.
Primary market analysis	Supply of and demand for new issues affects returns. Increases (decreases) in new issues tend to decrease (increase) relative yields.	When you expect rates to fall, you expect new issues and refinances to increase.
Liquidity and trading analysis	Liquidity drives bid-ask prices and yields. As liquidity increases, demand increases. As trading increases, prices increase and yields decrease.	Identify issues/sectors that you expect to increase in price from increased liquidity.
Secondary trading rationales	Reasons for trading.	Yield/spread pickup trades. Credit-upside trades. Credit-defense trades. New issue swaps. Sector-rotation trades. Curve-adjustment trades. Structure trades. Cash flow reinvestment.
Secondary trading constraints	Reasons for not trading.	Portfolio constraints. "Story" disagreement. Buy and hold. Seasonality.
Spread analysis	Analyze the various spreads. With increased rate volatility (uncertainty), spreads tend to increase and widen with maturity.	Mean-reversion analysis. Quality-spread analysis. Percentage yield spread analysis.
Structural analysis	Study the structure of bond issues: bullets, callable, sinking funds, and put options.	Determine which bond structures will perform best given your macro predictions.
Credit curve analysis	Study credit and yield curves. With increased rate volatility (uncertainty), spreads tend to increase and widen with maturity.	Credit spread curves tend to change with the economic cycle (i.e., narrow during upturns and widen during downturns).
Credit analysis	Upgrades cause reduced yields and increased prices. Downgrades cause increased yields and decreased prices.	Identify credit upgrade and downgrade candidates.
Asset allocation/ Sector analysis	Macro allocation is across sectors. Micro allocation is within a sector.	Identify sectors/firms expected to outperform.

Rationales for Not Trading

There are also circumstances under which managers will not trade or are prohibited from trading:

Trading constraints. Portfolio trading constraints are considered to be a major contributor to inefficiencies in the global corporate bond market. Examples include:

- Quality constraints. Some investors are limited to investing only in investment grade bonds, those rated BBB and above.
- Restrictions on structures (callables or convertibles not allowed) and foreign bonds.
- High-yield corporate exposure limits for insurance companies.
- Structure and quality restrictions for European investors.
- In some countries, commercial banks are restricted and can only own floating-rate securities.

Other factors that can contribute to inefficiencies include *story disagreement, buy and hold*, and *seasonality*.

Story disagreement refers to the lack of consensus between buy-side and sell-side analysts and strategists, which can lead to conflicting recommendations and uncertainty about optimal trading strategies.

Buy and hold represents an unwillingness to sell and recognize an accounting loss or the desire to keep turnover low. Lack of liquidity has also been cited as a reason for not trading.

Seasonality refers to the slowing of trading at the ends of months, quarters, and calendar years, when portfolio managers are preoccupied with various reports and filings.

KEY CONCEPTS

LOS 21.a

In **relative value analysis**, assets are compared along readily identifiable characteristics and value measures. For example, in comparing firms we can use measures such as P/E ratios for ranking. With bonds, some of the characteristics used include sector, issue, and structure, which are used to rank the bonds across and within categories by expected performance.

- In the **top-down approach**, the manager uses economy-wide projections to first allocate funds to different countries or currencies. Then the analyst determines what industries or sectors are expected to outperform and selects individual securities within those industries.
- The **bottom-up approach** starts at the *bottom*. The analyst selects undervalued issues.

Classic relative-value analysis combines the best bond investment opportunities using both the top-down and bottom-up approaches.

LOS 21.b

Cyclical changes relate to the number of new issues. Increases in the number of new bond issues are sometimes associated with narrower spreads and relatively strong returns.

Secular changes relate to the characteristics of bond issues. In all but the high-yield market, intermediate-term bullets dominate the corporate bond market. Bullet maturities are not callable, putable, or sinkable. Callable issues still dominate the high-yield segment, but this situation is expected to change as credit quality improves with lower interest financing and refinancing.

LOS 21.c

Some investors are willing to give up additional return by investing in issues that possess greater liquidity (e.g., larger-sized issues and government issues), other investors are willing to sacrifice liquidity for issues which offer a greater yield (e.g., smaller-sized issues and private placements).

LOS 21.d

Secondary trade rationales include the following:

- Yield/spread pickup trades are the most cited reason for secondary trades.
- Credit-upside trades reflect managers' expectations that an issuer will experience a quality upgrade that is not already reflected in the current spread.
- Credit-defense trades reflect managers' desires to reduce exposure to sectors where a credit downgrade is expected to occur.
- New issue swaps are trades into large, new issues, particularly on-the-run Treasuries that are often perceived to have superior liquidity.
- Sector rotation trades are undertaken to take advantage of sectors that are expected to outperform on a total return basis.
- Yield curve adjustment trades occur because of the desire to alter the duration of a portfolio to be favorably positioned with respect to anticipated yield curve changes.

- Structure trades refers to swaps into structures (callable, bullet, and put) that will have strong performance given an expected movement in volatility and yield curve shape.
- Cash flow reinvestment is a common reason for portfolio managers to trade in the secondary market, particularly when primary issues are scarce.

LOS 21.e

Relative Valuation Methodologies

Methodology	Description	Strategy
Total return analysis	Consider coupons (yield) as well as potential price increases or decreases.	Study past bond reactions to macroeconomic changes to project future returns.
Primary market analysis	Supply of and demand for new issues affects returns. Increases (decreases) in new issues tend to decrease (increase) relative yields.	When you expect rates to fall, you expect new issues and refinances to increase.
Liquidity and trading analysis	Liquidity drives bid-ask prices and yields. As liquidity increases, demand increases. As trading increases, prices increase and yields decrease.	Identify issues/sectors that you expect to increase in price from increased liquidity.
Secondary trading rationales	Reasons for trading.	Yield/spread pickup trades. Credit-upside trades. Credit-defense trades. New issue swaps. Sector-rotation trades. Curve-adjustment trades. Structure trades. Cash flow reinvestment.
Secondary trading constraints	Reasons for not trading.	Portfolio constraints. "Story" disagreement. Buy and hold. Seasonality.
Spread analysis	Analyze the various spreads. With increased rate volatility (uncertainty), spreads tend to increase and widen with maturity.	Mean-reversion analysis. Quality-spread analysis. Percentage yield spread analysis.
Structural analysis	Study the structure of bond issues: bullets, callable, sinking funds, and put options.	Determine which bond structures will perform best given your macro predictions.
Credit curve analysis	Study credit and yield curves. With increased rate volatility (uncertainty), spreads tend to increase and widen with maturity.	Credit spread curves tend to change with the economic cycle (i.e., narrow during upturns and widen during downturns).
Credit analysis	Upgrades cause reduced yields and increased prices. Downgrades cause increased yields and decreased prices.	Identify credit upgrade and downgrade candidates.
Asset allocation/ Sector analysis	Macro allocation is across sectors. Micro allocation is within a sector.	Identify sectors/firms expected to outperform.

Study Session 10

Cross-Reference to CFA Institute Assigned Reading #21 – Relative-Value Methodologies for Global Credit Bond Portfolio Management

CONCEPT CHECKERS

1. Although all are presented as rationales for secondary trading, which is probably the *most* common rationale?
    A. New issue swaps.
    B. Credit-upside trades.
    C. Yield/spread pickup trades.

2. There is an increase in secondary market trading based on cash flow reinvestment when:
    A. the yield curve is inverted.
    B. the yield curve is relatively flat.
    C. the primary supply is short or the composition of the primary market is not compatible with portfolio objectives.

3. Although the practice is declining, it is common for practitioners to compare the value of mortgage-backed and U.S. Agency securities with investment-grade corporate securities. Which of the following spreads is used for this purpose?
    A. Static spreads.
    B. Nominal spreads.
    C. Option-adjusted spreads.

4. Which of the following is not considered a spread tool widely used in the United States for individually issued corporate bonds?
    A. Swap spread analysis.
    B. Percent yield analysis.
    C. Quality spread analysis.

5. Failure to evaluate future performance on the basis of total return is a common criticism of which of the following rationales for trading?
    A. Credit-defense trades.
    B. Credit-upside trades.
    C. Yield/spread pickup trades.

6. Which of the following is considered the leading contributor to inefficiencies in the global corporate market?
    A. Portfolio constraints.
    B. The reluctance to trade if it will show a loss relative to book value.
    C. The decline in trading activities that occurs during periods when performance reports and government filings are being prepared.

7. Percentage yield analysis examines which of the following values as part of the relative value analytical process? The ratio of:
    A. corporate yields to government yields for securities of similar maturity.
    B. corporate yields to government yields for securities of similar duration.
    C. government yields to corporate yields for securities of similar duration.

For more questions related to this topic review, log in to your Schweser online account and launch SchweserPro™ QBank; and for video instruction covering each LOS in this topic review, log in to your Schweser online account and launch the OnDemand video lectures, if you have purchased these products.

ANSWERS – CONCEPT CHECKERS

1. **C** It has been estimated that more than half of all secondary trades reflect investor intentions to add additional yield.

2. **C** Portfolio managers must search the secondary markets when portfolio cash flows occur during interludes in the primary market or when the composition of the primary market is not compatible with portfolio objectives.

3. **C** To compare the volatility of sectors (mortgage-backed securities and U.S. Agencies), practitioners often value investment-grade corporate securities in terms of option-adjusted spreads. The static spread is only used when interest rate volatility is not a concern.

4. **A** Mean-reversion analysis, quality spread analysis, and percent yield analysis are commonly used spread tools. A swap spread is a credit spread analysis tool widely used in Europe and Asia for all types of bonds. In the United States, it is used for MBS, CMBS, agency, and ABS.

5. **C** Relative yield pickup trades are based on swapping bonds based on YTM and do not include consideration of future price/spread movements.

6. **A** Client-imposed portfolio constraints are the biggest contributor to bond market inefficiencies.

7. **B** Percentage yield analysis is a popular tool that compares the yields on corporates to the yields on treasuries, keeping duration more or less constant.

The following is a review of the Fixed-Income Portfolio Management (2) principles designed to address the learning outcome statements set forth by CFA Institute. Cross-Reference to CFA Institute Assigned Reading #22.

FIXED-INCOME PORTFOLIO MANAGEMENT—PART II

Study Session 11

EXAM FOCUS

This topic assignment covers a variety of themes, many of which are also discussed in other areas, as well as the effects of leverage on an investment, including calculations and measures of risk. There is an important discussion of currency hedging that applies to any type of investment, not just fixed income. Don't overlook it. Hedging fixed income is very important—what it can and cannot accomplish, as well as calculations. Also, be familiar with the credit derivatives discussed here—what does each do and how do they work. The sections on foreign bond duration and breakeven spread may look unusual but are just variations on the basics of duration and spread. There is a discussion of the manager selection process that will be repeated in other topic areas. That is not intended to be hard material so be familiar with it.

LEVERAGE

LOS 22.a: Evaluate the effect of leverage on portfolio duration and investment returns.

Leverage refers to the use of borrowed funds to purchase a portion of the securities in a portfolio. Its use affects both the return and duration of the portfolio.

Leverage Effects

If the return earned on the investment is greater than the financing cost of borrowed funds, the return to the investor will be favorably affected. Leverage is beneficial when the strategy earns a return greater than the cost of borrowing.

Although leverage can increase returns, it also has a downside. If the strategy return falls below the cost of borrowing, the loss to investors will be increased. So leverage magnifies both good and bad outcomes.

Additionally, as leverage increases, the dispersion of possible portfolio returns increases. In other words, as more borrowed funds are used, the variability of portfolio returns increases.

Some examples will help illustrate these relationships.

Example: The effect of leverage on return

A portfolio manager has a portfolio worth $100 million, $30 million of which is his own funds and $70 million is borrowed. If the return on the invested funds is 6% and the cost of borrowed funds is 5%, **calculate** the return on the portfolio.

Answer:

The gross profit on the portfolio is: $100 million × 6% = $6 million.

The cost of borrowed funds is: $70 million × 5% = $3.5 million.

The net profit on the portfolio is: $6 million – $3.5 million = $2.5 million.

The return on the equity invested (i.e., the portfolio) is thus:

$$\frac{\$2.5}{\$30} = 8.33\%$$

This calculation can also be approached with the following formula:

$$R_p = R_i + [(B/E) \times (R_i - c)]$$

where:
R_p = return on portfolio
R_i = return on invested assets
B = amount of leverage
E = amount of equity invested
c = cost of borrowed funds

The formula adds the return on the investment (the first component) to the net levered return (the second component in brackets).

Using the example above:

$$R_p = 6\% + [(70 / 30) \times (6\% - 5\%)] = 8.33\%$$

Practice the use of this formula by checking Figure 1. In the table, we use the same example as above, except that we allow more leverage to be used (than the $70 million above) and allow the return on invested assets to vary (from the 6% above).

Figure 1: Leveraged Returns

	Return on Invested Assets		
Leverage	4%	6%	8%
$70 million	1.67%	8.33%	15.00%
$170 million	–1.67%	11.67%	25.00%
$270 million	–5.00%	15.00%	35.00%

The body of the table shows the leveraged return at combinations of return and leverage. The rows show how leveraged returns increase when asset returns increase. The columns show how leveraged returns either increase or decrease with leverage, depending on whether the return is greater or less than the cost of borrowed funds.

For example, the first row shows the effects of asset returns on leveraged return holding leverage constant at $70 million. Assuming $70 million in leverage, the leveraged return increases from 1.67% to 15% as the return on assets increases from 4% to 8%. Likewise, holding the asset return constant at 4% (which is less than the cost of funds), we see in the first column that the leveraged return decreases from +1.67% to –5% as leverage increases from $70 million to $270 million.

In summary:

- As leverage increases, the variability of returns increases.
- As the investment return increases, the variability of returns increases.

The Effect of Leverage on Duration

Just as leverage increases the portfolio return variability, it also increases the duration, given that the duration of borrowed funds is typically less than the duration of invested funds.

> **Example: The effect of leverage on duration**
>
> Using the original example above, the manager's portfolio was worth $100 million, $30 million of which was his own funds (equity) and $70 million was borrowed. If the duration of the invested funds is 5.0 and the duration of borrowed funds is 1.0, **calculate** the duration of the equity.

Answer:

The duration can be calculated with the following formula:

$$D_E = \frac{D_i I - D_B B}{E}$$

where:
D_E = duration of equity
D_i = duration of invested assets
D_B = duration of borrowed funds
I = amount of invested funds
B = amount of borrowed funds
E = amount of equity invested

Using the provided information:

$$D_E = \frac{(5.0)100 - (1.0)70}{30} = 14.33$$

Note the use of leverage has resulted in the duration of the equity (14.33) being greater than the duration of invested assets (5.0).

REPURCHASE AGREEMENTS

LOS 22.b: Discuss the use of repurchase agreements (repos) to finance bond purchases and the factors that affect the repo rate.

To increase the leverage of their portfolios, portfolio managers sometimes borrow funds on a short-term basis using repurchase agreements. In a *repurchase agreement* (repo), the borrower (seller of the security) agrees to repurchase it from the buyer on an agreed upon date at an agreed upon price (repurchase price).

Although it is legally a sale and subsequent purchase of securities, a repurchase agreement is essentially a collateralized loan, where the difference between the sale and repurchase prices is the interest on the loan. The rate of interest on the repo is referred to as the *repo rate*.

For example, assume a portfolio manager uses a repo to finance a $5 million position. Assuming that the repo term is one day and the repo rate is 4%, the dollar interest can be computed as follows:

dollar interest = $5 million × 0.04 × (1 / 360) = $555.55

This means that the portfolio manager agrees to sell a Treasury security to the lender for $5 million and simultaneously agrees to repurchase the same security the next day for $5,000,555.55. The $555.55 is analogous to the interest on the loan. The portfolio manager gets the use of the $5 million for one day.

The manager (borrower) obtains funds at a cheap interest rate while the lender earns a return greater than the risk-free rate. Although the term of a repo is typically a day or so, they can be rolled over to extend the financing.

The lender in a repurchase agreement is exposed to credit risk, if the collateral remains in the borrower's custody. For instance, the borrower could:

- Sell the collateral.
- Fraudulently use it as collateral for another loan.
- Go bankrupt.

As a result of this risk, repos will be structured with different delivery scenarios:

1. The borrower is required to physically deliver the collateral to the lender. Physical delivery can be costly however.

2. The collateral is deposited in a custodial account at the borrower's clearing bank. This is a cost-effective way to reduce the fees associated with delivery.

3. The transfer of securities is executed electronically through the parties' banks. This is less expensive than physical delivery but does involve fees and transfer charges.

4. Delivery is sometimes not required if the borrower's credit risk is low, if the parties are familiar with one another, or if the transaction is short-term.

The Repo Rate

No single repo rate exists for all repurchase agreements. The particular repo rate depends upon a number of factors.

- The repo rate increases as the **credit risk** of the borrower increases (when delivery is not required).
- As the **quality** of the collateral increases, the repo rate declines.
- As the **term** of the repo increases, the repo rate increases. It is important to note that the repo rate is a function of the repo term, not the maturity of the collateral securities.
- **Delivery.** If collateral is physically delivered, then the repo rate will be lower. If the repo is held by the borrower's bank, the rate will be higher. If no delivery takes place, the rate will be even higher.
- **Collateral.** If the availability of the collateral is limited, the repo rate will be lower. The lender may be willing to accept a lower rate in order to obtain a security they need to make delivery on another agreement.
- The **federal funds rate**, the rate at which banks borrow funds from one another, is a benchmark for repo rates. The higher the federal funds rate, the higher the repo rate.
- As the demand for funds at financial institutions changes due to **seasonal factors**, so will the repo rate.

BOND RISK MEASURES

LOS 22.c: Critique the use of standard deviation, target semivariance, shortfall risk, and value at risk as measures of fixed-income portfolio risk.

Duration is used as a measure of the interest rate risk of a portfolio. The duration for a portfolio is just the weighted average of the duration of its individual bonds. The duration of a portfolio can be adjusted using derivative securities, as we will see later on.

The limitations of duration as a risk measure include the fact that it is not accurate for large yield changes and for bonds with negative convexity. As such, other measures of bond risk should be examined.

Standard Deviation

The standard deviation measures the dispersion of returns around the mean return and is the square root of the variance. Assuming a symmetrical, normal distribution of returns around the mean, 68.3% of the returns will occur within ± one standard deviation of the mean. For example, a normal distribution of investment returns with a mean of 8% and a standard deviation of 4% means that 68.3% of all observed returns lie between 4% and 12% (8 − 4 = 4% and 8 + 4 = 12%).

Drawbacks of Standard Deviation and Variance

The problems with standard deviation and variance are as follows:

- Bond returns are often not normally distributed around the mean. For example, bonds with options will have non-normal return distributions.
- The number of inputs (e.g., variances and covariances) increases significantly with larger portfolios. In fact, if N represents the number of bonds in a portfolio, the number of inputs necessary to estimate the standard deviation of a portfolio is equal to $[N(N + 1)] / 2$.
- Obtaining estimates for each of these inputs is problematic. Historically, calculated risk measures may not represent the risk measures that will be observed in the future. Remember from studying duration that bond prices become less sensitive to interest rate changes as the maturity date nears. Therefore, today's volatility will probably not be the same as tomorrow's volatility. Furthermore, a bond's options will change in their influence over time, making the estimation of future portfolio risk even more difficult.

Other measures of risk have been developed to specifically examine downside risk. Downside risk measures focus on the portion of a returns distribution that fall below some targeted return.

Semivariance

As its name implies, semivariance measures the dispersion of returns. Unlike its namesake (variance), semivariance does not measure the total dispersion of all returns above and below the mean. Instead, it measures only the dispersion of returns below a target return, which is the risk that most investors are concerned about.

Drawbacks of Semivariance

Despite its advantage, semivariance is not a commonly used risk measure for the following reasons:

- It is difficult to compute for a large bond portfolio. While computing the portfolio standard deviation is computationally straightforward, there is no easy way of doing so for semivariance.
- If investment returns are symmetric, the semivariance yields the same rankings as the variance and the variance is better understood.
- If investment returns are not symmetric, it can be quite difficult to forecast downside risk and the semivariance may not be a good indicator of future risk.
- Because the semivariance is estimated with only half the distribution, it uses a smaller sample size and is generally less accurate statistically.

Shortfall Risk

Whereas the semivariance measures the dispersion of returns below a specified target return, shortfall risk measures the *probability* that the actual return will be less than the target return. For example, the shortfall risk may be specified as: there is a 9.3% chance that returns will be less than the Treasury bill rate this year.

The primary criticism of the shortfall risk measure is:

- Shortfall risk does not consider the impact of outliers so the magnitude (dollar amount) of the shortfall below the target return is ignored. In the example above, we are given no information on how low returns could actually get below the Treasury bill return.

Value at Risk

The value at risk (VAR) provides the probability of a return less than a given amount over a specific time period. For example, VAR could be specified as, "There is a 5% probability that the loss on a bond portfolio will be $242,000 or more over the next month."

The primary criticism of VAR is:

- As in the shortfall risk measure, VAR does not provide the magnitude of losses that exceed that specified by VAR.

Futures Contracts

Interest rate futures are a cost-effective means for managing the dollar duration of a bond portfolio. There are interest rate futures contracts on securities of varying maturities, from 30 days to 30 years. The Chicago Board of Trade (CBOT) has a 30-year Treasury futures contract, on which any Treasury bond with a maturity or first call of at least 15 years is deliverable. The 30-year contract is very popular, and it is used in most examples and problems.

Just like bond prices, the prices of an interest rate futures contract will change when interest rates change. Also like a bond, the direction of the price change for a long position is opposite to the direction of the change in interest rates. Consequently, futures contracts can be utilized to lengthen or shorten portfolio duration simply by purchasing or shorting the contracts. As you will see, the focus of the next two LOS is dollar duration, which we will discuss shortly.

Cheapest to deliver (CTD) is a very descriptive term for a bond that the counterparty in the short position can deliver to satisfy the obligation of the futures contract. For example, many different bonds can be used to satisfy a CBOT 30-year Treasury bond futures contract. Furthermore, the short position has some choice with respect to the time of delivery. Note that these issues are not addressed in the LOS to follow so this discussion is just to help with your comprehension.

 Professor's Note: The option of choosing the bond to deliver on the futures contract is sometimes referred to as the "quality" option or "swap" option. The ability to choose the actual delivery day is referred to as the "timing" option. The "wild card" option is the right to announce, after the exchange has closed, your intent to deliver on the contract.

A **conversion factor** helps determine the price received at delivery by the party with the short position. The quoted price for the CTD is the product of the quoted futures price and the conversion factor. This will be demonstrated in the examples below. Each bond eligible for delivery has a conversion factor provided by the exchange, the computation of which is not important here.

ADVANTAGES OF INTEREST RATE FUTURES

LOS 22.d: Demonstrate the advantages of using futures instead of cash market instruments to alter portfolio risk.

There are three main advantages to using futures over cash market instruments. All three advantages are derived from the fact that there are low transactions costs and a great deal of depth in the futures market.

Compared to cash market instruments, futures:

1. Are more liquid.

2. Are less expensive.

3. Make short positions more readily obtainable, because the contracts can be more easily shorted than an actual bond.

DOLLAR DURATION

The **dollar duration** is the *dollar* change in the price of a bond, portfolio, or futures contract resulting from a 100 bps change in yield. The relationship between duration and dollar duration is straightforward.

For a given bond with an initial value:

duration = (%Δvalue) = (effective duration)(0.01)

Multiplying through by the market value of the bond or portfolio, we get dollar duration, represented by DD:

DD = ($Δvalue) = (effective duration)(0.01)(value)

The dollar duration of a futures contract is the change in the futures dollar value for a 100 bps interest rate change. The dollar duration of a portfolio can be adjusted by taking a position in futures contracts.

To **increase** dollar duration → **buy** futures contracts.

To **decrease** dollar duration → **sell** futures contracts.

DURATION MANAGEMENT

LOS 22.e: Formulate and evaluate an immunization strategy based on interest rate futures.

> **For the Exam:** Controlling, or hedging, interest rate risk is an important topic for the Level III exam. You should know the concept, the issues, and the calculations. It will be covered both here and in risk management (derivatives). The formulas here are based on DD and price of the CTD bond that underlies the contract. In derivatives, an alternate version based on duration and price of the contract will be used. You will need to know both, as you must use the formula for which inputs are given in any question. They are mathematically identical in the end so there is no discrepancy in the approaches. Know both.

Hedging or controlling interest rate risk can involve either buying or selling derivatives, depending on the objectives. One approach is to determine a target dollar duration, compare that to the existing dollar duration, and determine the dollar duration of futures to add or subtract to reach the target. Comparing this to the dollar duration of the futures makes it easy to determine the number of contracts. This can be expressed as:

$$DD_T = DD_P + DD_{Futures}$$

where:
DD_T = the target dollar duration of the portfolio plus futures
DD_P = the dollar duration of the portfolio before adding futures
$DD_{Futures}$ = the total dollar duration of the added futures contracts

Note that we denote the dollar duration of a single futures contract as DD_f.

- A positive DD of futures indicates increasing duration and buying contracts.
- A negative DD of futures indicates decreasing duration and selling contracts.

As an aside, once a given DD_T has been achieved, market conditions will probably change the portfolio's properties, and the manager will usually adjust the futures position to move the dollar duration of the portfolio (which now includes futures) back to DD_T.

It is quite simple to determine the number of contracts needed to achieve a dollar duration if you are given the dollar durations of the current portfolio, the target portfolio, and one futures contract.

Example: Achieving the target dollar duration

The manager of a bond portfolio expects an increase in interest rates, so duration should be reduced. The portfolio has a dollar duration of $32,000, and he would like to reduce it to $20,000. The manager chooses a futures contract with a dollar duration of $1,100. How can the manager achieve the target duration?

Answer:

$$\text{number of contracts} = \frac{DD_T - DD_P}{DD_f}$$

$$= \frac{\$20,000 - \$32,000}{\$1,100} = -10.91$$

The manager should short (sell) 11 contracts to reduce the dollar duration.

The Hedging Formula

While conceptually easy to understand, it is more common to work from duration rather than dollar duration and from the characteristics of the cheapest-to-deliver that underlies the contract.

Working from dollar durations, the number of contracts to construct a hedge is:

$$\text{number of contracts} = \frac{DD_T - DD_P}{DD_f}$$

A more common approach is to rewrite this formula and work directly from durations as:

$$\text{number of contracts} = \frac{(D_T - D_P)P_P}{D_{CTD}P_{CTD}}(\text{CTD conversion factor})$$

Example:

A French portfolio manager has a diversified portfolio of bonds totaling EUR 30,000,000 market value with a duration of 7.50. The manager is willing to adjust duration up or down 10% to 6.75 or 8.25 and the manager expects rates to fall. An available bond contract specifies delivery of EUR 100,000 par per contract and the contract price is EUR 125,000 (this is interpreted as meaning the forward price of the deliverable bond). The CTD has a duration of 6.2 and a conversion factor of 1.15.

Determine whether the manager should buy or sell contracts and **compute** the number of contracts to use.

Expecting a fall in rates the manager should increase duration to increase the price gain that will occur in the portfolio. The manager must buy bond contracts.

The number to buy is:

Number of contracts = $\{[(D_T - D_P)P_P] / (D_{CTD}P_{CTD})\}\ CF_{CTD}$

$= \{[(8.25 - 7.5) \times 30,000,000] / (6.2)(125,000)\} \times 1.15 = 33.39$

Buy 33 contracts priced at EUR 125,000.

> *Professor's Note: Practitioners and candidates who work with this material have pointed out the terminology used in this section of CFA text is odd.*
>
> *EUR 125,000 is the delivery price of a specific deliverable bond and CF must be used in the formula to allow for the reality that the deliverable bond can change. Because the contract price and CF are given in the question, both are used in the calculation.*
>
> *Your primary reading in derivatives will solve this in simpler fashion by providing the actual futures contract price and no CF. In this example it would be EUR 108,696. (This is EUR 125,000 / 1.15). EUR 108,696 can be used without CF to reach the same numeric solution: [(8.25 – 7.5) × 30,000,000] / [(6.2)(108,696)] = 33.39.*
>
> *I suggest you wait and pay more attention to the way this will be covered in the later, primary reading on contract hedging in derivatives where no CF is provided.*

Hedging Issues

For the Exam: The material on the next several pages is presented as necessary background material. It is not specifically addressed in any LOS. Do pay attention to basis and basis risk, cross hedge, and yield beta as they occur regularly on the exam.

Although calculating the number of contracts needed to increase or decrease interest rate risk exposure is straightforward, in practice the hedge may not work as planned. The following discusses some of the issues in hedging that may arise in practice.

Basis Risk and Cross Hedging

Price basis refers to the difference between the spot price and the futures price at delivery:

price basis = spot (cash) price – futures delivery price

Basis risk is the variability of the basis. It is an important consideration for hedges that will be lifted in the intermediate term (i.e., before delivery). Basis can change unexpectedly due to difference in the underlying bond and the futures contract.

In a **cross hedge**, the underlying security in the futures contract is not identical to the asset being hedged (e.g., using T-bond futures to hedge corporate bonds). A cross hedge can be either long or short. It must be used if no corresponding futures contract exists for a given position or, if a corresponding contract exists, its liquidity is too low to be effective.

The prices of the bond portfolio and the futures contract will vary over time with changes in interest rates. And since they are not perfectly correlated, they can move closer together or farther apart. In other words, the basis changes over time. If the basis is significantly different than expected at the horizon date for the investment, the hedge could be quite ineffective.

Thus, it is important to note that at the initiation of a hedge, a manager substitutes the uncertainty of the basis for the uncertainty of the price of the hedged security. In other words, the manager may think he has effectively hedged the risk of the bond with a futures contract, when in fact he has not.

When implementing a cross hedge, the manager should evaluate the differences in the relevant risk factor exposures of the bond and the futures contract. If the bond has greater sensitivity to interest rate changes, for example, more of the futures contract will be needed to effectively hedge the bond position.

The desired hedge ratio is given by:

$$\text{hedge ratio} = \frac{\text{exposure of bond to risk factor}}{\text{exposure of futures to risk factor}}$$

For example, if it was determined that 100 futures contracts would be needed to hedge a bond portfolio and the manager subsequently estimates that the hedge ratio is 1.2, the bond portfolio should be hedged with 120 contracts.

Note that the hedge ratio and hence the number of contracts should be estimated for the time at which the hedge is lifted (i.e., the hedge horizon), because this is when the manager wishes to lock in a value. The manager should also have an estimate of the price, because the effect of changes in risk will vary as price and yield vary.

Given that the pricing of the futures contract depends on the cheapest-to-deliver bond, the hedge ratio can also be expressed as:

$$(1) \quad \text{hedge ratio} = \frac{\text{exposure of bond to risk factor}}{\text{exposure of CTD to risk factor}} \times \frac{\text{exposure of CTD to risk factor}}{\text{exposure of futures to risk factor}}$$

In the formula above, the second term on the right-hand side represents the conversion factor for the CTD bond.

If we are examining interest rate risk as the risk factor and we wish to fully hedge the bond, the target dollar duration is zero. Thus, we can rewrite the formula for the number of contracts to hedge a bond from the numerical example above as:

$$(2) \quad \text{hedge ratio} = \frac{D_P P_P}{D_{CTD} P_{CTD}} (\text{CTD conversion factor})$$

> *Professor's Note: Some candidates have asserted the above formula from the CFA text is wrong because it must include a "−" sign in the numerator. Those candidates are wrong and it is important to your future success that you understand why. **Displaying or not displaying a "−" sign is irrelevant.***
>
> *This section is a theoretical discussion of the concept behind hedging. The portfolio can increase or decrease in value. Hedging adds something (contracts) to modify the net increase or decrease in value. The earlier applied formula for calculating the number of contracts uses the desired change in duration for the numerator. For a full hedge, the target duration is 0, and the desired change is $0 − D_P = −D_P$, Hence the comment by candidatures the above formula is wrong.*
>
> *However, this misses a more important point: to increase duration, buy contracts; to reduce duration, sell contracts. Targeting a 0 duration will be a reduction and will require selling contracts. Whether you show or do not show the calculation result as a − does not affect the correct solution. **Use the facts of the case to determine if you must increase duration and buy contracts or decrease duration and sell contracts. Then use a formula to determine the number of contracts to buy or sell.** Do not focus on irrelevant display issues.*

Yield Beta

Another complication that arises with cross hedges is that the spread in yields between the bond and the futures may not be constant. In the calculations up to now, we have assumed that the yield spread is constant (i.e., the yields change in unison so that the spread remains the same). To adjust for changes in the spread, the **yield beta** is obtained from a regression equation:

$$\text{yield on bond} = \alpha + \beta(\text{yield on CTD}) + e$$

The yield beta, β, shows the relationship between changes in the yields on the bond and the CTD. A yield beta of 0.80, for example, would imply that for a yield change of 100 bps on the CTD, the yield on the bond changes 80 bps. If the yield spread between the bond being hedged and the CTD issue is assumed to be constant, the yield beta must equal one.

To adjust formula (2) for fully hedging interest rate risk when yield spread is not constant, we must adjust the formula to incorporate the yield beta as follows:

$$\text{hedge ratio} = \frac{D_P P_P}{D_{CTD} P_{CTD}}(\text{CTD conversion factor})(\text{yield beta})$$

The formula states that if the yield on the hedged bond or portfolio is more volatile than that of the CTD (i.e., $\beta > 1$), then more futures contracts will be needed to hedge the bond than would be the case if yield spreads were constant. If the yield on the bond was less volatile, fewer contracts would be needed.

Evaluating Hedging Effectiveness

The effectiveness of hedging strategies should be evaluated so that future hedging will be more effective. There are three basic sources of hedging error. There can be an error in the:

1. Forecast of the basis at the time the hedge is lifted.

2. Estimated durations.

3. Estimated yield beta.

Estimating the duration of bonds with options can be particularly complicated and should be estimated with care.

LOS 22.f: Explain the use of interest rate swaps and options to alter portfolio cash flows and exposure to interest rate risk.

In an **interest rate swap**, one party typically pays a fixed rate of interest and the other party pays a floating rate. The principal typically acts only as a reference value and is not exchanged. The floating interest rate is based on London Interbank Offered Rate (LIBOR), Treasury bills, or some other benchmark.

Swaps can be used to convert a floating rate loan or bond into a fixed rate, or vice versa. They can also be used to alter the duration of a portfolio. Receiving fixed in a swap increases duration while paying fixed reduces duration. The duration of the floating side is negligible. Swaps are used to hedge interest rate risk because they are lower in cost than futures and other contracts.

> *Professor's Note: This is an important concept that was taught at Levels I and II. A swap can be replicated with a pair of capital market transactions. You own one and are short the other. In this case, a floating rate and fixed rate bond.*

> *Just remember that to calculate the duration of a swap, add the duration of the instrument that replicates what you receive and subtract the duration of the instrument that replicates what you pay. Thus, for a receive fixed and pay floating, add the duration of the fixed rate bond and subtract the duration of the floating rate bond.*

> *Also, remember that floating rate bonds have little duration.*

For the Exam: There are options on bond prices and options on interest rates (e.g., caps and floors).

1. Remember bond prices and interest rates have an inverse relationship. Suppose an investor wants protection from rising interest rates (i.e., declining bond prices). Either buying a call on interest rates or a buying put on bond prices will work.

2. Read any question or case to determine if it is referring to rates or prices.

3. There are also options on Treasury bond futures contracts. The application is the same as an option on the price of the bond because futures contact prices move (roughly) parallel with the price of the underlying bond.

Know the concepts and work practice questions to solidify what is expected.

Bond options are also written on interest rate futures contracts, rather than on a debt security. In a call option written on a Treasury futures contract, the buyer has the right to buy the futures contract at the strike price. If exercised, the seller would take a short position in the futures contract. In a put option written on a Treasury futures contract, the buyer has the right to sell the futures contract at the strike price.

The duration of an option depends on the duration of the underlying contract, the option delta, and the leverage. The option delta measures the change in price of the option relative to the change in the underlying contract. The leverage refers to the price of the underlying contract relative to the price of the option. Out-of-the-money options will be cheaper and hence provide more leverage than in-the-money options. However, out-of-the-money options will be less sensitive to the underlying contract and hence have a lower delta.

Combining these factors, the duration of a bond option is computed as:

$$\text{option delta} \times \text{duration of the underlying} \times \frac{\text{price of underlying}}{\text{price of option}}$$

The delta and duration of a call will be positive (it provides the right to go long), and the delta and duration of a put will be negative (it provides the right to go short).

Options can be used to establish a **protective put** or a covered call. In the former, the purchase of a put protects a bond investment from increases in interest rates. If interest rates fall, the bond investment will increase in value and the manager will let the put expire worthless. The cost of the put will, however, reduce the manager's return.

In a **covered call**, the manager believes that the upside and downside on a bond owned are limited and sells a call to earn extra income. If, however, interest rates fall, the covered call will be exercised against the manager and reduce his return. If interest rates rise, the loss on the bond will be buffered by the income from the sale of the call but can still be substantial. If the manager wants downside protection, better choices would be to hedge the bond or use a protective put.

There are also interest rate **caps** and **floors**. A call on price pays the call owner if the underlying price rises above the strike price. A cap on interest rates pays the cap owner if interest rates rise above a strike rate, and a cap normally specifies several pay dates, not just final expiration. It is normally purchased by a floating rate payer to provide protection against rising rates. A put on price pays the put owner if the underlying price falls below the strike price. A floor on interest rates pays the floor owner if interest rates fall below a strike rate, and a floor normally specifies several pay dates, not just final expiration. It is normally purchased by a floating rate receiver to provide protection against falling rates. A collar is a combination of a cap and floor, with one long and one short, usually buy the cap and sell the floor.

For example, a bank borrows short-term to lend long-term. To protect against an increase in short-term rates, the bank will buy a cap. If interest rates rise above the strike rate, the cap will provide a payment to the bank that mitigates the increased cost of borrowing. If interest rates fall, the bank will let the cap expire worthless and benefit from the lower rate.

The bank may finance the purchase of the cap by selling a floor. If, however, short-term rates fall below the floor's strike rate, the bank will owe a payment on the floor and the sale of the floor will adversely affect the bank.

On the other hand, an insurance company may have a long-term liability in the form of an annuity contract that calls for fixed payments (i.e., payments at a fixed rate). The proceeds from the sale of the annuity policy might be invested in a floating rate note. The risk of short-term interest rates falling is mitigated by buying a floor. If short-term rates fall below the strike rate, the floor will provide a payment that mitigates the lower return to the insurance company. If short-term rates rise, the insurance company will let the floor expire worthless and benefit from the higher rate.

The insurance company may finance the purchase of the floor by selling a cap. If, however, short-term rates rise above the cap's strike rate, the sale of the cap will reduce the insurance company's profits.

MANAGING DEFAULT RISK, CREDIT SPREAD RISK, AND DOWNGRADE RISK WITH DERIVATIVES

LOS 22.g: Compare default risk, credit spread risk, and downgrade risk and demonstrate the use of credit derivative instruments to address each risk in the context of a fixed-income portfolio.

Types of Credit Risk

There are three principal credit-related risks that can be addressed with credit derivative instruments:

Default risk is the risk that the issuer will not meet the obligations of the issue (i.e., pay interest and/or principal when due). This risk is unique in the sense that it results from a potential action—failure to pay—of the debt issuer.

Credit spread risk is the risk of an increase in the yield spread on an asset. Yield spread is the asset's yield minus the relevant risk-free benchmark. This risk is a function of potential changes in the market's collective evaluation of credit quality, as reflected by the spread.

Downgrade risk is the possibility that the credit rating of an asset/issuer is downgraded by a major credit-rating organization, such as Moody's. If the credit rating is downgraded, the price of the bond will fall as its yield rises.

Types of Credit Derivative Instruments

Credit derivatives are designed to transfer risk between the buyer and seller of the instrument. They fall into three broad categories: (1) *credit options,* (2) *credit forwards,* and (3) *credit swaps.*

Credit options. Credit options provide protection from adverse price movements related to credit events or changes in the underlying reference asset's spread over a risk-free rate. When the payoff is based on the underlying asset's price, the option is known as a binary credit option. When the payoff is based on the underlying asset's yield spread, the option is known as a credit spread option.

Credit options written on an asset. A binary credit put option will provide protection only if a specific **credit event** occurs, and if the value of the underlying asset is less than the option strike price. A credit event is typically a default or an adverse change in credit rating. The option value (OV) or payoff is:

$$OV = \max\,[(strike - value),\ 0]$$

> **Example: Using binary credit options to address risk**
>
> A portfolio manager holds 1,000 bonds with a face value of $1 million and fears that a negative credit event may occur. The portfolio manager purchases binary credit puts that are triggered if the bond is downgraded with a strike price at par. Subsequently a credit downgrade occurs, and the bonds decline in value to $900. What is the option value?
>
> **Answer:**
>
> $$OV = \max\,[(\text{strike} - \text{value}),\, 0] = (\$1{,}000 - 900) = \$100$$
>
> If protection were purchased on the entire position, the overall payoff would be $100,000 (= $100 × 1,000), less the cost of purchasing the options. Remember, a positive payoff is contingent upon both a credit event occurring, and the option being in-the-money. A decline in value alone will not trigger a payoff.

Credit spread options. A credit spread call option will provide protection if the reference asset's spread (at option maturity) over the relevant risk-free benchmark increases beyond the strike spread. The increase in the spread beyond the strike spread (i.e., the option being in-the-money) constitutes an identifiable credit event, in and of itself. The OV or payoff is:

$$OV = \max\,[(\text{actual spread} - \text{strike spread}) \times \text{notional} \times \text{risk factor},\, 0]$$

> **Example: Using credit spread options to address risk**
>
> A portfolio manager holds 1,000 bonds with a face value of $1 million. The current spread over a comparable U.S. Treasury is 200 basis points. The portfolio manager purchases credit spread calls with a strike price of 250 basis points, notional principal of $1 million, and a risk factor of 10. At the option's maturity, the bond price is $900, implying a spread of 350 basis points. What is the option value?
>
> **Answer:**
>
> $$OV = \max\,[(0.035 - 0.025) \times \$1\text{ million} \times 10,\, 0] = \$100{,}000$$
>
> The size of the notional principal and the risk factor are calibrated to the level of protection desired by the portfolio manager. In this case, the level of protection was the same as that derived from the binary credit option.

A credit spread put option is also where the underlying is the credit spread, but it is used when the credit spread is predicted to decrease.

Credit forwards. Credit spread forwards are forward contracts wherein the payment at settlement is a function of the credit spread over the benchmark at the time the contract matures. The value (FV) or payoff to the buyer of a credit spread forward is:

FV = (spread at maturity – contract spread) × notional × risk factor

This is a zero sum game in that for one party to gain, the other party to the contract must lose. If the spread at maturity is less than the contract spread, the forward buyer (often the portfolio manager) will have to pay the forward seller.

Example: Using credit spread forwards to address risk

A portfolio manager holds 1,000 bonds with a face value of $1 million. The current spread over a comparable U.S. Treasury is 200 basis points. The portfolio manager purchases a credit spread forward with notional principal of $1 million, a contract spread of 250 basis points, and a risk factor of 10. At the contract's maturity, the bond price is $900, implying a spread of 350 basis points, what is the value of the forward?

Answer:

FV = [(0.035 – 0.025) × $1 million × 10] = $100,000

Once again, the size of the notional principal and the risk factor are calibrated to the level of protection desired by the portfolio manager. The resulting level of protection was the same as that derived in the previous option examples.

Credit swaps. Credit swaps describe a category of products in the swap family, all of which provide some form of credit risk transfer. Our focus here will be on **credit default swaps** which can be viewed as protection, or insurance, against default on an underlying credit instrument (called the reference asset or reference entity when referring to the issuer).

To obtain the requisite insurance, the protection buyer agrees to pay the protection seller a periodic fee in exchange for a commitment to stand behind an underlying bond or loan should its issuer experience a credit event, such as default. A credit default swap agreement will contain a list of credit events that apply to the agreement.

The terms of a credit swap are custom-designed to meet the needs of the counterparties. They can be cash settled or there can be physical delivery, which generally means the buyer of the swap delivers the reference asset to the counterparty for a cash payment.

Example: Using credit default swaps to address risk

The Rose Foundation enters into a 2-year credit default swap on a notional principal of $10 million of 5-year bonds issued by the Crescent Corporation. The swap specifies an annual premium of 55 basis points and cash settlement. Assume that the Crescent Corporation defaults at the end of the first year, and the bonds are trading at 60 cents to the dollar. **Describe** the cash flows associated with the credit default swap.

Answer:

The Rose Foundation would pay $55,000 (0.0055 × $10 million) at the beginning of the first year to the seller of the credit default swap. If Crescent defaults after one year, the Rose Foundation will receive a payment of $4,000,000 [(1 − 0.6) × $10 million)]. This payment compensates Rose for the decline in value of the bonds.

Note that in all cases, the rules for the calculation of the cash payouts for these credit derivative instruments must be agreed upon when the instrument is created. Of particular importance is the definition of what constitutes a credit event that will trigger payment and the size of the resulting payment. The buyer will only realize adequate protection from a specific type of credit risk if these parameters are correctly specified.

INTERNATIONAL BOND EXCESS RETURNS

LOS 22.h: Explain the potential sources of excess return for an international bond portfolio.

The phrase *excess return* implies active management. That is, instead of passively overseeing the portfolio, the manager of a bond portfolio actively seeks out sources of additional return beyond that merely compensating for the level of risk. In this LOS, we discuss six of the potential sources of excess return on international bonds: (1) market selection, (2) currency selection, (3) duration management, (4) sector selection, (5) credit analysis, and (6) markets outside the benchmark.

Market selection involves selecting appropriate national bond markets. The manager must determine which bond markets offer the best overall opportunities for value enhancement.

Currency selection. The manager must determine the amount of active currency management versus the amount of currency hedging he will employ. The manager should remain unhedged or employ hedging strategies to capture value only if she feels confident in her ability to forecast interest rate changes and their resulting impact on exchange rates. Due to the complexities and required expertise, currency management is often treated as a separately managed function.

Duration management. Once the manager has determined what sectors (i.e., countries) will be held, she must determine the optimal maturities. That is, anticipating shifts or twists, the manager will often utilize segments of the yield curve to add value. Limited maturity offerings in some markets can be overcome by employing fixed-income derivatives.

Sector selection. This is directly analogous to domestic bond portfolio management. Due to increasing ranges of maturities, ratings, and bond types (e.g., corporate, government), the international bond portfolio manager is now able to add value through credit analysis of entire sectors. (Note that sector selection refers to entire sectors, not individual securities.)

Credit analysis refers to recognizing value-added opportunities through credit analysis of individual securities.

Markets outside the benchmark. Large foreign bond indices are usually composed of sovereign (government) issues. With the increasing availability of corporate issues, the manager may try to add value through enhanced indexing by adding corporates to an indexed foreign bond portfolio.

INTERNATIONAL BOND DURATIONS

LOS 22.i: Evaluate 1) the change in value for a foreign bond when domestic interest rates change and 2) the bond's contribution to duration in a domestic portfolio, given the duration of the foreign bond and the country beta.

Duration is based on the assumption of parallel yield curve shifts. While the assumption is unrealistic, duration-based analysis still produces useful results in *domestic-only* bond portfolios because rate changes across the bonds in the portfolio tend to be similar. When foreign bonds are added to the portfolio, the results deteriorate. Foreign bond interest rates and domestic rates are not likely to move by approximately the same amount, but there may be a stable relationship between the movement.

Yield beta measures the relationship between change in one set of rates (foreign) and another set (domestic). The change in value of the foreign bond will depend on its duration and change in foreign rates. But how that foreign bond changes in value when the investor's domestic rates change will also need to consider the yield beta relationship.

$$\Delta \text{yield}_{\text{foreign}} = \beta(\Delta \text{yield}_{\text{domestic}}) + e$$

Example: Applying the country beta

Suppose the country (yield) beta for Japan is 0.45 for a British investor and the duration of a Japanese bond is 6.0. **Estimate** the change in the price of the Japanese bond given a 100 bps change in the domestic interest rate of the British investor.

Answer:

For a 100 bps change in the domestic rate, the Japanese bond's yield will change (0.45) (100 bp) = 45 bps. Multiplying the estimated change in the Japanese rate by the Japanese bond's duration gives the estimated change in the Japanese bond's price.

$$\%\Delta_{\text{price}} = \text{duration} \times \Delta y \times \beta_{\text{yield}}$$

$$\%\Delta_{\text{price}} = 6 \times (0.01 \times 0.45) = 0.027 = 2.7\%$$

Duration Contribution

The duration of a foreign bond must also be adjusted when we calculate its *contribution* to the portfolio duration. Remember that the contribution of a domestic bond to the duration of a purely domestic portfolio is the bond's weight in the portfolio multiplied by its duration. Likewise, the duration contribution for a foreign bond to a portfolio is its *standardized* duration multiplied by its weight in the portfolio.

Example: Duration contribution of a foreign bond

The duration of an Australian bond is 6.0 and the country beta is 1.15. A U.S. portfolio manager has $50,000 in the Australian bond in an otherwise domestic portfolio with a total value of $1,000,000. **Calculate** the Australian bond's duration contribution to the portfolio.

Answer:

First, the bond's *standardized* duration can be estimated as $6 \times 1.15 = 6.90$. Multiplying the bond's *standardized* duration of 6.90 by its weight in the portfolio (5%) gives the bond's contribution to portfolio duration:

$$\text{duration contribution} = \text{weight} \times \text{duration}$$
$$= 0.05 \times 6.90 = 0.35$$

As with a purely domestic portfolio, the duration of a portfolio containing both domestic and foreign bonds can be estimated as the *sum* of the individual bond duration contributions.

Example: Portfolio duration

Assume you have a portfolio consisting of two bonds. 75% of the portfolio is in a U.S. dollar-denominated bond with a duration of 5.0. 25% of the portfolio is in a foreign bond with a duration of 8.0 and a country beta of 1.2. **Compute** the duration of this portfolio from a U.S. perspective.

Answer:

contribution of domestic bond	= 0.75 × 5	= 3.75
contribution of foreign bond	= 0.25 × 8 × 1.2	= 2.40
portfolio duration	= 3.75 + 2.4	= 6.15

THE HEDGING DECISION

LOS 22.j: Recommend and justify whether to hedge or not hedge currency risk in an international bond investment.

A domestic (d) investor in a foreign (f) bond (or any other asset) is exposed to both change in value of the bond (or asset) measured in the foreign currency and change in value of the foreign currency. The investor can accept the risk of the foreign currency and earn its change in value from initial spot exchange rate (S_0) to ending spot exchange rate (S_T). Alternatively, the investor can hedge the foreign currency risk by selling the foreign currency forward at f_0. Hedging does not mean the currency return is 0. The hedged currency return is the change from S_0 to f_0 (i.e., the forward premium or discount). (Hedging is often not perfect but that is an issue discussed elsewhere.)

The relationship in free markets between S_0 and f_0 is determined by interest rate parity (IRP). IRP simplifies and dictates the forward premium or discount is approximately the difference in the initial periodic interest rates for d and f. As a review, the formulas are shown here:

Interest Rate Parity

$$F = S_0 \left(\frac{1 + c_d}{1 + c_f} \right)$$

where:
F = the forward exchange rate (domestic per foreign)
S_0 = the current spot exchange rate (domestic per foreign)
c_d = the domestic short-term rate
c_f = the foreign short-term rate

The *approximate* forward premium or discount is the difference in short-term rates:

$$f_{d,f} = \frac{(F - S_0)}{S_0} \approx c_d - c_f$$

This means that:

- If the foreign rate is higher than the investor's domestic rate, the foreign currency will trade at a forward discount and selling the foreign currency forward to hedge the currency risk will earn a negative currency return.
- If the foreign rate is lower than the investor's domestic rate, the foreign currency will trade at a forward premium and selling the foreign currency forward to hedge the currency risk will earn a positive currency return.

Example: Calculating a forward differential

Suppose that the U.S. dollar is trading at a spot rate of $1.50 per £1.00, and 1-year U.S. dollar Eurocurrency deposits are yielding 6.50%, while 1-year pound sterling Eurocurrency deposits are yielding 5.75%. **Calculate** the equilibrium 1-year forward rate and the pound sterling forward premium or discount.

Answer:

We use IRP to determine the implied forward exchange rate:

$$F = S_0 \left(\frac{1 + c_d}{1 + c_f} \right) = 1.50 \left(\frac{1.065}{1.0575} \right) = 1.51064 \, \text{USD} / \text{GBP}$$

Once the implied forward exchange rate is calculated, we can calculate the premium or discount using IRP. We can also approximate the premium or discount as the interest rate differential between the two countries.

$$f_{d,f} = \frac{F - S_0}{S_0} = \frac{1.51064 - 1.50}{1.50} = 0.71\%$$

or

$$f_{d,f} \approx c_d - c_f = 6.5 - 5.75 \approx 0.75\% \text{ (approximation)}$$

Currency Hedging Techniques

For the Exam: This material is important, highly testable, and simpler than it looks. It returns to an earlier topic of a domestic investor who invests in foreign securities, thus taking on foreign currency risk. The focus here is calculating the contribution of currency to return and approaches to hedging. As is common in the CFA curriculum, the notation and terminology can differ from other sections. The term LMR will again be used as the return of the investment denominated in the foreign currency of the investment and LCR as the percent change in value of the foreign currency. Some important assumptions:

- The investor's precise return is (1 + LCR) (1 + LMR) − 1, but adding LCR and LMR is a close approximation and makes the underlying issues more clear. The focus here is the additive approximation.
- The material has nothing to do with fixed income per se. The LMR could be the return on a bond, stock, or building, for example. This is a discussion of hedging currency and the return created by hedging currency. Other related issues will be explored in other study sessions.
- Even perfect currency hedging does not lock in zero LCR but instead locks in the initial basis, the difference in initial spot and forward price. Don't ever forget this.
- When IRP holds, arbitrage dictates that initial basis is determined by the relative interest rates of the two currencies and the hedge (LCR) will earn a return equal to adding the interest rate of the currency bought forward and losing the interest rate of the currency sold forward. (This is the simple addition approximation which is the focus of this section).

The exam is not going to test derivation so what you should conclude and know from this coming material is:

- Invest in a foreign asset, don't hedge, and earn LMR + LCR
- Invest in a foreign asset and (forward) hedge the currency. This means invest in the foreign asset and sell the foreign currency forward. Earn the LMR + the investor's domestic interest rate − the foreign currency interest rate because the LCR hedged will equal investor's domestic interest rate − the foreign currency interest rate. Generally, it is impossible to construct a perfect hedge, as you would need to know in advance the ending value of the foreign currency asset to know how much currency to sell forward. On the exam you would sell beginning value unless directed otherwise.
- This means that when selecting among foreign markets, the market with the highest MRP (LMR − that market's risk-free rate) will end up providing the best currency hedged return.
- Invest in a foreign asset and proxy hedge the currency. This means invest in the foreign asset and sell a third currency (Z) forward. This is riskier and depends on the foreign currency and Z being highly correlated. It might be done if the foreign currency is difficult to hedge directly.
- Invest in a foreign asset and cross hedge the currency. This means invest in the foreign asset and sell the foreign currency forward to buy a different currency (X) forward. This is taking active risk based on an expectation X will be the better performing currency.

The approaches to hedging the currency risk in an international bond investment are: (1) the *forward hedge*, (2) the *proxy hedge*, and (3) the *cross hedge*.

The forward hedge. The forward hedge is used to eliminate (most of) the currency risk. Utilizing a forward hedge assumes forward contracts are available and actively traded on the foreign currency in terms of the domestic currency. If so, the manager enters a forward contract to sell the foreign currency at the current forward rate.

The proxy hedge. In a proxy hedge, the manager enters a forward contract between the *domestic currency and a second foreign currency* that is correlated with the first foreign currency (i.e., the currency in which the bond is denominated). Gains or losses on the forward contract are expected to at least partially offset losses or gains in the domestic return on the bond. Proxy hedges are utilized when forward contracts on the first foreign currency are not actively traded or hedging the first foreign currency is relatively expensive.

Notice that in currency hedging, the proxy hedge is what we would usually refer to as a *cross hedge* in other financial transactions. In other words, the manager can't construct a hedge in the long asset, so he hedges using another, correlated asset.

The cross hedge. In a currency cross hedge, the manager enters into a contract to deliver the original foreign currency (i.e., the currency of the bond) for a third currency. Again, it is hoped that gains or losses on the forward contract will at least partially offset losses or gains in the domestic return on the bond. In other words, the manager takes steps to eliminate the currency risk of the bond by replacing it with the risk of another currency. The currency cross hedge, therefore, is a means of *changing* the risk exposure rather than eliminating it.

Foreign Bond Returns

The return on an investment in a foreign bond can be broken down into its nominal local return and the currency return implied by the forward currency differential:

$$R_b \approx R_l + R_c$$

where:
R_b = the domestic return on the foreign bond
R_l = the local return on the foreign bond (i.e., in its local currency)
R_c = the expected (by the market) currency return; the forward premium or discount

We can decompose the relationship using IRP, which demonstrates that the forward premium or discount depends upon the interest rate differential:

$$R_b = R_l + R_c \Rightarrow \text{Since } R_c \approx i_d - i_f$$

$$R_b = R_l + R_c \approx R_l + (i_d - i_f) \Rightarrow i_d + (R_l - i_f)$$

So, as shown by decomposing the return, as long as the bonds are similar in maturity and other risk characteristics, choosing between them is determined solely by the bond that offers the greatest excess return denominated in its local currency.

The Hedging Decision

Professor's Note: An important implication of this is that the ranking of returns on fully hedged international investments depends only on the individual investment's risk premiums. That is, when comparing fully hedged strategies, the investment that offers the highest excess return over the risk-free rate in its local currency will provide the highest fully hedged return. Remember this material is about hedging the currency and the LCR could be for a bond, stock, or building, and so forth.

We explore the hedging decision by first determining the optimal bond to purchase and then determining whether to hedge or not.

Example: Selecting the right international bond

Using only the following data on two foreign bonds with the same risk characteristics (e.g., maturity, credit risk), **determine** which bond should be purchased, if the currency risk of either can be fully hedged with a forward contract.

Country	Nominal Return	Risk-Free Rate
i	4.75%	3.25%
j	5.25%	3.80%

Answer:

Because their maturities and other risk characteristics are similar and an investment in either can be hedged using a forward contract, we can determine the better bond to purchase by calculating their excess returns:

Bond i: 4.75% – 3.25% = 1.50%

Bond j: 5.25% – 3.80% = 1.45%

Bond i offers the higher excess return, so given the ability to fully hedge, the manager should select Bond i.

Example: To hedge or not to hedge

A U.S. manager is considering a foreign bond. The U.S. risk-free rate (i.e., the domestic rate) is 4% and the risk-free rate in the foreign country (i.e., the local rate) is 4.8%. The manager expects the dollar to appreciate only 0.4% over the expected holding period. Based on this information and assuming the ability to hedge with forward contracts, **determine** whether the manager should hedge the position or leave it unhedged.

Answer:

Start by calculating the forward differential expected by the market for the foreign currency:

$$f \approx i_d - i_f = 4.0\% - 4.8\% = -0.8\%$$

This means that a forward currency hedge would lock in 0.8% depreciation in the foreign currency.

Now compare this to what the manager thinks will happen to the foreign currency. The manager expects the USD to appreciate 0.4%, which is equivalent to saying the manager expects the foreign currency to depreciate approximately 0.4%. Comparing the 0.8% loss that will occur on a hedge of the foreign currency with the manager's expectation that unhedged the loss will only be 0.4%, it is better to remain unhedged on the currency.

Notice the manager is still ahead. Staying in the United States, the return would be only 4.0%. Investing in the foreign market will earn 4.8% and an expected currency loss of 0.4%, for a total return of approximately 4.4%.

Example: To hedge or not to hedge (cont.)

Continue to assume the U.S. risk-free rate is 4% and the risk-free rate in the foreign country is 4.8%, but the manager expects the dollar to appreciate 1.0%, which is equivalent to saying the foreign currency will depreciate approximately 1% over the expected holding period. Based only on this information, **determine** whether the manager should hedge the position or leave it unhedged.

Answer:

The forward market hedge would continue to lock in a 0.8% loss on the foreign currency. However, the manager now expects the foreign currency to fall approximately 1.0%. Hedging for a loss of 0.8% is now preferable. The manager should sell the foreign currency forward.

Notice that in this case, it turns out the manager would do just as well to stay in the U.S. investment earning 4.0%. The foreign investment will earn 4.8% but lose 0.8% on the currency hedge for a total return of 4.0% as well.

BREAKEVEN SPREAD ANALYSIS

LOS 22.k: Describe how breakeven spread analysis can be used to evaluate the risk in seeking yield advantages across international bond markets.

Breakeven spread is the change in spread that would make the return on two bonds equal. For any other change in spread, one of the bonds will have superior return. Calculating breakeven requires:

- Making assumptions to calculate the initial return difference between the two bonds.
- Using duration to calculate the change in spread between the two bonds that will produce a relative change in price that will offset the initial return difference.

A typical analysis begins with a strategy expected to produce a higher return and calculating the *spread widening* that will offset that return advantage. If the assumptions do not specify which bond will change in price and the two bond durations are different, the higher duration is used. Using the higher duration produces a smaller spread widening and is considered the more conservative assumption.

> **Example: Breakeven analysis**
>
> A portfolio manager is performing a breakeven analysis to determine the shift in interest rates that would generate a capital loss sufficient to eliminate the yield advantage of the foreign bond. **Determine** the breakeven change in the yield of the foreign bond if the intended holding period is three months.
>
> | Bond | Nominal Return | Duration |
> |------|----------------|----------|
> | i (domestic) | 4.75% | 4.5 |
> | j (foreign) | 5.25% | 6.3 |
>
> **Answer:**
>
> The foreign bond is currently at an annual yield advantage of 50 bps, which equates to a quarterly advantage of 12.5 bps.
>
> As long as the foreign bond price does not decline relative to the domestic bond price by more than 12.5 bp, the foreign bond will provide the higher realized return. The basic duration and price relationship can be used to find the yield spread change at which point the higher yield bond is no longer superior. A complication is that the two bonds have different durations, and the spread change can occur if either the higher yield bond's yield increases (and its price declines 12.5 bp) or the lower yield bond's yield declines (and its price increases 12.5 bp). The convention is to use the higher of the two durations to ensure the higher yield bond ends up with the superior realized return.

Simply insert the relative price loss for the higher yield bond that is tolerable and solve for spread change:

% change in relative price = $-D_S \, \Delta S$

-12.5 bp $= -6.3 \, \Delta S$

$\Delta S = 1.98$ bp increase in spread

Alternatively:

$\Delta S = \%$ change in relative price $/ -D_S$

-12.5 bp $/ -6.3 = \Delta S$

$\Delta S = 1.98$ bp increase in spread

The conclusion is that the yield on the foreign bond would have to increase a little under 2 bps over the holding period for the decrease in its price (i.e., the capital loss) to completely wipe out its yield advantage. The manager can compare this breakeven event against her interest rate expectations and currency expectations to assess whether the yield advantage warrants investment in the foreign bond.

Professor's Note: This section has described one specific application of breakeven analysis. More generally, breakeven starts with an expected difference in return between two investments and then examines one factor that could change. The question is how much could that factor change before it overwhelms the initial difference in return. You will probably find practice questions that look at this more general approach.

EMERGING MARKET DEBT

LOS 22.l: Discuss the advantages and risks of investing in emerging market debt.

In actively managing a fixed-income portfolio, managers often utilize a **core-plus approach**. In a core-plus approach, the manager holds a *core* of investment grade debt and then invests in bonds perceived to add the potential for generating added return. Emerging market debt (EMD) is frequently utilized to add value in a core-plus strategy.

Advantages of investing in EMD include:

- Generally provides a diversification benefit.
- Increased quality in emerging market sovereign bonds. In addition, emerging market governments can implement fiscal and/or monetary policies to offset potentially negative events and they have access to major worldwide lenders (e.g., World Bank, International Monetary Fund).
- Increased resiliency; the ability to recover from value-siphoning events. When EMD markets have been hit by some event, they tend to bounce back offering the potential for high returns.
- An undiversified index, like the major EMD index [i.e., the Emerging Markets Bond Index Plus (EMBI+)], offers return-enhancing potential.

Risks associated with EMD include:

- Unlike emerging market governments, emerging market corporations do not have the tools available to help offset negative events.
- EMD returns can be highly volatile with negatively skewed distributions.
- A lack of transparency and regulations gives emerging market sovereign debt higher credit risk than sovereign debt in developed markets.
- Under-developed legal systems that do not protect against actions taken by governments. For example, there is little protection provided (i.e., lack of seniority protection) for prior debt holders when emerging market governments add to their debt.
- A lack of standardized covenants, which forces managers to carefully study each issue.
- Political risk (a.k.a. geopolitical risk).
  - Political instability.
  - Changes in taxation or other regulations.
  - International investors may not be able to convert the local currency to their domestic currency, due to restrictions imposed by emerging market governments.
  - Relaxed regulations on bankruptcy that serve to increase its likelihood.
  - Imposed changes in the exchange rate (e.g., pegging).
- Lack of diversification within the EMBI+ index, which is concentrated in Latin American debt (e.g., Brazil, Mexico).

SELECTING A FIXED-INCOME MANAGER

LOS 22.m: Discuss the criteria for selecting a fixed-income manager.

The due diligence required to identify managers who can consistently generate superior returns (i.e., positive alpha), entails thoroughly analyzing the managers' organization and personnel as well as trading practices. Because the vast majority of the typical fixed-income portfolio is managed actively, the focus should be on active managers. Past performance, however, should not be used as an indicator of future success.

Criteria that should be utilized in determining the *optimal mix* of active managers *include style analysis, selection bets, investment processes,* and *alpha correlations.*

Style analysis. The majority of active returns can be explained by the managers' selected style. The primary concerns associated with researching the managers' styles include not only the styles employed but any additional risk exposures due to style.

Selection bets. Selection bets include credit spread analysis (i.e., which sectors or securities will experience spread changes) and the identification of over- and undervalued securities. By decomposing the manager's excess returns, the sponsor can determine the manager's ability to generate superior returns from selection bets.

Investment processes. This step includes investigating the total investment processes of the managers. What type of research is performed? How is alpha attained? Who makes decisions and how are they made (e.g., committee, individual)? This step typically entails interviewing several members of the organization.

Alpha correlations. Alphas should also be *diversified*. That is, if the alphas of the various managers are highly correlated, not only will there be significant volatility in the overall alpha, but the alphas will tend to be all positive or negative at the same time. The sponsor should attempt to find the mix of active managers that optimizes the average alpha with the alpha volatility.

You may have noticed that the process for determining the best mix of fixed-income active managers is much the same as that for selecting the best mix of equity portfolio managers. The one consideration that distinguishes the two is the need for a low-fee strategy. That is, fees are an important consideration in selecting any active manager, but the ratio of fees to alpha is usually higher for fixed-income managers.

KEY CONCEPTS

LOS 22.a

Leverage is only beneficial when the strategy earns a return greater than the cost of borrowing.

Although leverage can increase returns, it also has a downside. If the strategy return falls below the cost of borrowing, the loss to investors will be increased. So leverage magnifies both good and bad outcomes.

leveraged return: $R_p = R_i + [(B/E) \times (R_i - c)]$

LOS 22.b

To increase the leverage of their portfolios, portfolio managers sometimes borrow funds on a short-term basis using repurchase agreements. In a **repurchase agreement** (or **repo**), the borrower (seller of the security) agrees to repurchase it from the buyer on an agreed-upon date at an agreed-upon price (repurchase price). Although it is legally a sale and subsequent purchase of securities, a repurchase agreement is essentially a collateralized loan, where the difference between the sale and repurchase prices is the interest on the loan. The rate of interest on the repo is referred to as the *repo rate*.

The lender in a repurchase agreement is exposed to credit risk if the collateral remains in the borrower's custody. For instance, the borrower could sell the collateral, fraudulently use it as collateral for another loan, or go bankrupt.

The repo rate decreases as the credit risk decreases, as the quality of the collateral increases, as the term of the repo decreases, if collateral is physically delivered, if the availability of the collateral is limited, and as the federal funds rate decreases.

LOS 22.c

Standard deviation measures the dispersion of returns around the mean.

Drawbacks of Standard Deviation and Variance
• Bond returns are often not normally distributed around the mean.
• The number of inputs (e.g., variances and covariances) increases significantly with larger portfolios.
• Obtaining estimates for each of these inputs is problematic.

Semivariance measures the dispersion of returns below a target return.

Drawbacks of Semivariance
• It is difficult to compute for a large bond portfolio.
• If investment returns are symmetric, the semivariance yields the same rankings as the variance and the variance is better understood.
• If investment returns are not symmetric, it can be quite difficult to forecast downside risk and the semivariance may not be a good indicator of future risk.
• Because the semivariance is estimated with only half the distribution, it is estimated with less accuracy.

Shortfall risk measures the *probability* that the actual return or value will be less than the target return or value.

Drawback of Shortfall Risk
- Shortfall risk does not consider the impact of outliers so the magnitude (dollar amount) of the shortfall below the target return is ignored.

The value at risk (VAR) provides the probability of a return less than a given amount over a specific time period.

Drawback of VAR
- VAR does not provide the magnitude of losses that exceed that specified by VAR.

LOS 22.d

The main advantages to using futures over cash market instruments are that they are more liquid, less expensive, and make short positions more readily obtainable because the contracts can be more easily shorted.

The general rules for using futures contracts to control interest rate risk are:
- Long futures position → increase in duration.
- Short futures position → decrease in duration.

LOS 22.e

To increase duration, buy contracts. To decrease duration, sell contracts. The number of contracts can be calculated as:

$$\text{number of contracts} = \frac{(D_T - D_P)P_P}{D_{CTD}P_{CTD}}\left(\text{CTD conversion factor}\right)$$

Dollar duration (DD) can also be used:

$$\text{number of contracts} = \frac{DD_T - DD_P}{DD_f}$$

Remember, if a yield beta is given, include it as a multiplication.

LOS 22.f

In volatile interest rate environments, floating rate assets and liabilities are subject to cash flow risk, and fixed rate assets and liabilities are subject to market value risk. Anticipating rising interest rates the holder of a fixed-rate asset might want to swap into a floating rate to increase cash received as well as minimize the decline in market value. The holder of a floating rate liability would want to swap into a fixed rate to minimize the increase in cash paid and to maximize the decline in market value. Interest rate put options (floors) are used to protect floating rate assets against falling interest rates. Interest rate calls (caps) are used to protect floating rate liabilities against rising interest rates. An option on a swap (i.e., a swaption) provides the holder the option to enter into a swap before, during, or after a change in interest rates.

$$\text{duration of an option} = \text{option delta} \times \text{duration of the underlying} \times \frac{\text{price of the underlying}}{\text{price of the option}}$$

LOS 22.g

Default risk is the risk that the issuer will not make timely payments of principal and/or interest. This risk can be effectively hedged through the use of credit swaps and credit options.

Credit spread risk is the risk that the market's collective assessment of an issue's credit quality will change, resulting in an increase in the yield spread. This risk can be managed with credit options and credit forwards.

Downgrade risk reflects the possibility that the credit rating of an asset/issuer will be downgraded by a major credit-rating organization. This risk can be managed through the use of credit swaps and credit options.

When the payoff is based on the underlying asset's price, the option is known as a **binary credit option**. When the payoff is based on the underlying asset's yield spread, the option is known as a **credit spread option**.

A **binary credit put option** will provide protection if a specific **credit event** occurs, and if the value of the underlying asset is less than the option strike price. A credit event is typically a default or an adverse change in credit rating. The option value (OV) is:

$$OV = \max\,[(\text{strike} - \text{value}),\, 0]$$

A **credit spread call option** will provide protection if the reference asset's spread over the relevant risk-free benchmark increases beyond the strike spread. The option value (OV) is:

$$OV = \max\,[(\text{actual spread} - \text{strike spread}) \times \text{notional} \times \text{risk factor},\, 0]$$

Credit spread forwards are forward contracts wherein the payment at settlement is a function of the credit spread over the benchmark at the time the contract matures. The value (FV) or payoff to the buyer of a credit spread forward is:

$$FV = (\text{spread at maturity} - \text{contract spread}) \times \text{notional} \times \text{risk factor}$$

This is a zero sum game in that for one party to gain, the other party to the contract must lose. If the spread at maturity is less than the contract spread, the forward buyer (often the portfolio manager) will have to pay the forward seller.

Credit default swaps can be viewed as protection against default on an underlying credit instrument (called the reference asset or reference entity when referring to the issuer).

LOS 22.h

Market selection. The manager must determine which bond markets offer the best overall opportunities for value enhancement.

Currency selection. The manager must determine the amount of active currency management versus the amount of currency hedging he will employ.

Duration management. The manager must determine the optimal maturities. Anticipating shifts or twists, the manager will often utilize segments of the yield curve to add value.

Sector selection. Adding value through credit analysis of entire sectors.

Credit analysis refers to recognizing value-added opportunities through credit analysis of individual securities.

Markets outside the benchmark. The manager may try to add value through enhanced indexing by adding bonds not in the index.

LOS 22.i
The relationship (i.e., correlation) between yields on the domestic and foreign bonds can be determined with:

$$\text{yield}_{\text{foreign}} = \beta(\text{yield}_{\text{domestic}}) + e$$

In the regression, β is the *country beta* or *yield beta*, which measures the sensitivity of the yield on the foreign bond to changes in the yield on the domestic bond. Multiplying the country beta times the change in the domestic rate gives the manager the estimated change in the foreign yield. Then, multiplying the change in the foreign yield by the bond's duration gives the estimated change in the foreign bond's price.

The duration contribution for a foreign bond to a portfolio is its duration multiplied by its weight in the portfolio and the country beta.

LOS 22.j
We can *approximate* the forward premium or discount (i.e., the *currency differential*) as the difference in short-term rates:

$$f_{d,f} = \frac{(F - S_0)}{S_0} \approx c_d - c_f$$

The decision of whether or not to hedge a foreign bond is based upon interest rate parity and the manager's expectations for the foreign currency. The difference between the domestic and foreign risk-free interest rates reflects interest rate parity. If the manager expects the foreign currency to appreciate more or depreciate less than interest rate parity implies, the position should not be hedged.

LOS 22.k
Note that in performing a breakeven analysis, the manager must assume a *set time horizon* and measure the yield change in the bond with the *higher duration*.

The breakeven spread tells us by how much the spread between the yields of two bonds will have to widen to produce a loss in relative price performance that will offset the initial yield advantage of the higher yield bond.

% change in relative price = $-D_S \Delta S$, and solve ΔS

or

ΔS = % change in relative price / $-D_S$

LOS 22.l

Advantages of investing in emerging market debt (EMD) include:

- Increased quality in emerging market sovereign bonds.
- Increased resiliency; the ability to recover from value-siphoning events.
- Lack of diversification in the major EMD index offers return-enhancing potential.

Risks associated with EMD include:

- Unlike emerging market governments, emerging market corporations do not have the tools available to help offset negative events.
- Highly volatile returns with negatively skewed distributions.
- A lack of transparency and regulations.
- Underdeveloped legal systems that do not protect against actions taken by governments.
- A lack of standardized covenants.
- Political risk.

LOS 22.m

Style analysis. The majority of active returns can be explained by the manager's selected style.

Selection bets. Selection bets include credit spread analysis (i.e., which sectors or securities will experience spread changes) and the identification of over- and undervalued securities.

Investment processes. This step includes investigating the total investment processes of the managers.

Alpha correlations. Alphas should also be diversified. That is, if the alphas of the various managers are highly correlated, not only will there be significant volatility in the overall alpha, but the alphas will tend to be all positive or negative at the same time.

CONCEPT CHECKERS

1. A portfolio manager has a portfolio worth $160 million, $40 million of which is his own funds and $120 million is borrowed. If the return on the invested funds is 7%, and the cost of borrowed funds is 4%, the return on the portfolio is *closest* to:
    A. 11.0%.
    B. 12.0%.
    C. 16.0%.

2. A manager's portfolio is worth $160 million, $40 million of which is his own funds and $120 million of which is borrowed. If the duration of the invested funds is 4.2, and the duration of borrowed funds is 0.8, the duration of the equity invested is *closest* to:
    A. 3.6.
    B. 5.0.
    C. 14.4.

3. Which of the responses *best* describes the relationship between the repo rate and the term of the repo and delivery of the security? Lower repo rates are associated with:

	Term of the repo	Delivery of the security
A.	Intermediate	Held by borrower's bank
B.	Longer	No delivery
C.	Shorter	Physically delivered

4. If the target return for AA Bond Investors, Inc. is 15% and 15 out of 60 return observations fall *below* the target return percentage, then shortfall risk is:
    A. 15%.
    B. 20%.
    C. 25%.

5. Which of the following downside risk measures takes into consideration the effects of outliers below the target return?
    A. Value at risk.
    B. Shortfall risk.
    C. Semivariance.

6. Which of the following is *least likely* to be considered a characteristic of futures, relative to the underlying cash market?
    A. More liquid.
    B. Harder to short.
    C. Less expensive.

7. The effective duration of the futures contract is 3.25. The futures contract has a face value of $100,000 and is currently trading at 102.5. What is the expected change in value for a 75 basis point increase in interest rates?
    A. –$2,437.50.
    B. –$2,498.44.
    C. –$3,250.00.

8. An investor's portfolio has a duration of 10.0 and a market value of £15,550,000. His target duration is 14.47. The relevant pound sterling futures contract has a price of £23,519, a duration of 15 with a conversion factor of 0.97. To achieve his target duration, he should:
   A. sell 191 contracts.
   B. sell 197 contracts.
   C. buy 191 contracts.

9. To hedge a bond portfolio against an increase in interest rates, which of the following options positions will be the *best* choice to hedge the downside risk while leaving as much of the upside potential intact?
   A. A collar.
   B. Long puts.
   C. Long calls.

10. There are three principal credit-related risks to which a portfolio manager is exposed and can be addressed with the appropriate derivative securities. For example, a manager owns Bond Q, and is concerned that the firm's management is about to take an action that will affect the value of Bond Q adversely. This describes:
   A. downgrade risk, and this can be most effectively managed with credit spread options or credit forward contracts.
   B. spread risk, and this can be most effectively managed with credit spread options or swaps.
   C. default risk, and this can be most effectively managed with binary credit options or swaps.

11. There are three principal credit-related risks to which a portfolio manager is exposed and can be addressed with the appropriate derivative securities. For example, a manager owns Bond R, and is concerned that market forces may result in a change that will affect the value of Bond R adversely. This describes:
   A. downgrade risk, and this can be most effectively managed with credit binary options or credit forward contracts.
   B. spread risk, and this can be most effectively managed with credit spread options or credit forward contracts.
   C. default risk, and this can be most effectively managed with credit spread options or swaps.

12. There are three principal credit-related risks to which a portfolio manager is exposed and can be addressed with the appropriate derivative securities. For example, a manager owns Bond S, and is concerned that the actions of a third party may result in a change that will affect the value of Bond S adversely. This describes:
   A. downgrade risk, and this can be most effectively managed with binary credit options or swaps.
   B. spread risk, and this can be most effectively managed with credit spread options or swaps.
   C. default risk, and this can be most effectively managed with binary credit options or credit spread options.

13. When considering potential sources of excess return for an international bond portfolio manager, which of the following statements is *most correct*?
    A. Market selection refers to nations in which investments are to occur, currency selection refers to whether or not currency exposures are actively managed or hedged, and sector selection refers to industries, ratings categories, maturity ranges, et cetera.
    B. Sector selection refers to nations in which investments are to occur, currency selection refers to whether or not currency exposures are actively managed or hedged, and market selection refers to industries, ratings categories, maturity ranges, et cetera.
    C. Currency selection refers to nations in which investments are to occur, and sector selection refers to industries, ratings categories, maturity ranges, et cetera.

14. A Canadian bond represents 10% of an international bond portfolio. It has a duration of 7 and a yield beta of 1.2. If domestic interest rates change by 50 basis points, what is the estimated percentage price change for the bond, and what is its duration contribution to the portfolio?

	Price change	Duration contribution
A.	3.5%	0.70
B.	4.2%	0.84
C.	8.4%	0.42

15. An international bond portfolio manager is considering two bonds for investment. The bonds are comparable in terms of risk characteristics, and the following information applies:

Country	Nominal Return	Risk-Free Rate	Exchange Rate #/D
A	9.75%	8.50%	3.00
B	4.75%	3.25%	5.00
Domestic	n/a	5.75	n/a

    You expect Currency A to depreciate against the domestic currency by 2.6%, and you expect Currency B to appreciate against the domestic currency by 2.6%. On a fully hedged basis, which bond should be selected, and, assuming that this bond is selected, should the bond's currency exposure be hedged?
    A. Bond A; hedge.
    B. Bond A; do not hedge.
    C. Bond B; do not hedge.

16. A portfolio manager with investable funds is considering two alternatives:

Bond	Nominal Yield	Duration
Australian Bond	7.65%	6.5
New Zealand Bond	6.85%	5.3

If the target holding period is six months, by how much would either of the yields on these two bonds have to change to offset the current yield advantage of the Australian Bond?
A. Australian increase by 6 bp, New Zealand decrease by 8 bp.
B. Australian decrease by 6 bp, New Zealand increase by 8 bp.
C. Australian increase by 12 bp, New Zealand decrease by 15 bp.

17. From the perspective of an international bond portfolio manager, which of the following is the *least likely* rationale for an allocation to emerging market debt (EMD) securities?
A. EMD credit quality has been improving.
B. Holding EMD issues results in reduced currency risk exposure.
C. EMD issuers are recovering from adverse events more quickly than in the past.

18. With respect to emerging market debt (EMD), one of the main risks to the foreign bondholder is political risk. Which of the following is *least likely* to be a type of political risk?
A. Potential changes in tax and/or regulatory policy.
B. A lack of standardized debt covenants for EMD securities.
C. The possibility that investment capital cannot be repatriated to the investor's home country.

19. Factors that should be evaluated during the due diligence process when selecting a fixed-income portfolio manager include:
A. style analysis, selection ability, investment process, and beta correlations.
B. style analysis, selection ability, investment process, and alpha correlations.
C. style analysis, selection ability, risk management process, and alpha correlations.

For more questions related to this topic review, log in to your Schweser online account and launch SchweserPro™ QBank; and for video instruction covering each LOS in this topic review, log in to your Schweser online account and launch the OnDemand video lectures, if you have purchased these products.

ANSWERS – CONCEPT CHECKERS

1. **C** The gross profit on the portfolio is: $160 million × 7% = $11.2 million.

   The cost of borrowed funds is: $120 million × 4% = $4.8 million.

   The net profit on the portfolio is: $11.2 million − $4.8 million = $6.4 million.

   The return on the equity invested (i.e., the portfolio) is thus: $6.4 / $40 = 16.0%.

   Alternatively, the problem can be solved as: 7% + [(120 / 40) × (7% − 4%)] = 16.0%.

2. **C** The duration of equity can be calculated with the following formula:

   $$D_E = \frac{D_i I - D_B B}{E}$$

   Using the values in the problem:

   $$D_E = \frac{(4.2)160 - (0.8)120}{40} = 14.40$$

3. **C** The repo rate decreases: as the credit risk decreases; as the quality of the collateral increases; as the term of the repo decreases; if collateral is physically delivered, if the availability of the collateral is limited: and as the federal funds rate decreases.

4. **C** Shortfall risk is the ratio of number of observations that fall *below* the target return to the total number of observations. Shortfall risk = 15 / 60 = 25%.

5. **C** Like the variance, the semivariance measures the dispersion of returns. Unlike the variance, semivariance does not measure the total dispersion of all returns above and below the mean. Instead it only measures the dispersion of returns below a target return.

   Of the responses, only the semivariance takes into consideration the effects of outliers below the target return. By measuring all returns in the left hand side of the distribution, outliers are considered by the semivariance. None of the other methods evaluate outliers.

6. **B** The advantages to using futures over cash market instruments are that they are more liquid, less expensive, and make short positions more readily obtainable because the contracts can be more easily shorted. There is a great deal of depth in the futures market which explains their liquidity and low cost.

7. **B** −3.25 × 0.0075 × $102,500 = −$2,498.44

8. **C** To increase duration, contracts must be purchased. Only one of the answer choices is a buy and there is no reason to make a calculation.

$$\text{number of contracts} = \frac{(D_T - D_P)P_P}{D_{CTD}P_{CTD}} \times CF_{CTD}$$

$$= \frac{(14.47 - 10.0)15,550,000}{15 \times 23,519} \times 0.97$$
$$= 191.12$$
$$= 191 \text{ contracts to buy}$$

9. **B** Using a long put with the bond portfolio (a protective put) will provide downside protection below the option strike price but will leave most of the upside potential intact.

10. **C** Although there are obviously many actions that a firm's management could take to the detriment of the bondholders, of the three principal credit-related risks, this most accurately describes default risk. In this event, the firm's management fails to pay principal or interest when due, causing the issue to default. Default risk can be best managed with binary credit put options or credit default swaps.

11. **B** Market forces come to bear on bonds via required yields. The credit-related risk most closely associated with market forces is credit spread risk, which is the difference between the yield on the reference asset (Bond R in this case), and the appropriate risk-free benchmark. If the spread increases, reflecting a deterioration in the market's assessment of the creditworthiness of the issue or issuer, the value of Bond R will be adversely affected. Credit spread risk can be best managed with credit spread options or credit spread forward contracts.

12. **A** The type of credit-related risk most closely associated with the actions of a third party is downgrade risk. In this case, a major rating agency reduces its assessment of the issue/issuer's credit quality, and the value of the bond is adversely affected. This type of credit risk can be best managed with binary credit options or swaps. In the case of both instruments, the specified credit event is a downgrade below some level.

13. **A** There are at least six potential sources of excess return. Market selection concerns determining which national bond markets may afford the best opportunities. Currency selection concerns currency exposure management: should we hedge our exposures or should we actively manage our exposures? Duration management refers to managing interest rate risk and exposure so as to take advantage of any anticipated changes in rates. Sector selection involves seeking out the best performing industries, ratings categories, maturity ranges and other sector classifications. Credit analysis concerns the evaluation of credit qualities in an attempt to identify securities that may experience positive credit quality changes. The degree to which we are willing to deviate from our benchmark, which is often referred to as enhanced indexing.

14. **B** The estimated price change is:

$$\%\Delta_{price} = \text{duration} \times \Delta y \times \beta = 7 \times 0.005 \times 1.2 = 4.2\%$$

The duration contribution is:

$$DC = \text{weighting} \times \text{duration} \times \beta = 0.10 \times 7 \times 1.2 = 0.84$$

15. **C**   Assuming a comparable level of risk and a fully hedged position, the bond selection is based upon the bond's excess return:

Bond A excess return = 9.75 – 8.50 = 1.25%

Bond B excess return = 4.75 – 3.25 = 1.50%

Bond B should be selected under the assumption that the position will be fully hedged.

Once Bond B has been selected, if the hedging decision is revisited, the decision will depend upon the change in currency values implied by the differential in the risk-free rates, relative to the portfolio manager's expectations.

Change in Currency B implied by the interest rate differential = 5.75 – 3.25 = +2.50%. Because you expect Currency B to appreciate by 2.60%, you should not hedge.

16. **A**   The current yield advantage to the Australian Bond is 7.65 – 6.85 = 0.8% or 80 bp. Because the target holding period is six months, this represents 40 bp over the investment horizon. Next, we calculate the required change for each bond:

$$\Delta y_{AU} = \frac{-0.40\%}{-6.5} = 0.06\% \rightarrow \text{The yield would need to increase by 6 bp.}$$

$$\Delta y_{NZ} = \frac{0.40\%}{-5.3} = -0.08\% \rightarrow \text{The yield would need to decrease by 8 bp.}$$

In either case, the yield advantage is offset by the spread widening.

17. **B**   Emerging market currencies can be extremely volatile, especially during negative market events. Thus, even if the choice is between a bond in a developed country/currency and an EMD issue, the currency risk is most likely to be greater for the EMD issue. The other points are valid rationales for an allocation to EMD.

18. **B**   A lack of standardized debt covenants is certainly an issue, and creates risks for the EMD holder. If the covenants were changed arbitrarily, that could constitute political risk. However, the lack of standardization itself is not political risk. The other points are all forms of political risk.

19. **B**   Four principal factors that should be evaluated during the due diligence process surrounding the selection of a fixed-income portfolio manager are (1) style analysis (which includes portfolio management policy), (2) security selection ability, (3) investment process (which includes how research is conducted and decisions are made), and (4) the correlation of the manager's alpha with other current and prospective managers.

You have now finished the Fixed-Income topic area. To get immediate feedback on how effective your study has been for this material, log in to your Schweser online account and take the self-test for this topic area. Questions are more exam-like than typical Concept Checkers or QBank questions; a score of less than 70% indicates that your study likely needs improvement. These tests are timed and allow three minutes per question.

FORMULAS

market volatility: $\sigma_t^2 = \beta\sigma_{t-1}^2 + (1-\beta)\varepsilon_t^2$

factor model based market return: $R_i = \alpha_i + \beta_{i,1}F_1 + \beta_{i,2}F_2 + \varepsilon_i$

factor model based market variance: $\sigma_i^2 = \beta_{i,1}^2\sigma_{F_1}^2 + \beta_{i,2}^2\sigma_{F_2}^2 + 2\beta_{i,1}\beta_{i,2}\text{Cov}\left(F_1,F_2\right) + \sigma_{\varepsilon,i}^2$

covariance of returns between two markets, C and D:

$$\text{Cov}\left(C,D\right) = \beta_{C,1}\beta_{D,1}\sigma_{F_1}^2 + \beta_{C,2}\beta_{D,2}\sigma_{F_2}^2 + (\beta_{C,1}\beta_{D,2} + \beta_{C,2}\beta_{D,1})\text{Cov}\left(F_1,F_2\right)$$

variance of a market, C:

$$\sigma_C^2 = \beta_{C,1}^2\sigma_{F_1}^2 + \beta_{C,2}^2\sigma_{F_2}^2 + 2\beta_{C,1}\beta_{C,2}\text{Cov}\left(F_1,F_2\right) + \sigma_{\varepsilon,C}^2$$

price of a stock at time 0: $P_0 = \dfrac{\text{Div}_1}{\hat{R}_i - g} \Rightarrow \hat{R}_i = \dfrac{\text{Div}_1}{P_0} + g$

Grinold-Kroner expected return on equity: $\hat{R}_i = \dfrac{\text{Div}_1}{P_0} + i + g - \Delta S + \Delta\left(\dfrac{P}{E}\right)$

expected bond return:

$\hat{R}_B = $ real risk-free rate + inflation risk premium + default risk premium + illiquidity risk premium + maturity risk premium + tax premium

ICAPM: $\hat{R}_i = R_F + \beta_i\left(\hat{R}_M - R_F\right)$

beta for stock i: $\beta_i = \dfrac{\text{Cov}\left(i,m\right)}{\sigma_M^2} = \dfrac{\rho_{i,M}\sigma_i\sigma_M}{\sigma_M^2} = \dfrac{\rho_{i,M}\sigma_i}{\sigma_M}$

correlation of stock i with the market: $\rho_{i,M} = \dfrac{\text{Cov}\left(i,m\right)}{\sigma_i\,\sigma_M} \Rightarrow \text{Cov}(i,m) = \rho_{i,M}\sigma_i\sigma_M$

equity risk premium for market *i*: $\text{ERP}_i = \rho_{i,M}\sigma_i\left(\dfrac{\text{ERP}_M}{\sigma_M}\right)$
where:
$\rho_i = 1.0$ for a fully segmented market

target interest rate to achieve neutral rate:

$$r_{target} = r_{neutral} + \left[0.5\left(\text{GDP}_{expected} - \text{GDP}_{trend}\right) + 0.5\left(i_{expected} - i_{target}\right)\right]$$

Cobb-Douglas function (% change): $\dfrac{\Delta Y}{Y} = \dfrac{\Delta A}{A} + \alpha\dfrac{\Delta K}{K} + (1-\alpha)\dfrac{\Delta L}{L}$

Solow residual = $\%\Delta\text{TFP} = \%\Delta Y - \alpha(\%\Delta K) - (1 - \alpha)(\%\Delta L)$

H-model: $V_0 = \dfrac{D_0}{r - g_L}\left[(1 + g_L) + \dfrac{N}{2}(g_s - g_L)\right]$

constant growth model: $V_0 = \dfrac{D_1}{r - \overline{g}}$

Fed model: $\dfrac{\text{S\&P earnings yield}}{\text{Treasury yield}}$

Yardeni model: $\dfrac{E_1}{P_0} = Y_B - d(\text{LTEG})$ $\qquad V_0 = \dfrac{E_1}{Y_B - d(\text{LTEG})}$

P/10-year MA(E): $\dfrac{\text{current level of the S\&P}}{\text{average S\&P earnings over last ten years (adjusted for inflation)}}$

Tobin's q $= \dfrac{\text{asset market value}}{\text{asset replacement cost}} = \dfrac{\text{market value of debt + equity}}{\text{asset replacement cost}}$

equity q $= \dfrac{\text{market value of equity}}{\text{replacement value of net worth}} = \dfrac{\text{\# outstanding shares} \times \text{price per share}}{\text{replacement value of assets} - \text{liabilities}}$

$U_P = \hat{R}_P - 0.005(A)\left(\sigma_P^2\right)$

Roy's Safety-First Measure (RSF): $\text{RSF} = \dfrac{\hat{R}_P - R_{MAR}}{\sigma_P}$

If $S_i > S_p \times \rho_{i,p}$ adding the investment will improve the portfolio Sharpe ratio

where:
S_i $\quad$ = Sharpe ratio of proposed investment
S_p $\quad$ = current portfolio Sharpe ratio
$\rho_{i,p}$ $\quad$ = correlation of the returns on the proposed investment with the portfolio returns

$S_i = \dfrac{\hat{R}_i - R_F}{\sigma_i}$

Foreign Asset Return and Risk:

$R_{DC} = (1 + R_{FC})(1 + R_{FX}) - 1 = R_{FC} + R_{FX} + (R_{FC})(R_{FX})$

$R_{DC} = \displaystyle\sum_{i=1}^{n} w_i(R_{DC,i})$

$\sigma^2(R_{DC}) \approx \sigma^2(R_{FC}) + \sigma^2(R_{FX}) + 2\sigma(R_{FC})\sigma(R_{FX})\rho(R_{FC}, R_{FX})$

$\sigma(R_{DC}) = \sigma(R_{FX})(1 + R_{FC})$

where:
R_{FC} = the return on a foreign currency denominated risk-free asset

portfolio effective duration: $D_p = \sum_{i=1}^{n} w_i D_i = w_1 D_1 + w_2 D_2 + w_3 D_3 + ... + w_n D_n$

contribution of bond or sector i to the portfolio duration $= w_i D_i$

dollar duration of a bond or portfolio:

$DD = (\$\Delta value) = (effective\ duration)(0.01)(value)$

portfolio dollar duration: $DD_P = \sum_{i=1}^{n} DD_i = DD_1 + DD_2 + DD_3 + ... + DD_n$

$$rebalancing\ ratio = \frac{target\ DD}{new\ DD}$$

return of a leveraged portfolio:

$$R_P = R_i + [(B\ /\ E) \times (R_i - c)]$$

leveraged equity duration (may also be referred to as portfolio duration):

$$D_E = \frac{D_i I - D_B B}{E}$$

dollar interest on a repo $= (loan\ amount)(repo\ rate)\left(\dfrac{repo\ term}{360}\right)$

number of contracts to adjust portfolio duration:

$$= \frac{(D_T - D_P)P_P}{D_{CTD}P_{CTD}}(CTD\ conversion\ factor)$$

$$= \frac{DD_T - DD_P}{DD_f}$$

if yield beta is given include it as a multiplier in the previous calculation

$OV = max\ [(strike - value),\ 0]$

$OV = max\ [(actual\ spread - strike\ spread) \times notional \times risk\ factor,\ 0]$

payoff to a credit spread forward:

FV = (spread at maturity – contract spread) × notional × risk factor

forward premium or discount: $f_{d,f} = \dfrac{(F - S_0)}{S_0} \approx c_d - c_f$

breakeven spread analysis:

% change in relative price = $-D_S \, \Delta S$

ΔS = % change in relative price / $-D_S$

return on a bond denominated in a foreign currency:

$R_b = R_l + R_c \approx R_l + (i_d - i_f) \Rightarrow i_d + (R_l - i_f)$

duration of an option $=$ option delta $\times$ duration of the underlying $\times \dfrac{\text{price of the underlying}}{\text{price of the option}}$

Index

A

active management 203

active management by larger risk factor mismatches 203

adjusting dollar duration 219

adjustments to the immunized portfolio 213

advantages of interest rate futures 266

aligning risk exposures 206

ALM approach 107

ALM strategic asset allocation 85

alpha correlations 290, 295

alpha research 1

alternative investments 92

anchoring trap 5

appraisal (smoothed) data 3

asset allocation steps 100

asset class returns 33

asset/liability management (ALM) 85

asynchronism 3

B

banks 123

barbell strategy 228

base currency 144

basis risk 270

beta research 1

bid/asked price 144

bid/offered 144

binary 170

Black-Litterman approach 104

Black-Litterman (constrained) model (BL) 105

bond-equivalent yield 210, 211

bond index as a benchmark 200

bond indexing strategies 201

bond options 273

bond portfolio benchmarks 200

bond risk measures 264

bond structures 250

bottom-up approach 245

bottom-up forecast 63

breakeven spread analysis 287

bullet strategy 227

bullet structures 251

business cycle 18, 19

business spending 22

buy and hold 254

C

CAL 102

callable bonds 251

call risk 227

capital allocation line (CAL) 118

capital flows approach 37

capital market expectations 1

capital stock 56

cap risk 227

caps 274

carry trade 158

cash flow matching 229

cash flow reinvestment trades 248

cash instruments 33

cell matching 206

cheapest to deliver (CTD) 266

checklist approach 32

classical immunization 211

classical single-period immunization 212

CML 102

Cobb-Douglas production function (CD) 56

coincident indicators 32

collar 170

combination matching 231

commercial paper 33

common stock 35

composite 32

conditional return correlations 98

conditioning information 5

confirming evidence trap 5

constant growth model 10

consumer and business spending 22

consumer spending 22

contagion 28

contingent claim risk 227

contingent immunization 223

conversion factor 266

corner portfolio 112, 113

covered call 274

covered interest rate parity 158

credit analysis 252, 279, 294

credit default swaps 277, 293

credit-defense trades 248

credit derivative instruments 275

credit forwards 277

credit options 275

credit risk 205

credit risk-free bonds 33

credit risky bonds 34

Notes

Notes

Notes

Notes

Notes

Notes

Notes

Notes

Notes

Notes

Notes

Notes

Notes

Notes

Notes

Notes

Notes